Musical Theatre Choreography

Reflections On My Artistic Process For Staging Musicals

Musical Theatre Choreography
Reflections On My Artistic Process For Staging Musicals
All Rights Reserved.
Copyright © 2020 Linda Sabo
v8.0 r1.0

The opinions expressed in this manuscript are solely the opinions of the author and do not represent the opinions or thoughts of the publisher. The author has represented and warranted full ownership and/or legal right to publish all the materials in this book.

This book may not be reproduced, transmitted, or stored in whole or in part by any means, including graphic, electronic, or mechanical without the express written consent of the publisher except in the case of brief quotations embodied in critical articles and reviews.

Farnham Academy Press

ISBN: 978-0-578-22139-7

Library of Congress Control Number: 2019908914

Cover Photo © 2020 Scott Muthersbaugh. All rights reserved - used with permission.

PRINTED IN THE UNITED STATES OF AMERICA

Use Your QR App
To Learn More Today

Dedication

To Fritz, because he always believed in me…

To my mother, because without her I would never have become a dancer…

To my father, because he shared with me his love of movie musicals…

To my children, because they inspire me and give me hope.

Table of Contents

Foreword — i

Special Thanks and Acknowledgements — v

Tables — vii
Illustrations — vii
Lyric Permissions — ix

Preface — xi

Introduction — xiii

PART ONE — 1
Telling the Story

Chapter 1 — 3
I Could Write a Book
The Musical Theatre Choreographer as Dramatist

Chapter 2 — 24
In the Beginning...
Starting a Choreography Project

Chapter 3 — 36
A Brand New World
Working With The Director's Overall Vision

Chapter 4 — 47
Gotta Find My Purpose
Why is *This* Song in *This* Musical in *This* Spot?

Chapter 5 — 56
What's the Buzz?
Staging Exposition to Give Important Background Information

Chapter 6 — 71
On My Own
Staging the *Who, What, When, Where* and *Why* of the
Inner Monologue and Solo Song

Chapter 7 — 87
Were Thine That Special Face?
Staging Character Development and Relationship

Chapter 8 — 105
Muddy Water
Choreography or Staging? Or Both?

Chapter 9 — 128
Aftershocks
Additional Useful Tips for Teachers
of Undergraduate Choreographers

A Postscript to Part One
A Glimpse of the Weave

PART TWO — 137
The Development of Choreographic Theory and Teaching Practice
A Chronology of the Development of Theatre Dance and a Review of Prominent Literature in Modern and Musical Theatre Choreographic Pedagogy

Overture for Part 2 — 139

Choreographers Teaching Choreography — 141

Early Musical Entertainment in the Colonies — 144

Early Documentation of Modern Dance Choreography Technique — 152

Early Documentation of Popular and Musical Theatre Dance Forms — 154

Academic Dance and Early Analysis — 160

Dance in the Musicals of the 1940s and 1950s — 169

Existing Texts of Musical Theatre Choreography Pedagogy — 174

Appendices to Part One — 185

Bibliography — 216

FOREWORD

Christmas of 1960 was the first time I saw *Peter Pan*, starring Mary Martin, on television. I was Hooked ☺. I made my parents buy me the LP and I wore out the album—and my parents—memorizing every line and performing every role. I grew up in Princeton, New Jersey and 275 miles away in McKeesport, Pennsylvania another little girl was letting this production inform who she would become, memorizing every line and ruining her life for the better! That little girl was Linda Chiaverini Sabo.

When Linda arrived at Elon University 20 years ago she already had a full career as a performer and educator. After years of professional work as an actor and dancer, she created a musical theatre program with Brent Wagner at Syracuse University, continued to choreograph professionally, and taught musical theatre and dance majors at academic institutions like the University of Michigan, Iowa State University, and Interlochen National Music Camp, as well as at professional schools and dance companies around the country.

While at ELON she was the director and choreographer for seventeen productions (some of my favorite being *1940's Radio Hour, The Light in the Piazza, She Loves Me* and *110 in the Shade*), and she and I joyfully created twelve productions together (some of our favorites were *Sweeney Todd, Children of Eden, The Secret Garden, Titanic* and *Jekyll and Hyde*).

When I direct, Linda is my favorite choreographer. The love of music theatre is in her blood. In musicals, when a character can no longer express what they desire in words, they sing. And if singing cannot satisfy the need they dance. The beauty of storytelling through dance is that it is not bound like language to nationality and culture. Linda's storytelling through dance always takes the audience on a truthful and emotional journey to further the plot and to "enlist empathy and understanding for the characters and their experiences."

I took that last part from her book…the book you are about to read.

Musical Theatre Choreography:
Reflections on my artistic process for staging musicals

is an essential handbook for aspiring and experienced choreographers and directors. Linda Sabo's clear and practical approach uses well-defined methods for choreographing any production. This book—needed for a long time— presents theoretical ideas to consider and practical solutions to apply when choreographing and staging musicals. In Part One she sets out to demystify the process by clearly organizing and unfolding a course in development and progression starting with analyzing the libretto and then taking the reader through various ways of approaching staging with the *purpose* of the songs clearly in mind. Each chapter ends with in-class assignments and/or homework making this book an excellent guide for teachers and students. In Part Two she explores the evolution of the theatre choreographer and historical information about teaching with passion and detail.

This book is for all of us – every choreographer, director, and actor who wants to learn more about their craft. It is for all of us who found our passion and our light when we experienced our first musical be it *The Phantom of the Opera…* or *Peter Pan* ☺.

Catherine McNeela

Catherine McNeela is Founder and Director of the Music Theatre Program at Elon University where she also served as Chair of the Performing Arts Department for twelve of her twenty-five-year tenure. Catherine is a member of Actors Equity Association and has performed professionally throughout the U.S., Canada, and Europe in more than one-hundred plays, musicals and operas. She has directed almost as many musical productions while training kick-ass singers and actors as she established Elon's now nationally known program. Catherine is a proud recipient of the Daniels-Danieley Award for Excellence in Teaching and the William S. Long Endowed Professorship.

Special Thanks and Acknowledgements

To Dr. Kathy Lyday, Professor of English at Elon University for lending her love of theatre and her meticulous eye and ear for grammar to the editing of this book.

To my dear friend and former student, Broadway performer Johnny Stellard, for investing his time, editing skills, and musical theatre knowledge into shaping and inspiring this book.

To my former UNCG Professors Ann Dils, the late Jan Van Dyke, Susan Stinson, Jill Green, and Larry Lavender for nurturing this old dog with new tricks for both dance and writing. I am so grateful to them for giving me a late-in-life opportunity to gain more knowledge and insight into the nature of dance and art and to allow me to create an inroad for theatre dance to be considered and studied alongside modern dance.

To my extended family for always being right where I know I can find them, with arms wide open. My family is my anchor. Each of them contributed to who I am and what is in this book.

To all of my colleagues and teachers, past and present, who have shared their skills and their hearts with me, but most of all to my two main partners in crime over these past many years, Brent Wagner and Catherine McNeela, who have shared with me their extraordinary knowledge of music and acting, and their considerable expertise creating musical theatre, deepening my own understanding and appreciation for these art forms. I will remember mostly the fun we have had doing it, and for that I am most grateful.

To every student I have ever taught. You have taught me more. I am in awe of your abilities, yes, but also of your drive and your love for what you do. You have provided me the use of your lived bodies, extending them to my own in empathy and expectation…and love… so that we could create together. I have made art with you and the artistic theories and philosophies that drive this text are because of you. It has been a joyous forty year process and I love you all.

The photographs in this book represent my more recent work at Elon University. This has more to do with technology than anything else and does not diminish the artistic and personal influence of the commercial work I have done or of those early days and my work at Syracuse University. In my mind, that was only yesterday.

TABLES

Table 1. Comparison of Elements used in Play and Libretto Analysis

Table 2. Comparison chart: Brechtian Influences Seen in *A Chorus Line*

ILLUSTRATIONS

Figure 1. Opening look of *110 In the Shade*. Scenic Design by David Minkoff, Lighting by Bill Webb, Costumes by Matt Emig. Elon University Archives, 2010.

Figure 2. Abstraction and realism in *110 In the Shade*. Elon University Archives, 2010.

Figure 3. Foreshadowing romance in *110 In the Shade*. Elon University Archives, 2010.

Figure 4. Wagon area during the day, *110 In the Shade*. Elon University Archives, 2010.

Figure 5. Using projections to evoke history in *Rags*. Performer, Kendra Goehring, Scenic Design by Dale Becherer, Lighting & Projections by Bill Webb, Costumes by Tracy Justus. Elon University Archives, 2002

Figure 6. Unit set. *Jane Eyre, the musical*. Scenic Design by Dale Becherer, Lighting Design by Katherine Lowery Frazier. Elon University Archives, 2005.

Figure 7. Ensemble as narrators, characters, and symbolic aspects of main characters in *Jane Eyre, the musical*. Elon University Archives, 2005.

Figure 8. Ensemble as the tormented Bertha's damaged mind in *Jane Eyre, the musical*. Elon University Archives, 2005.

Figure 9. Close up of ensemble. *Jane Eyre, the musical*. Elon University Archives, 2005.

Figure 10. Ensemble character development in opening number from *110 in the Shade,* Elon University Archives, 2010.

Figure 11. Ensemble character introduction in *110 in the Shade.* Elon University, 2010.

Figure 12. More character development in opening from *110 In the Shade.* Elon University, 2010.

Figure 13. A "crossover" of ensemble to picnic grounds further establishing ensemble characters and relationships in *110 in the Shade.* Elon University Archives, 2010.

Figure 14. Utilizing moving pieces in "Façade" from *Jekyll & Hyde.* Directed by Catherine McNeela, Scenic Design by Dale Becherer, Lighting by Bill Webb. Elon University Archives, 2006.

Figure 15. "Façade" from *Jekyll & Hyde.* Elon University Archives, 2006.

Figure. 16. John Adams alone in the empty chamber, "Is Anybody There?" from *1776.* Performer Ryan Burch, Scenic Design by Natalie Hart, Lighting by Bill Webb, Costumes by Karl Green. Elon University Archives, 2014.

Figure 17. John leaves the chamber and advances on the audience. "Is Anybody There?" from *1776.* Elon University Archives, 2014.

Figure 18. Overall scenic structure in *The Light in the Piazza.* Scenic Design by Natalie Hart, Lighting by Bill Webb, Photographer Scott Muthersbaugh. Elon University Archives, 2016.

Figure 19. Ensemble as people on the street and building movers in "Let's Walk" from The *Light in the Piazza.* Photographer Scott Muthersbaugh. Elon University Archives, 2016.

Figure 20. Entrance of the Third Class Passengers in *Titanic* at Elon. Directed by Catherine McNeela, Scenic Design by Gateway Playhouse, Lighting by Bill Webb. Tony Spielberg ©, 2014.

Figure 21. Entrance of 2nd Class Passengers in *Titanic* at Elon. Tony Spielberg©, 2014.

Figure 22. Entrance of 2nd Class Passengers, full stage view from *Titanic*. Tony Spielberg©, 2014.

Figure 23. Set placement for entrance of 1ˢᵗ Class Passengers in *Titanic*. Tony Spielberg©, 2014.

Figure 24. Dinner with the 1ˢᵗ class passengers in *Titanic*. Tony Spielberg©, 2014.

Figure 25. Entertainment for 1ˢᵗ class passengers on deck in *Titanic*. Tony Spielberg©, 2014.

Figure 26. After dinner dancing below deck—3rd class passengers in *Titanic*. Tony Spielberg©, 2014.

Figure 27. End of opening sequence as the boat leaves shore in *Titanic*. Tony Spielberg©, 2014.

LYRIC PERMISSIONS

"Maria" by Leonard Bernstein and Stephen Sondheim
© Copyright 1956, 1957, 1958, 1959 by Amberson Holdings LLC
and Stephen Sondheim
Copyright renewed Leonard Bernstein Music Publishing Company LLC, publisher
Boosey & Hawkes, agent for rental
International copyright secured
All Rights Reserved. Used with Permission

GONNA BE ANOTHER HOT DAY (from *110 In the Shade*)
Music by Harvey Schmidt
Words by Tom Jones
Copyright© 1964 (Renewed) CHAPPELL & CO., INC.
All Rights Reserved
Used by Permission of ALFRED MUSIC

ANYTHING FOR HIM (from *Kiss of the Spiderwoman*)
Lyrics by Fred Ebb
Music by John Kander
Copyright© 1992, 1993 KANDER & EBB, INC..
All Rights on behalf of KANDER & EBB, INC.
Administered by WARNER-TAMERLANE PUBLISHING CORP.
All Rights Reserved
Used by Permission of ALFRED MUSIC

PREFACE

My decision to write a text focusing on the craft of musical theatre choreography developed over time for a number of reasons, not the least being my own need for such guidance when I began working professionally as a choreographer. As an educator who has offered such training in the past, I have noticed a dearth of specialized texts on this subject as well as poor representation in academia of training programs for choreographing or directing musicals. In addition, I hope to address the lack of legitimacy I have encountered throughout my career that has been relegated to dancing in musicals, to the evolution of its artistry, and to the raised standards for dancers and performers in this genre. By aligning musical theatre choreography with modern dance choreography and pointing out pedagogical convergences and traditional tools that can be useful in the development of dances in both genres, I hope to focus on its legitimacy as an art form. By pointing out the dissimilarities between these two genres and identifying the specialized demands of crafting artistic and script-serving theatre dance and staging, I hope to differentiate musical theatre choreography as a separate and bona fide art form and suggest that universities recognize it as such by offering training possibilities for future musical theatre choreographers.

As schools begin to add courses for directors and choreographers of musicals or develop graduate programs that emphasize directing or choreographing in this genre, such as The School of Theatre at Penn State's unique Master of Fine Arts Program "Directing for Musical Theatre," more texts that target this line of study will be necessary. I am only one choreographer sharing a personal method I have developed over many years as a starting place. There are hundreds of others, however, with a wealth of ideas and methods that can be useful to novice musical theatre dancemakers. Perhaps this text will encourage other MT professionals to follow suit and document or perhaps even codify their own artistic journeys when choreographing for musicals. This text documents the theories that underlie my practice as a choreographer.

INTRODUCTION

About Me

My own background in dance is varied. As a child I studied dance from the age of three through high school with Ken and Jean Phifer, a married couple who owned a local dance studio in the town where I grew up. Their school taught all forms of dance, and over the years I came to love my teachers and viewed them not only as educators, but also as entertainers. They were effortless dancers and innate performers who loved dance in all its incarnations and who had a close affinity with many styles of music. I believe it was this diversity in their teaching that nurtured my own affinity for musical theatre dance and other popular forms. In college I studied predominantly classical dance forms and became a serious student of modern dance, modern dance choreography, and ballet technique while "modern jazz" and tap, my previous mainstays, remained conspicuously in the background. These more theatrical forms were taught occasionally as "styles," as was character, folk, and flamenco, but not as ongoing technique courses. By the 1960s, modern dance had become well established as an art form through the groundwork lain—from the early 1900s through the 1950s--by dancers Isadora Duncan, the Denishawn dancers, Doris Humphrey, Martha Graham, Charles Weidman, Hanya Holm, and their progeny. Modern dance found recognition and a home in academia through the pioneering efforts of Martha Hill at Bennington and Margaret H'Doubler at the University of Wisconsin during the 1930s and 40s. I began my own professional training at the Boston Conservatory in 1967 on the heels of founder Jan Veen, (formerly Hans Weiner of Austria), who passed away that same year, leaving the Conservatory program in the hands of co-Chairs former ballerina Ruth Ambrose and jazzman Robert Gilman. Besides Veen's former students who taught his Laban/Dalcroze/Wigman-influenced modern technique, also teaching modern dance at the Conservatory during that time were Renate Schoettelius and Ray Harrison. Each also had German roots, Schoettelius was born in Germany and first studied modern there, and Harrison was a former student and dancer for Hanya Holm. Harrison was strictly American, however, and like Holm had one foot in the ballet and modern world and the other in Broadway musicals. His choreography was stunning and challenging and fused modern dance with more popular stylistic elements and dance genres. There were always Graham teachers, also, and a variety of guest artists and visiting professors. I was trained in several styles of modern dance and took daily ballet lessons, dance composition, and an imposing collection of dance related courses, such as Labanotation, Kinesiology, Music Theory, Score Analysis, and Art History, with a variety of teachers. But because of my love of theatre music and solid theatrical roots, I maintained powerful leanings toward theatre and theatre dance. My artistic identity didn't really start to come together until several years after college, however, when I began receiving requests to choreograph for musical theatre productions while I was a performer in New York. No one taught musical theatre choreography then, but by then I had taken enough time to assimilate various dance techniques with my eclectic interests in theatre, musical theatre, and dance. I was prepared to learn through the "trial and error" method—on my own.

And so, after a short time living and working in (and out of) Manhattan as a performer, I began to be hired as the choreographer or assistant choreographer for summer stock productions and even small projects in the City. I got my feet wet and liked it and began to tire of the daily grind of auditions and out of town engagements. I wanted to choreograph but not live the New York City lifestyle, and eventually found a position at Syracuse University working alongside director Brent Wagner as he fashioned a musical theatre performance program to match the existing BFA degree in musical theatre. It was during my ten year tenure at Syracuse that I had the opportunity to work alongside this scholarly director and composer from whom I learned a great deal about the genre, its history, and its music, and was able to work with talented and committed students who provided me the materials for endless "practice" in teaching and choreographing. Over forty-five years of professional and academic experience as a teacher, director, choreographer, performer, and lifelong student has given me a unique perspective on life, art, and teaching young artists. I have directed and choreographed both professionally and academically, and many of my former colleagues and students enjoy successful careers as musical theatre, dance, theatre, film, and television professionals, and it is particularly gratifying to know that many of them are teachers now themselves. Most recently, I have been a member of the music theatre faculty at Elon University in North Carolina.

About my purpose

Becoming a well-rounded musical theatre *performer* who is a strong singer, dancer, and actor is obviously a complex, strenuous and protracted undertaking. People who teach and work with these triple threat performers must also be diverse in their theatrical background and interests, even though they may have specialized fields. Mine was dance, but I studied acting and other theatre and music subjects, did a great deal of backstage apprenticeship and work, and performed as an actress and a dancer. Today, ensembles in musicals no longer exclusively separate the dancers from the singers, although in many shows there will be "featured dancers" who are more technically trained and versatile movers.

Musical theatre choreography has indisputably evolved over the years, and in many cases choreographers develop methods of working and philosophical approaches that should be documented but rarely are. Textual information is limited, and what has been written is generally more practical than theoretical (see pp. 174-182 of this text). Choreography has been passed down, however, through assistants, dance captains and dancers, and many important works have been archived in live performances by Lee Theodore's *American Dance Machine* (Gruen, 1978) and even more extensively through current technology. But the number of *texts* on the technical and theoretical elements of staging dance and movement for musicals is minimal compared to those written for choreographers of modern and contemporary dance.

It is my belief that musical theatre choreographers are best equipped by first studying and understanding traditional modern dance composition techniques, including extensive improvisation work. Add to that knowledge some theoretical ideas and methods of working with diverse musical and dance styles—from a *dramaturgical* point of view—and we begin to address the needs and purposes of dance in musicals. After discussing theoretical ideas in each chapter of Part One, I offer suggestions for assignments that may be of use to aspiring choreographers and directors. In Part Two, I attempt to review the scope of literature and representative articles that have been published on both topics, modern dance composition and musical theatre choreography, and while doing so, concisely trace the history of modern dance choreographic pedagogy, aligning it with concurrent trends happening within the American musical theatre.

PART ONE
TELLING THE STORY

Chapter 1
I Could Write a Book
The Musical Theatre Choreographer as Dramatist

Three important tasks for the Musical Theatre (MT) choreographer are:

- To use dance to convey information, i.e. place, time, situation, emotional state, relationship, personality, motivation, etc.,

- To fashion movement as a storytelling device to further the plot or fit seamlessly into the story, and

- To enlist empathy and understanding for the characters and their experiences (while remaining entertaining and engaging).

These functions are every bit as complex and require as much research, invention and artistry as dances created in any other dance genre. Note that the duties mentioned above are strikingly similar to those of a playwright who uses words instead of movement to accomplish these same things.

The story of a musical is already written by the librettist, composer, and lyricist, and therefore comes to the choreographer with a set of "givens" or existing features which then need to be developed for the stage by each of its artistic collaborators. Dances, however, are *not* already "written," but remaining within the limitations presented by the playwright, will be *created* by the choreographer to become a part of the script itself, or in a musical what is known as the libretto. In 1943, composer Richard Rodgers and lyricist/librettist Oscar Hammerstein II wrote what is thought to be the first completely integrated musical with *Oklahoma!*, a musical that began what we call "The Golden Age." The move toward integration of the music and the script started earlier, however, with composers such as Jerome Kern, and actually took root in 1927 with Kern and Hammerstein's classic work *Show Boat.* A light switch was flipped with *Oklahoma!*, however, when Rodgers' and Hammerstein's mission to keep the book absolutely central was established; after that, other music theatre artists followed suit and the standard changed. Now no other artistic element in a musical makes a move without first ensuring that it serves the script. Since that time, by creating original material that is integral to the telling of story, composers and lyricists came to be thought of as dramatists. In *Oklahoma!* Choreographer

Agnes de Mille seamlessly integrated her dances and staging into the action and created character and situation-specific movement that actually helped forward the plot. Because of *her* groundbreaking advances, foundational experiments of those who came before her, and the innovations of other forward-thinking dance artists who continued this move toward the integration of dance in musicals, musical theatre choreographers are now *expected* to create dances that serve the script and help to tell the playwright's story. The choreographer, like the librettist, composer, and lyricist, is now positioned as dramatist, as well.

Analyzing the Libretto

Normally I have already heard the music of a musical by the time I decide to direct or choreograph it. I will discuss that more in a subsequent chapter. However, when I am considering any musical, the first steps I take are to read it and listen to the music to get a complete understanding of it. After the musical is chosen, I read the libretto while listening to the score several times to develop a thorough knowledge of its needs and a personal connection to it. I then begin to research the original production and any revivals it may have had, after which I conduct historical period research on what it was like to live during the time in which the musical takes place. (Throughout these chapters I will keep coming back to the historical background of the shows I am discussing, which is absolutely necessary information for the choreographer to work with as (s)he creates choreography for any musical.) After I have a solid knowledge of the show's history, a clear snapshot of its creators, and its cultural context, I get down to the task of knowing and understanding the play as a literary work.

Play analysis is a course I would put in the curriculum of any program training musical theatre choreographers. Many university drama programs already have such a course in place so, when possible, choreographers interested in working in musicals should take advantage of it, even as an out-of-major elective. Furthermore, there are texts and articles written by theatre and musical theatre scholars on the topics of play and music analysis that demonstrate ways to discover the innermost workings of a libretto and score. Seek out and study whatever you can to deepen your understanding of the material, even if you think you already understand it. As to the methods you employ to analyze the elements of a musical, that will eventually be your choice, or of your own creation. To start with, however, use mine or your teacher's method because they will give you specific ideas for how to begin.

Throughout this text, I will use my own work in a variety of musicals to illustrate or examine theoretical points being discussed, in the way I use this first play *110 in the Shade* (*110*) to discuss plot analysis. In this chapter, after summarizing the plot of *110* following the stages of plot development mentioned below, I will discuss the play itself in terms of Aaron Frankel's *basic elements of a musical* to help determine the style (Frankel 5-24). In Chapter 4 of this text, which deals with purpose, I will share with readers a sample of my own "walk-through" analysis of each scene and song, as mentioned above. Creating such documents for yourself will provide a roadmap, of sorts, to make certain you stay on task when choreographing a musical.

Analyzing the Plot

Both *The Rainmaker* and its musical version, *110 in the Shade,* are perfect examples of classic literary plot construction. As both playwright and librettist of the musical, N. Richard Nash followed closely the structure of his original play, which resulted in a musical as seamlessly constructed. A **plot** is the sequence of events of the story being told and traditionally speaking, narrative plot construction holds the following elements: **exposition, rising action (or conflict), climax or turning point, falling action, *denouement*, and resolution.** To illustrate how Nash's musical follows this pattern I will work through the plot of *110*, inserting explanations of these plot devices along the way. It helps if you have some previous familiarity with either the play, the film or the musical. All are easy to find (see Appendix D).

Plot Analysis--*110 in the Shade* (Nash, 1963)

In **Scene 1** of this musical we first meet the sheriff (File) and the townspeople and discover during the opening sequence that we are in front of a train station near a water tower in Three Point, Texas in 1936 when this area might have been part of the American Dust Bowl. The townspeople are hoping for rain to end the drought. In the complete opening sequence, we meet File and realize he will figure as a main character in the story as will the two Curry boys—Lizzie's older brother Noah and her younger brother Jim (in his early 20s)—and their father, H.C., who all come to the depot to eagerly await the arrival of Lizzie. Lizzie is the middle child in her late 20s or early 30s but has been a motherly figure for the boys, especially Jim, since their mother passed. From the lyrics, we know that this is a close knit family and Lizzie is the loving and caring center of their home. Through dialogue we also discover that Lizzie is approaching "spinsterhood," which for Lizzie is a horrible fate because she wants so badly to have a family of her own and to share a different kind of love with a husband than she shares with her father and brothers. Ever the antagonist, her older brother Noah feels she has to begin to accept the fact that she will not have that opportunity, but H.C. and Jimmy are still optimistic and insist that File is a good prospect for Lizzie. Lizzie doesn't feel she is pretty or interesting to men and does not know how to be attractive to them. She doesn't like the idea of being "set up" by her brothers or acting flirty, even though she does have feelings for File. Still, the men decide to pay File a visit and ask him to join them for lunch later that day at the town picnic, leaving Lizzie alone with her thoughts. Through song, Lizzie makes known her profound desire to have a fulfilling family life; she describes what she has to offer and pleads, "Love, don't turn away"!

*All of the above can be considered **exposition** and also plot introduction—whether or not Lizzie will find a husband. By the end of Scene 1, we know what we need to know about the characters and both the plot and the subplot are set in motion. We move now into the development stage of the musical.*

In **Scene 2** the Curry men visit File in the Sheriff's office and through song persuade him to at least try to join them later at the park for lunch to "play a little poker," but of course, it is really to get him to taste Lizzie's cooking. Before they leave, File tells them to keep an eye out for a con man heading into the area—a man who promises he can make rain for a hundred dollars.

During the set change there is a musical crossover where we see the families heading to the picnic grounds, singing a slow reprise of the opening number. Jim and Noah run into Snookie, the pretty girl who always wears a little red hat and who Jimmy likes very much. This subplot figures into the show importantly by showing a flirty, ultra-feminine, and seemingly frivolous girl who, by contrast, shows us clearly the kind of girl that Lizzie is not. At the same time, it is made known that this is the kind of girl who gets men to fall for her: someone who seems superficial and who acts helpless and flighty, again unlike Lizzie who is smart, emotionally deep, and down to earth. Noah, who is antagonistic to anything even slightly outside the realm of conventionality and common sense, also expresses his concern that Jimmy will get himself into trouble with Snookie because he isn't smart enough to make mature decisions. Noah's defeatist attitude toward Jimmy's dreams parallels his attitude toward Lizzie's.

*Scene 2 and the following crossover contain **rising action,** setting up a meeting/confrontation between Lizzie and File, foreshadowing Starbuck's imminent entrance into the town, and introducing the **sub-plot**, which is whether or not Jimmy will be able to handle himself intelligently with Starbuck and Snookie.*

Regarding the kinds of conflicts presented in the play, Nash really covered the gamut. Lizzie is conflicted with herself, with Starbuck, File, and Noah, with society's ideas of what women need, and finally with fate, which may not end up in her favor. The town also has a conflict with nature. There is a drought. There is enough conflict to go around, but the major conflicts, of course, are Lizzie's own opinion of herself and the absence of rain, the latter of which is actually just a metaphor for Lizzie's conflict. Boiled down to the nitty gritty, the main conflict is Lizzie's lack of self-belief and self-regard. The rising action continues in **Scene 3**:

> At the park, we see the main plot begin to develop as more conflict enters the story in the person of the charismatic Starbuck who arrives and convinces everyone he can make it rain. Lizzie is disgusted by Starbuck's claims and also by his ultra-confident demeanor and tells him so. It is obvious, however, that she is drawn to him, partly because of her frenzied state of mind regarding her future, partly because of her nervousness about meeting File and failing to be desirable to him, and partly because she is attracted to Starbuck and does not understand those feelings. The song "You're Not Foolin' Me," is an argument that allows Starbuck to see the depth of Lizzie's intelligence and passion, and allows her to glimpse at the insecurities in him that cause him to be the way he is. Also during this scene, except for Noah and Lizzie, most of the town accepts Starbuck's claims, and H.C. gives him the $100 to make rain.

The conflict and sexual tension between these two must come out in this scene so it can build to the climax of the story in Act 2. In the next scene we see Lizzie's growing agitation with herself and how she is beginning to recognize her own sexual nature.

> In the song "Raunchy," Lizzie teasingly tells her father how she is sick and tired of being the "good girl" all the time and that she is going to change and become more flirty and superficial in order to do better with men. File walks in at the end of the number to see her strutting around and acting silly with her friends. She falls down to the ground laughing as the number ends, but when she opens her eyes he is staring down at her. She is, of course, mortified at her own outrageous behavior.
>
> Nevertheless, during the following scene they have a heart to heart talk during which he tells her how his wife left him for another man and that he no longer trusts women or relationships. In the ballad "A Man and a Woman," Lizzie tells him that love doesn't always have to end up that way and for a moment they connect, foreshadowing the possibility of something happening between them. Feeling she is becoming too serious, however, she abruptly changes tactics and begins flirting with him and acting, in his words, "ridiculous"; her behavior angers him and he leaves. In a desperate state of mind, unsure of how she can ever make this right, seeing Snookie making ground with Jimmy, and feeling even more alone and hopeless than ever, she sings the song "Old Maid," ending Act I on her knees in anguish praying, "Oh God don't let me live and die alone." It is important to see the depth of Lizzie's desperation to understand how it motivates her to turn to Starbuck in Act II.

> Act 2 begins the evening of the picnic and the whole town is in a romantically lit clearing in the park behind the bandstand where there is music and dancing. This scene opens with a couples' dance as the ensemble sings, "Everything Beautiful Happens at Night," foreshadowing the scene to follow between Starbuck and Lizzie. Jim and Snookie are together and everyone is partnered off. Lizzie isn't at the dance but later is again chided by her brother about the unlikelihood of her ever finding a partner, another event that pushes her toward finding some sort of affirmation of her desirability from Starbuck.

*All of the above continues the **rising action**, and a rising desperation in Lizzie to make something happen in her life. The opening of Act 2 foreshadows and prepares the audience for her upcoming sexual encounter with Starbuck by creating a highly romantic atmosphere causing Lizzie to feel even more alone and in an impulsive frame of mind.*

> The following scene opens with her approaching Starbuck's wagon, ostensibly to bring him a blanket. During the scene their differences are strongly pointed up in the songs they sing to each other: Starbuck the dreamer, lover of fantasy and adventure sings about the perfect woman "Melisande," and Lizzie who just wants "someone to talk to" and someone to love her describes "Simple Little Things" as being enough for her. All of her "dreams" are based in reality, all of his in fantasy. Even so, they are drawn to each other and as he pursues her he takes down her hair and forces her to confront herself as a woman, challenging her to say simply that she is pretty, whether or not she believes it. Although this does not come easily, when Lizzie can finally voice these words she is able to let down completely and be with him, regardless of whether or not it is forever or if it is the sensible or even moral thing to do.

*This scene marks the **climax** of the play, not because Lizzie has found a husband, but because there is a **turning point** in how she sees herself. She now can recognize her self-worth as a woman because, like the fictional Melisande might have done, she took a "fantastical" leap of faith and accepted that she could be desirable to the handsome and exciting Starbuck. The sub-plot of Jimmy and Snookie also resolves itself a scene later as we discover that Jimmy, although young, is not hopelessly stupid and can make good choices and handle himself in a mature fashion. It turns out he transforms Snookie a bit, as well.*

The *falling action:*

> …begins when File, searching for Starbuck, realizes that Lizzie is trying to hide him. Starbuck enters and File pulls out his gun to arrest him. Lizzie gets between them and talks File into

I Could Write a Book

> allowing Starbuck to leave. File consents, but before Starbuck exits he stops and asks Lizzie to leave with him, prompting File to say "Lizzie, don't go."

The **denouement** or conclusion begins here:

> Both men sing contrasting verses of "Wonderful Music" urging Lizzie to choose: Starbuck is offering her a life of fantasy and adventure, File is offering her just those "simple little things" she sang about earlier in the act. She chooses File, of course, Starbuck leaves on an upbeat note, and the **resolution** plays out as it begins to rain. The townspeople reprise "The Rain Song" from Act 1 and the show ends.

For me, writing through the plot in this fashion not only cements the story and sequence of events in my mind, but it also begins to help me notice my own interpretation of the events and my personal feelings for the characters and the choices they make. Dealing with *details* and *specificities* when creating art and interpreting them in your own way is important to making your personal contribution to the spirit of the production.

Determining the Style through Interpreting the Elements

Aaron Frankel, in his text *Writing the Broadway Musical,* uses most of the traditional play analysis guidelines stated above to analyze the examples he uses in his text, but *before* he gets to that, he devotes a chapter to "The Basic Elements of a Musical" which he categorizes as **Seed, Story, Spirit, Sound and Look, Point of View,** which make up **Style** (Frankel 5-24). In my own initial analysis of the songs in a musical, I find these categories most useful, particularly in developing concept, which we will discuss more in Chapter 3.

Now the following is really helpful, so read closely. The **story**, which should condense easily to a sentence, is *not* the plot but holds the plot together and *must always* begin with a conflict between persons, not between ideas; ask the question "*who* does *what* to whom?" (9). The plot is the detailed unfolding of the story. For *110 in the Shade,* the **story** could be stated as: "a man changes a woman's life," or "a man changes how a woman feels about herself" or, more specifically, "a man gives a woman a sense of self-worth" or "a sense of possibilities." Starbuck, the con man and the "rainmaker" is the catalyst or driving force in the play. He makes things happen that affect everyone in this small rural town, so the **story** can be more broadly stated as "a man gives a woman a sense of self-worth, and a dying town a sense of hope." In fact, I think I will choose the latter as my statement of the ***story*** of *110 In the Shade*.

In terms of Frankel's basic elements (5-24), we will continue to examine my own interpretations here to get an overall sense of the work before detailing each scene. I recommend this step, or a variation of it, to help choreographers formulate their own interpretation of the style of the musical.

Seed: A seed is planted in the mind(s) of the original creator(s), making this a very personal part of the process. What moves someone toward this project? In this case, Nash first approached composer Harvey Schmidt and lyricist Tom Jones (*The Fantasticks! I Do, I Do*) about writing a musical version of his play *The Rainmaker.* Former Texans, both Schmidt and Jones related to the people and the place and loved the emotionality of the characters in the original play (Yurgaitis, 2003). They felt that it had the potential to be "opened up" beyond the fourth wall (between the stage and the audience) and made to "sing," terms Frankel uses to contrast straight plays and musicals. Frankel differentiates between *picture theatre* (the story is "framed" within four walls and the actors work within that, or behind the fourth wall), and *platform theatre* where the actors' energy connects with the audience directly. Rather than endeavoring to *represent* a real life event, musical theatre, like platform theatre, *presents* a theatre event (Frankel 6). Throughout my career I have heard the word "presentational" theatre used a great deal, particularly in a negative sense and in connection to musical theatre. Presentational is simply a question of style that is important for directors and choreographers of musical theatre to understand, but certainly not to dwell on or overthink. It does not mean there is a special way you need to work with actors because the form takes care of itself. The nature of music, song, and dance places them squarely upon this *platform* stage. It *is* presentational, without anyone needing to "direct" it that way. The acting is still truthful, not overacted or indicated, but the energy level is higher. Frankel says that musical theatre may be getting more real, but it is not becoming more realistic: "A realistic play closes in on its subject, while a musical book opens up its subject, freeing it to become less literal" (7). Case in point: the play *The Rainmaker* has 7 characters and 2 settings while the musical *110 In the Shade* had 45 in the original cast with 6 settings and a 20 piece orchestra. The addition of the music opens up the presentation:

> The difference is the fourth wall. Retained, it encloses and intensifies, which serves the gradual, microscopic method of realism. Removed, it releases and expands, which serves the swift, telescopic method of musicals. (7)

Music allows the energy to release itself through song and dance, which translates to great physical energy and heightened reality. The body is most alive when performing in this way. In addition, by incorporating the nonliteral and abstract nature of music and dance, emotionality is also released and expanded making meaning more profound because it is deeply *felt* rather than just intellectually understood.

Story: We have already stated the **story** of *110 In the Shade* in a number of ways, but as I wrote earlier, I will use: *"a man gives a woman a sense of self-worth, and a dying town a sense of hope,"* except that I need more active and concrete verbs to lend more precise action to the characters, such as *"a man awakens a woman's sense of self-worth, and revives a dying town's sense of hope."* Directors often use "verbing," and choreographers might also practice it when preparing to choreograph, applying it either to specific characters or the ensemble as a whole. Verbing clarifies what is motivating the characters and driving the story forward; how the story is happening. Frankel notes that the only way an audience will care about the story and take sides is through the *specific actions* of the characters (9). The actors need to be credible, of course, but their motives and actions must also be compelling in order for the audience to begin to care about them, which is really the only way a play can impact its audience. Both "awakens" and "revives" are more specific verbs than "gives" and begin to breathe life into your work.

Spirit: When I first start talking with my designers (as director of the show or as part of the creative team), I describe my initial reactions and feelings about the show, which helps to begin the process of collaboration. At these beginning stages I may be more familiar with the show than they are, particularly in academic settings when designers are working on several productions during the school year. As a choreographer, the more I can give them in terms of what I am visualizing for specific songs, the better springboard they will have to begin formulating their own ideas to express and expand mine. When they do begin sharing their research and responses, often it has to do with textures, colors, architecture, and artifacts of the period involved. Language, of course, has power so when interpreting the spirit of a show, all of the feeling and ideas of the team should be discussed openly and thoroughly talked through. I often like to start with words or fragments of phrases that strike me as I read through the show, listen to the music, hear from my designers, or just visualize a dance. Here are some of the words we all contributed during early production meetings to help us determine the **spirit** of <u>110 In the Shade</u>: *down-home, genuine, romantic, funny, fun, earthen, simple folk, slowed down, neighborly, seductive, melodic, calico, wood, windmills, fanciful, wooden picnic tables, coca cola, hoedowns, green turning brown, musically moving, overalls, deck of cards, tablecloths, picnic baskets, dusty, countrified, desperate, hopeful, worn down buildings, tin roofs, lean-to's, horseshoes, holsters, compassionate and invested, reality versus fantasy, drought and desperation, cotton, cowboy hats and boots*, and so on. Try applying this same response game to individual numbers, particularly production numbers, at the beginning of the choreography process. Listening to the music in context with the play for the first time, you will begin to have responses… some even full-blown.

Tangent. *To my mind, one of Broadway's most inventive choreographers was Tommy Tune. His work seemed to be either stream of consciousness reactions to the script from which he chose the most unexpected possibilities; OR, contradictorily he incorporated the first thing that came into his head full-blown, and it just happened to always be far outside the box and usually very compelling. I wonder that he became a director so he could more easily incorporate his unconventional choreographic ideas into a production without a director saying, "Too far out. I can't see it!" Because Tune was the director/choreographer of <u>A Day in Hollywood, A Night in the Ukraine</u>, for instance, he and his co-choreographer Thommie Walsh were able to incorporate their own vision throughout, for better or worse, such as the catwalk idea to introduce those early musical stars. A male and female dancer entered and exited throughout Act 1, dancing on a raised catwalk-like platform positioned across the upstage area. We know only what stars they depict by the bottom half of their costume, as we see them only from waist down! This minimalistic approach to the addition of dance in the first act of this show was one of the smartest, most creative concepts I can remember seeing in a Broadway musical. Talk about telling the story through dance in brilliant collaboration between director/choreographers and their scenic and costume designers. True collaboration. I went on this tangent to emphasize the use of your imagination and the importance of not limiting it or disregarding your initial thoughts and reactions to a project. Rather, let them be your springboard to what might be your most innovative work.*

Regarding your designers, count on and expect from them hands-on, visual research in the way of photos, slides, videos, etc., particularly at the beginning of the process. Interesting to me is the way designers express themselves emotionally—usually less through words than through objects and images. The director and the choreographer talk about their feelings; the designers, who have emotional responses just as strong, express their passion in the amount and kind of research they do, their interpretations of the research, and the objects, images, renderings, and models they bring into the meetings. I was particularly captivated by designer David Minkoff's scenic design for my 2010 production of *110 in the Shade*. It was a simple, gentle, beautiful, and visually effective setting for this work (see figs. 1-4). While the play itself is written in the style of realism, its meanings are steeped in metaphor. The time period, place, and situation are all dictated by the playwright, but the musical elements and the undercurrent of allegory allow for the involvement of the abstract—almost calling out for it. Added to this were limitations of offstage storage space and my desire to have the show move easily in and out of environments. What I loved most about this design was its appropriate merging of the realistic with the abstract, the beautiful lines it gave to visual presentation of the scenes, its easy simplicity, and use of textures and shapes to help set the time period. This setting was designed by an artist invested in the play, in the team's combined vision of the play, and in the limitations presented by space and budget. His presentations to me were through his medium—always something actual—something I could see, hear, touch, smell, or taste. It makes sense that designers work this way, and it is a perfect complement to a choreographer's often fragmented ideas that come at the initial stage of any project. Designers research aspects of the show you may not have researched yet yourself, such as the architecture of the period or the condition of the landscape, and from that research pull textures, shapes, and colors that they will incorporate into their design. Their research will enrich yours, and what they do with the environment and costumes will be vital aspects of your own work. The final realization begins with your creative team's initial vision generated by their sensual responses to the libretto and score, the story being told, and the way the playwright presents it. Mixing of the literal with the abstract, the predominant use of wood, cotton, earth tones, and using what is natural, ordinary, unpretentious, and down-to-earth. These things created the spirit and style of our production.

Figure 1. Opening look of *110 In the Shade*. Elon University Archives, 2010.

Figure 2. Abstraction and realism in *110 In the Shade.* Elon University Archives, 2010.

Figure 3. Foreshadowing romance in *110 In the Shade.* Elon University Archives, 2010.

Figure 4. Wagon area during the day, *110 In the Shade.* Elon University Archives, 2010.

Point of View: When I am directing or creating choreography for a show, it is important for me to understand the point of view of the creators of the work, to analyze my own point of view, and then to help the actors communicate each character's point of view. The movement I create for any show will be based on the world view of the characters performing it. I believe the point of view of the authors of *110 In the Shade* might be considered by some to be a bit old-fashioned today. This musical was created in 1963 in America, depicting a small Texas town in 1936. When placing movement on any one of the characters at any time during the musical these facts must be honored, unless the concept for the show is to present the play in a different period. It is entirely possible that when Schmidt and Jones joined Nash in creating *110 in the Shade*, they saw it out of slightly different eyes than they might have even a decade later, after the women's movement took hold. What we expect of women now is in deep contrast to what was expected of them in 1963, and certainly even more so in 1936. I like to keep historical circumstances in mind when interpreting and creating movement for any musical. When I choose to present a play, I try to honor the historical context of the work and respect it, even if I do not agree with it. That being said, an author's intent is always open for interpretation and every reader, audience member, or choreographer will come to a work with their own background, beliefs, and sensibilities. I believe that plays are open to the interpretation of directors who will decide the *way* they will tell the story. So, as choreographers, we must always be ready to adapt our points of view to those of the director. Make certain you and your director are of the same mind and that the entire creative team is working from the *same* point of view. Maintaining unity of purpose for any production is your major obligation as a member of the artistic team.

ESSENTIAL SKILLS FOR MUSICAL THEATRE CHOREOGRAPHERS

Besides the ability to analyze and support a libretto with movement that continues the task of telling the story, I have enumerated below a skill-set useful to choreographers of musicals. Feel free to add to this if you like.

1. *The Skill to Collaborate:* Musical theatre choreography requires meetings with collaborators and an allegiance to realizing the overriding vision of the show's director. Be open to all input, consider it carefully. Rejoice in the differences between you and your collaborators and take as much delight in their successes as you would in your own. And, *always* give credit where credit is due. Just remember one prevailing principle: Regardless of how expert a director is at creating a mutually gratifying collaborative environment and maintaining an atmosphere of equality among a show's creative team, ultimately, the director's word is the final decisive note on all artistic choices made during the mounting of a musical. The director's singular vision is the most dependable way to provide a production with coherence and unity of concept. If you find that you don't like working that way, then make arrangements to start directing your own musicals.

2. *The Skill (and love) of Conducting Research:* In another vein, the "dancer" part of the choreographer needs to have a working knowledge of historically accurate musical and dance styles and preferably unfailing musicality. For some choreographers of concert dance genres, this kind of service feels more like servitude or suppression of their creativity. For others, it can represent tremendous freedom or even a kind of artistic sanctuary. Regardless, it is about creating movement that *tells a story*, and is most often about people living in a particular place at a particular time, as in *West Side Story* (NYC in the 1950s). Sometimes it is about a mythical place, set in a particular era or time period like *Camelot* (Great Britain during The Middle Ages). Sometimes it is about lions in The Pride Lands of Africa, or sailors in the South Pacific during WWII, an Italian film director in the 1960's, or a kindly research doctor in 19th century England who discovers a potion that unleashes his inner demon. While the choreographer will need to have a working knowledge of dances from the time period and/or place of the musical, the movement will always be dictated by the style of each individual song. Sometimes they all stay within a particular period of time and place, such as Bernstein's 1950's bebop/Latin-laced, jittery jazz of *West Side Story*; or the musical style can change from dance to dance, as in Bernstein's eclectic score for *Wonderful Town*, which boasts a myriad of dance styles, such as a swing dance, the Conga, the Irish

Jig, a bluesy ballet and even the whimsically fabricated "Wrong Note Rag." Important nuances of characters and their stories can be revealed through the movement they perform. Like music, movement or the non-literal can often do this in more profound and meaningful ways than through what is spoken or even sung. If you choreograph for musicals, you must love to do research dictated by the particulars laid out in the libretto. It will guide and specify everything you create.

3. *The Skills of a Trained Dancer:* Some say that the postmodern age now allows art to be anything and everything. This approach is freeing and has led to new and meaningful pathways in all of the arts. The future of art *should* be wide open. However, we do learn, build on, and break away from what has come before, and learning to work with the techniques of different historical periods of art very often leads artists to new ground. So, established techniques are important, to a degree. The time-honored techniques of dance and choreography give its practitioners a deeper well of knowledge and methods to choose from. Also, trained dancers can find and develop what the body can do in more ways than the untrained body. Again, the caveat is that new dance techniques arise and what we consider "technical dance" continues to change. It is obvious I am conflicted around this point, but the history of successful choreographers shows that most were formally trained technical dancers. As a dancer who no longer has her technique to create with, I will say that choreographing now is like creating a piano concerto without a piano. It can be done, but both kinesthetic and long-term memory become the stabilizing factors rather than the lived body. Also, musicals are special in some ways. In order for an existing work to be presented as intended, or even at all, there are always technical requirements to consider, often even different skills for different musicals. So, since the style of songs in musicals runs the gamut and non-dancing-directors have and do often accomplish excellent staging, musicals most often need a broader knowledge of technical dance in order to elevate large group songs and production numbers into the realm of dance. Other goals are to make them innovative and challenging, and emotionally and psychologically affective within the parameters of the story. In order to function fully as a dance stylist in a highly eclectic musical domain, to work with and challenge highly trained dancers, and to contribute a working language to the broad range of musicals in today's market, comprehensive choreographers really should be trained dancers.

4. *Basic Skills and Knowledge of Music & Acting:* Choreographers should have at least a rudimentary knowledge of:

   - Basic play, song, script and score analysis
   - Acting methods and techniques
   - Music theory, and even some understanding of vocal technique and the needs of singers. It is always useful to be able to talk to actors and singers using their jargon, which speeds the process and specifies your points.

5. *Historical Knowledge:* A choreographer's knowledge of musical theatre should span its evolutionary forms—roughly from the early 1800's through now—which are the various forms of variety entertainment, (e.g. minstrelsy, vaudeville, the revue, and burlesque), as well as the book musical and the various styles of presentation dictated by its era of inception, (e.g. the pre-golden age musical, the film musical, parody, the concept musical, the jukebox musical, etc.). Information from these forms are needed, particularly if you are choreographing a classic musical, for which you will often call on a staging convention you would be aware of only if you've studied or seen it done and understood its derivation. Besides an historical knowledge of the range of musical theatre forms, a solid background in the work of both early and contemporary songwriters is important as well as how movement can and does conform to musical styles. This last trait is the proof of a choreographer's musicality, which I think of as an unfailing rhythmic sense and the ability to embody music and interpret it appropriately. This comes from living with the genre, listening, watching, reading, working with—essentially immersing yourself in the many forms and styles of musical theatre. Growing up in the 1950s and 60s, I never attended an actual minstrel, burlesque or vaudeville show, but films made from the early 1930s on, and television during the decades I spent in elementary and high school, were brimming with historical information about these musical forms--the comedy as well as the song and dance. I may not have known it at the time, but those films became part of my personal research library that I would refer to for the rest of my life. Musical comedy became a part of me.

6. *The Skills of a Trained Choreographer:* Without improvisatory skills in the elemental areas that make up dance (time/force/space), choreographers would need to rely primarily on derivative and learned movement, and might never develop their own approach to solving a movement problem or inventing a more personalized movement vocabulary. Facility with

improvisation, knowledge of one's own movement proclivities and of existing ideas in dance composition, artistic design, spatial design, and rhythmic variation can give inexperienced choreographers a starting place with "rules" to follow and to break and the opportunity to forge continuity with the past while encouraging the art form to progress. Much like learning a foundational ballet or modern technique before taking a jazz class, choreographers should also allow themselves a strong foundation in modern dance composition and improvisation.

7. *The Skills of a Teacher:* In my younger days, I equated demonstrating movement with teaching and often gave it more importance than necessary. Yes, demonstrating is a prominent aspect of teaching, particularly when giving new material or working with styles, but truly any assistant can demonstrate a movement and be technically correct. Demonstrating is the nuts and bolts of dancing, showing the actual/factual movement, per se. It doesn't necessarily include precise nuances of style, quality of movement, aspects of character, or musicality. A *great* demonstrator, your hand-picked assistant, will include all of these more esoteric aspects in their demonstration of your movements, but even that demonstration—I guarantee—will never replace your verbal descriptions of what you intend the movement to convey, nor the comments and corrections you give to your dancers to cajole a strong performance out of them. Teaching means to show someone the way, to guide, to pass on knowledge. As a choreographer, you must accomplish each of these things effectively if the dancers you choose are to interpret your work with uniform and strong technique, musicality and style, in character, and in the precise way you would like it to come across. And remember this, bullying seldom works because doing something brought about by knowledge always trumps doing something brought about by fear. Bullying has been used by some of our most revered choreographers, but it is never the constructive option.

8. *The Skills of a Performer:* Musical theatre choreographers benefit also from having, at some time, performed in musicals as actors/singers/dancers. Having performed, I can put myself in the dancers' shoes and see rehearsals from their perspective, which helps me to pull challenging work from them or to understand why my methods may *not* be working. As a young choreographer I could demonstrate all of my own movement, and while I was creating it I had the habit of putting on the characters myself, which allowed me to "feel" the rightness or wrongness of the movement. Even now, movement memory and the kinesthetic sense I have developed

as a dancer help me to know what I can expect from my dancers and how far I should push them to conquer challenging work. Creating staging and choreography also demands attention to the fact that the performer is most often singing, and close collaboration with the musical director at key points in the process will assure you both that neither the vocal or dance performances will suffer. Often this is the time when the ability to give and take is so necessary, which leads me, naturally, to the next point.

9. *The Skill to Serve and be Flexible:* Finally, the "skill" I found to be the most vital to develop throughout my career, wherever I have worked, is the ability to be flexible, not just in body, but in temperament. This ability is normally not something one is born with. On the contrary, most of us are not. It is something, however, that can be developed through experience—but it is an ongoing process, to be sure. Each show has its own dynamic, just as each relationship between colleagues has its own distinct and subtle undercurrent. Regardless, within the creative team itself the overriding concern of each designer, including the dance designer, is to first serve the director's vision, followed by the need to integrate and balance his work equally alongside each of the musical's collaborating art forms. Concert dance choreographers have more complete autonomy in this regard and actually have more sway over their designs because they are created solely to serve the dance. Rather than the choreographer modifying or conforming a dance idea to serve the needs of the scenic or costume design, it makes the most sense that designers for concert dance works re-imagine their ideas, when possible, to accommodate the work of the choreographer. In a musical, although consensus in choice-making is usually arrived at before the rehearsal process begins, choreographers often need to structure or restructure choreography around scenic elements, modifying aspects of it for better dance design, safety issues, or technical considerations. Placement of dancers or issues of timing may need to conform to lighting considerations; and any number of modifications may have to be made to conform to the desires of the director. I have been asked to change steps, restage for a different number of performers, re-choreograph for different props or elimination of props, rework my ideas for a dance to accommodate the movement ability of the performer, and more. Choreographers of musicals learn to pick their battles. For me, the bottom line is always to ask myself, "Am I telling the story in the fashion desired by the director?" If I answer this question in the affirmative and feel strongly about what I have been asked to change, I might go to battle. That being said, I also know that after years of working as a creative artist, there are *many* ways to say something through dance. Simply being pushed to take a step farther into my

own creativity, I often come up with something surprising; something I like even better than my original idea. While temperament is the only personality trait I expand upon as a trait that MT choreographers *must* possess, there are many I feel one *should* possess to make everyone else's life easier and the process more enjoyable. Some of these are a sense of humor, patience, integrity, generosity of spirit, patience, good taste, the ability to count a dance phrase in an understandable fashion, and consistency. And, of course, we all love working with someone who is charismatic, which most often comes from a strong belief in self. Coming from someone who has worked through a haze of self-doubt on and off for most of my life, my advice is to not waste precious time on bothering with such an exercise. If you have done your work and you are prepared to create your dances, believe in yourself and be confident. Own your space, and take charge of your rehearsal. Your dancers will appreciate this quality in you more than you can know.

In the following chapters, I will discuss some of the activities inherent in beginning a choreography project. I will also introduce certain theoretical ideas regarding how "givens," or given circumstances presented in the libretto and score of a musical, might dictate the needs of the choreography. Theory is proposed and discussed largely through examples of specific issues or challenges I have encountered in my own work, or that I have analyzed and interpreted in the work of others. This information may guide neophyte musical theatre choreographers or provide an opportunity for experienced choreographers to analyze the elements of *who, what, when, where and why*, while they complete choreographic and staging assignments *in context* with the rest of the show. Although some of the individual assignments do not require actual dance-making, they do require a great deal of background work, including close readings of the libretto, script analysis, special knowledge and analysis of librettos and scores, a consideration of assigned design elements, and sufficient rehearsal with the choreographers' casts and accompanists. Choreography students should be expected to make specific choices in context with the rest of the script and be asked to justify each choice made from the beginning to the end of their process. Working this way on one number can progress to larger chunks from shows in subsequent courses, so that when presented with an entire musical, students will have already developed and have in place a personal system for how to approach the process of analysis and creation.

Assignments – Chapter 1

Note to teachers: For ease of process and to keep the assignment consistent across the class, my suggestion is to not work with original musicals. All musicals assigned should have been previously produced with fully realized scores, published librettos, and audio recordings of the original productions.

Out of class assignment

1. Choose or accept from your instructor the assignment of a musical you will work with throughout the first half of this course. Imagine that you have been hired to choreograph the production; your instructor will act as director.

2. Read the libretto of the musical. Write a plot summary separating the plot divisions described in this chapter. Be sure to delineate exposition, rising action (or conflict), climax or turning point, falling action, denouement, and resolution. Describe what you understand about the story and what, if any, visual images you had as you read it; what you know about the characters; how the score serves the script, etc. Try to encompass as much as you can in the way of knowledge given to you by the writers. What is the story to be told?

3. Analyze the elements of the show in the manner shown in this chapter using the breakdown of seed, story, spirit, sound, look, and point of view. Discuss concept with your "director."

Chapter 2
In the Beginning...
Starting a Choreography Project

Architecture starts when you carefully put two bricks together. There it begins.
Ludwig Mies van der Rohe, American Architect

Beginning A Concert Dance Work Versus A Musical Theatre Project

In stark contrast to beginning musical theatre choreography, beginning a concert dance work is to depart on a less communal and more lonesome journey. It is also one that for me personally is more frightening because it is less specified, which is why I believe examining those differences here might be a good place to start.

So, what do I dance about when I am not told what to make a dance about? Modern dance pioneer Doris Humphrey said "anything," and believed that the most trivial thing could make the most engaging dance, even a dying swan, *but* it must always take on great significance to the choreographer. She wrote:

> The choreographer must behave as though the theme were of the highest significance, for if he does not, the fire goes out, the piece becomes routine and the public will know that nothing has happened when it is finally on view. (Humphrey 28)

That being said, it is also pertinent to note here that Humphrey was somewhat of an elitist when it came to what to dance about. Although my copy of her text has become my personal "velveteen rabbit," I admittedly shun some of her elitist comments and associate them to her time, the newness of modern dance, and the passion these early moderns had for their work. Nevertheless, bigotry among these artists existed, and not just in artistic terms. For instance, although Isadora often insisted that she was a revolutionary fighting constantly for the oppressed (Duncan 10), historian Patricia Vertinsky wrote:

> At the same time, Isadora always followed her heart rather than her head in political as well as personal matters and in many respects remained wedded to an attitude of entitlement that was typical of her generation. Like Rudolf

Laban, she was vitriolic about jazz, "negro dancing" and its "convulsive sexuality" as demonstrated for example by Josephine Baker in her highly successful performances in Harlem and later at the *Folies Bergère* in Paris. Isadora's feminism excluded not only all people of color but also all those who failed to match the eugenic claims of racial hygiene. (Vertinsky 33)

Dance scholar Julia I. Foulkes also discusses the exclusionary politics of the early moderns toward ethnic bodies (more specifically Ruth St. Denis), whether they danced their own or the white modern aesthetic, as well as their negative attitude toward dance used for entertainment (Foulkes 2002). Knowledge of such attitudes dilutes the altruism we associate with the pioneers of modern dance—the rebels who fought against the rigid expectations and elitism of ballet. For instance, in a section of her book regarding source material, Humphrey addresses the commercial "independent choreographer," whom she painstakingly qualifies as one who works for money instead of art, either out of choice, or because it's the best they can do:

> The luxury of doing as they please is not for those hard-working and highly skilled directors…Nevertheless, the taint of commercialism pervades them all in varying degrees, and the inevitable necessity for conforming to the demands of the situation damages the individuality of the choreographer and possibly prevents a contribution which might otherwise be more genuine and imaginative…because there are certain personalities…who feel most comfortable in a setting *where they are told what to do* (my emphasis). To these individuals freedom is a frightening specter, shunned and unloved. Also, of course, there are choreographers who have no ideas of their own. (Humphrey 29)

Well, there you are. According to this philosophy, not only does someone like me spend a great deal of my artistic life working squarely within a field disdained by Humphrey (my hero), but I am also one of those "certain personalities" Humphrey refers to who is comfortable being "told what to do," which I admit to as a choreographer of musicals. According to Humphrey, working in musical theatre, (a field that carries the "taint of commercialism"), also causes me to miss opportunities to do authentic and imaginative work, either because I won't or I can't.

First of all, I revere Doris Humphrey unconditionally, so I harbor no bad feelings about her harsh assessment of popular art forms. Her legacy is an important part of my own development as a dance artist. However, as someone who works with concert dance forms as well as in musical theatre, I can only defend my proclivity for musical theatre choreography by saying that I love the cooperation between disciplines that is always in play within musicals. I prefer interpreting music that tells a story more than I prefer making dances any other way. Musical theatre dance is dependent upon its music. Like classic jazz dance, it exists *because* of its music. I love the music of musicals and like working within that dependency. I enjoy the "limitations" it often insists I work within, but I also relish the innumerable ways I can do that while expressing myself creatively. For me, the integration of so many art forms that is inherent in musical theatre, combined with its egalitarian and classless accessibility to a huge demographic, gets to the heart of things like nothing else can. And, maybe that is also the difference in a nut-shell: I am most concerned with "the heart" as a responder to art.

The dance hierarchy still exists today, and *that* fact is at the heart of why I am writing this book. In writing down the procedures I call upon to create musical theatre choreography, I hope to reveal the artistry, authenticity, and imagination needed to accomplish it effectively. I hope also to shed light on the ways it is like modern dance choreography, and when the two forms part ways. I am grateful to Humphrey and other "moderns" I have studied and danced with, but I have a profound problem with elitism of any kind, particularly when it is practiced by an assemblage of artists who exist because they despised and rebelled against the elitism of others. I ask only that we consider the possibility that what makes art *popular* is what also makes it meaningful and worthwhile. As a culture, a society, and as individuals, popular art has tremendous impact on who we are. It shapes us.

Having expressed myself thus, this (predominantly) musical theatre choreographer will now (paradoxically) discuss choreographic method differences between these two dance genres in their beginning stages to examine how certain concert choreography practices can be useful to an MT choreographer. For instance, how can beginning a dance *without* a clear idea and absolutely *no* boundaries be a very good thing?

A Method Of Starting Without A Method

In her book *The Creative Habit,* choreographer Twyla Tharp (discussing concert dance) suggests a variety of ways to develop an idea—possibilities she calls "scratching" for ideas. "Scratching is what you do when you can't wait for the thunderbolt to hit you," she says (98). She also feels that most artists should have a plan of action: "The most productive artists I know," she wrote, "have a plan in mind when they get down to work. They know what they want to accomplish, how to do it, and what to do if the process falls off track" (118). UNCG dance Professor Larry Lavender gave the best advice for someone with my background (i.e., need for control, know everything beforehand, don't leave anything to chance, etc.), and that is to *force* myself to work without any plan at all—just get into a room with my dancers and try things. Play around. Scratch for ideas. He insisted that I do not necessarily have to know anything when I begin except who my dancers are and that I might like to start making a dance.

Lavender also offers a few ideas on how to tweak the process such as, of course, the prompting of dancers to improvise movement phrases utilizing traditional tools, like dynamics, phrasing, design, etc. (Lavender and Sullivan 2008) or decisions about how much to, or not to, collaborate with my dancers on inventing movement ideas (Butterworth 2004). Manipulating space in unconventional ways to extend movement potential was a jolting exercise for someone used to making dances for already established scenic givens. Prompting my dancers with the implausible directive to use center stage as their "offstage" and to start the same dance again from there made my head spin a little, but my dancers loved the idea and gleefully dove into it headfirst! Also, structuring a dance without any accompaniment and then performing it to a variety of accompaniment choices changes a dance in profound ways that might not otherwise ever be known. For someone used to making dances that exist only *because* of the music, this prompt was the most interesting and fun for me to play with. My dancers loved becoming a part of this process of discovery, and I fancied how much freedom I was learning to work with and accept. The concept of starting to make a dance without an idea, musical accompaniment, or some other boundary was initially difficult for me, but I did it anyway. When I approach dances with this open-hearted attitude, or even only a glimmer of an idea, even in a musical, a dance begins to build itself in an unstoppable and inevitable way. Pieces gradually fall into place. Working with a variety of teachers who taught me to tackle projects in a variety of atypical ways, I came to trust that I have enough structural knowledge gained through study and experience to finesse random discoveries into tightly organized and cohesive movement statements. Structure again, but without preconceptions. Inspiration comes *from* activity, not waiting to be inspired *to create* an activity.

Clearly, the possible paths to a concert dance work are limitless, and in that way, making dances for the concert stage is more challenging than creating choreography for a specific musical play. Working on concert dances, however, gave me the knowledge and practice to carry over to my musical theatre choreography; I developed the confidence to loosen control, leave some things to chance and to allow more input from my dancers, which is endlessly inspiring. Tharp writes:

> It's tempting to try to rein in the unruliness of the creative process, especially at the start. Planning lets you impose order on the chaotic process of making

something new, but when it's taken too far you get locked into a status quo, and creative thinking is about breaking free from the status quo, even from one you made yourself....It's vital to know the difference between good planning and too much planning." (122).

By working in a medium that gives me limitless freedom, no "givens" and no limitations, I believe that, paradoxically, I am able to develop a deeper understanding of how to work more creatively within the tight musical theatre structure. Also, my concept about collaboration with my dancers has broadened, as well as how it feels to work against the traditional perspective of musical theatre choreographers as authoritarian figures. Because musical theatre dance is so closely tied to historical and highly specific stylistic expectations, choreographers of musicals most likely can never relinquish complete authority. If and when it is possible, however, there can be joy and fulfillment in allowing the voices of your colleagues to enter your work and enrich it.

In-Class Assignment. *Work through some free improvisation prompts exploring movement elements: space, time, force, stressing Laban's breakdown of movement dynamics. Gradually work into an "assignment" for a short solo dance study and also a group study that can be worked on in pairs or trios. Provide prompts for these studies to manipulate them in a variety of ways.*

Beginning Choreography For A Musical

Getting a new musical theatre project off the ground can either be an exhilarating time for me, or it can induce a state of self-doubting inertia. My state of mind is dependent upon the level of confidence I feel toward the material. Through experience, I know that my confidence will grow exponentially as I proceed through important stages of discovery. In collaboration with my director and designers, the concept will become clearly established and my vision of the end product will begin to take shape.

The first order of business is primarily a left-brain task of getting to know the material and beginning to organize it in my mind. Below are the pre-production steps I usually take to research and prepare a show for rehearsals. Know that your path will always be somewhat dependent upon the schedule of your collaborators and venue of employment. Subsequently, I will go on to discuss aspects of this process from my point of view.

Suggested order of activities to begin a new musical theatre choreography project.

This order is not written in stone, and many of these activities will be ongoing and will often overlap throughout the creative process. I usually begin by becoming familiar with music, but this is a personal choice. Reading the libretto first makes sense, too.

1. Music study:
   a. Listen to the music alone—don't think too much but note how you feel about it. If this is an original show, you may be listening to piano-only version of the songs that come directly from the composer; if not, use the cast recording, but be aware that the orchestration in your production may vary from the original, depending upon your orchestra size.
   b. Listen to all of the songs without the lyrics so that you hear and respond to accompaniment only; record those responses.
   c. List and analyze all of the songs in terms of type, purpose, etc.
   d. Plan, initially, which songs the choreographer will be responsible for. Often the director will want to stage some of the ballads or smaller numbers alone. This could change somewhat later.

2. Libretto study:
   a. Read the script alone.
   b. Listen to music again, this time thinking of it in context.
   c. Read the script inserting the songs appropriately.
   d. Create a scene/song breakdown for the show. Write up a plot summary and beginning analysis; if you are doing only the choreography, ask your director to share his analysis with you or collaborate on preparing it so your ideas are unified. (See plot analysis example in Chapter 1.)

3. Historical Study:
   a. Research the history of the show, original and subsequent productions, writer/composer/lyricist; artists working on original production, reviews written about it, and other information.
   b. Research the historical context of the play: time, place, cultural/social setting; customs of locale and period.
   c. Study the social and folk dances of the era, if appropriate and necessary.
   d. Gather images of whatever seems appropriate to the musical to help you to visualize the time period, social customs, landscape, architecture, artifacts, etc. In the past this part of the process was time consuming and less productive. Now with the internet (and YouTube), choreographers can continue to research easily before *and* during the process.

4. Initial Meetings:
   a. One on one meeting with **director**; discussions of style and overall vision.
   b. One on one meeting with **musical director**; discuss questions about score and orchestrations preliminary talk about dance numbers. This is a good time to ask about anything troubling, that you need assistance with or changes in the score you should know about.
   c. Preliminary production meetings to brainstorm concept or how to facilitate directorial vision.
   d. Meetings with **assistants** to discuss dance auditions; create announcements, requirements, and information to send out before auditions and during rehearsals.

5. Ongoing Meetings:
   a. With the director, choreographer, and designers meet until final designs have been approved.
   b. With the designer to finalize designs as far before the first rehearsal as possible. Stage manager can create a mock-up of the set and stage placement of furniture or set pieces can be established.
   c. With the prop master to review a preliminary list of props. Props will also be added by the director and choreographer during the initial staging rehearsals but the production team will set a deadline for new props to be added. Normally, this is after all the creative work is set and rehearsals move into the clean and run stage.

To be sure, when working to meet deadlines and stay within budgets, employers will expect me to employ the most efficient and businesslike qualities. In such situations being a quick study is important, and making decisions regarding concept and style will rely more on previous knowledge of the musical or type of musical. Skill for crafting dances becomes very important now, and the ability to create effective movement following a more formulaic process allows me to generate work effectively and quickly in order to complete the task in a limited amount of time. Time, on the other hand, allows an artist to use the creative process to explore and discover. When time is not available, I must rely on past research and have less chance to examine and work with new dance vocabularies and styles that are outside of my knowledge base. I no longer jump into projects empty-handed or armed only with the obvious, a luxury I did not possess at the beginning of my career. I know that my students will often be in the position of creating movement for a musical in a week—or two if they are lucky—as will many young choreographers who are thankful for a job. Whether they can *construct* a dance only from the materials stored in their cache of choreographic knowledge and experience (certainly not a bad thing to do, and often necessary), or grant themselves the freedom to set a few malleable boundaries and *allow* the dance to take shape under their guidance and moment to moment inspiration, is dependent upon time, which is dependent upon who they are working for. Regardless of the conditions of the job, each one is a valuable learning experience.

A pragmatic choreographer will be ready to embrace either situation, and with each experience continue to refine his/her craft, become more confident, and with luck, develop a rich artistic imagination. However, ample time given to the creative process is important to perfecting and polishing the elements of one's craft in order to learn how to generate a product that shows a level of sophistication in theme, structure, and content. Taking time early in my career as I developed choreographic methods assured my facility with them later. This facility in crafting dances ensures the ability to work quickly and effectively when necessary. Thankfully, not all productions are like summer stock and have only a week to set staging and rehearse. Academic theatre gives me longer periods of time during which I can better discover, choose, craft, refine, and polish my choreography. In musicals, time spent crafting small individual moments of a large ensemble piece is time spent discovering seemingly insignificant kernels of physical, musical, and dramatic ideas (that may have otherwise been overlooked or discarded) into elements that increase and intensify the amount and type of information you offer an audience, improving the overall artistry of the storytelling. Although no one seems to know for sure who originally coined the phrase, "God is in the detail," I like to think of it as my own personal mantra, in action if not in word. As many theatre professionals have, I had to grow into it through trial and error and learning along the way; and that is why making specific choices and working for detail is something I try hard to get across to my students. To begin with this one important philosophy and learn at least this one thing from *my* experience may put them many jumps ahead of the game. Undertaking these developmental and information-gathering stages in a less time-driven and more creative fashion is the fun part of my work spent in collaboration with my colleagues.

But more on detail will come in time. First things first and, for me, the first thing that draws me into a new musical theatre project is, inevitably, the music.

Inspiration From The Composer And Lyricist

When beginning a new directing or choreography project for musicals, before anything else I listen to the music. Whether it is an established play with a cast recording or an original work with limited resources, my personal entry into the world of a musical is through its music, and my initial response to it will normally deepen as my familiarity with it increases. Despite the move to the primacy of the book that began with *Show Boat*, it is the score of a musical that I initially fall in love with and that takes me on the story's emotional journey. In the modern musical the music *serves* the story, but without the music the story is never as personal, affecting, complete, or compelling. The music helps me relate to a work in a more intimate way, even if the story is completely foreign to my own life experience.

My initial encounter with the Charles Strouse/Stephen Schwartz score of the musical *Rags* (1986), for instance, exemplifies these ideas as it was originally the score that was the reason I chose to work on that musical rather than my simpatico with the story. The libretto of *Rags* (Stein, 1986) follows a young Russian immigrant woman and her son on their fantastic journey in a new world beginning with her ocean voyage to Ellis Island, working in a sweatshop in New York, enduring the death of her friend in the Triangle Factory Fire, the ultimate estrangement from her politically corrupt husband, and an espousal of her own beliefs. As a member of a much later and more entitled generation, the most immediate way I had to relate to the loss, fear and isolation suffered by turn of the century immigrants traveling to America and depicted in Joe Stein's libretto for this musical was through the score. Rebecca's song on the deck of the ship that carried her to Ellis Island, "Children of the Wind," soundly captures the enormity of her loss of homeland, of the aloneness and vulnerability she and her son experienced in their passage, of her hopes for their future and, most compelling for me, of her fear as a young mother of going alone with her son to a place that would be stripped of any of the familiarity or the close relationships of her native country (see fig. 5). But her vision of America, though later thwarted, was one filled with extraordinary hopefulness, a feeling most likely shared by the thousands of others traveling to America during that time. It is interesting that Strouse and Schwartz chose to write this song not as a standard 32 bar theatre song, but in the verse/refrain structure closer to the traditional popular song format. There are three melodies, however, combined in the following format: verse, verse, chorus (or refrain), bridge, chorus. The halting, jerky and somewhat disjointed melodies of the first two verses that make up "Children of the Wind" support Rebecca's stream of consciousness memories of the fear and despair that drove her from her homeland and that continue to "haunt her dreams" (Strouse and Schwartz, 1986 and 1991).

Figure 5. Using projections to evoke history in *Rags*. Elon University Archives, 2002.

In the Beginning...

The profound sense of loss, as well as the pride and hope Rebecca feels, are both present in the soaring and moving melody of the repeated refrains: the first time for the loss of her previously lived background and pride in the traditions of her former life and the second for the hope she feels that she and her family will now be safe and free. These two choruses are separated by a "bridge," or a new melody, which moves us from the despair of her memories to the hope she has for her future. I was able to enter into the psychological and emotional realities of her story fully because of this song, so I allowed it to continue to guide me throughout the process. I wanted my cast and our audiences to relate to *Rags* with that same sense of understanding and empathy; therefore, the choices I made throughout the creative process were always guided by my own initial sense of connection to *that* story, Rebecca's story—a story remarkably similar to my grandparents' stories. But, although these stories resulted in my own present reality as an American citizen, they had little to do with me and my present life circumstances, so I relied on the music to move me from an intellectual understanding to an emotional connection.

Assignment: *Bring a song from a musical in to class. This should be a song that you know well, that drew you in some way toward a strong passion or connection you have with the story of the musical it is in. Play it for the class and describe for them the structure of the song, what it is saying, and how you relate to it.*

Cementing The Story

My next steps are normally to 1) read the libretto alone, 2) listen to the music again apart from the libretto, keeping the context of the songs in mind, and 3) listen again to the score *while* performing a closer reading of the libretto, which demands that I enter into the vision of the librettist more purposefully and experience the story in a more holistic way. I try to allow myself to have an overall response during this first experience of reading and listening, so I do not dwell on any one part or aspect of the script, but read and listen to it in real time and with attention to how I am responding to the story and what moments stand out to me, stay with me or affect me the most deeply. Inevitably, I will visualize what I am reading. Like many visual artists, it is impossible for me not to see things in my head as I listen or read; it is the primary way in which I experience the world. I allow the visualizations to occur, but do not write them down or make special notes of them at this point. I find they will return when they are strong enough or feel "right" enough. Responses will mature and morph as I learn more about the material, the cast, the space, etc., so now is the time for me, as the choreographer, to simply experience the work and notice what I am feeling and learning about it.

I have always known that the immigrant experience determined my own existence and my personal history, but it was only as I became more and more familiar with this score and then experienced it as an extension of the characters in *Rags* and their stories, that I was able to truly connect emotionally to what my grandparents experienced in order to live in America. I listened to the score over and over after reading the libretto and realized that I was discovering points of entry into that world through *all* of the songs, not just "Children of the Wind." I uncovered my own family's connections to the material by recollecting my relatives' stories and shared remembrances of their early days in America. I found myself wishing I had asked them more questions as I was growing up and I became drawn to the Ellis Island website, researching it for more information about my own background. Through this masterpiece of a score I discovered empathy and points of entry. I was careful to allow those early feelings to continue to guide the course of my directorial and choreographic journey.

Finally, since I was also the director of this production, I was (naturally) in sympathy with—and readily supported—my major choreographic choices for all the songs. (I love when that happens!) In this case, I was hoping to create a personal link to the epic nature of this story with the use of projections. Covering a stage-width semi-circular cyclorama and huge fragmented sections of stretched cloth, were photographs of immigrants taken throughout the early part of the 19th century. These projections were employed primarily during the musical numbers throughout the show in order to "up" the emotional ante in an attempt to elicit more audience empathy for the story and for the characters. Seeing factual historical images of early American immigrants while the actors were reliving their experiences in song was a powerful emotional reminder to the audience of the poverty, backbreaking labor and many other arduous conditions of struggle of many of their own ancestors. Sentimental? Well, yes, admittedly so but, like Oscar Hammerstein, I believe "There's nothing wrong with sentiment. …The things people are sentimental about are the fundamental things in life" (Hammerstein II quoted in Kislan 142). Unless an artist has become so jaded that he works only in order to complete a task, it is really the artist's *feelings* and sense of self that initiate a work and that compel an artist to create.

I believe the intellect guides the *process* of creation, but what guides the intellect is the artist's emotional connection to what is being created. The heart must always keep beating to keep the whole body alive. It can happen, of course, after many years of working in the arts or of learning to create "on demand" that, at times, the passion will seem lessened. In my experience, this happens but only *until* I actually begin to work on the project. Regardless of an occasional initial sense of apathy or ennui, the drive to create always returns upon engaging with the material. As a director and choreographer, once I know I will be involved creatively with certain material, I tune into it in a highly personal way. Only after my initial gut response has been recognized, and lived with long enough to determine an overall vision for the show, do I feel it is safe to fully engage my intellect/technique/craft and allow the structural work to begin. The initial vision must remain clear enough, and feel "right" enough, to hold firmly in place throughout the chaos inherent in the ensuing collaborations, choice-making, and staging of a musical production.

Assignments – Chapter 2

<u>Out of Class Assignment</u>

1. Working with your assigned musical, listen to the score (as many times as you like).

2. Read the libretto again, taking notice of stage directions and notes given by the librettist, whether you decide to use them or not.

3. Listen to the score **as** you read the libretto, jotting down any thoughts you have as you read. During or after this listening/reading assignment, free-write your thoughts about the show and what you hear in the score and how it affects you emotionally. What images does it conjure? What is your connection to it? What are elements you feel are important to address as the choreographer?

Chapter 3
A Brand New World
Working With The Director's Overall Vision

Assuming I am acting as choreographer only and am not also directing a production, after an initial analysis of the libretto and before beginning to work with the songs in any specific way, I meet with the director and we talk about that "c" word…or the director's *concept*. Sometimes I meet with the director and scenic designer as they are brainstorming ideas, or sometimes I will meet later with just the director. A concept, at least the way I think of it, has to do with the director's overall vision for the show, its treatment, its *mise en scéne*. This usually entails *all of the visual aspects* of a stage show and how they will be brought together to tell the story. Directors must be able to articulate their initial ideas to the musical director, the choreographer, and all of the designers. Just as importantly, they must also be good at listening to their collaborators' ideas with an open heart and mind and, when appropriate, use those ideas to enhance their own. If you have already done your own analysis of the show, you will most likely have begun to visualize it in your own way. If you are lucky, it will jive with your director's and designer's visions, but if it does not, you will need to put it aside until you have an opportunity to direct the show yourself.

During production meetings at the beginning of the process, designers will usually present preliminary sketches for costumes and scenic elements so that everyone's earliest reactions to the play can enter the discussion. This is the time for choreographers to present ideas and brainstorm with all of the collaborators. During these early meetings, the concept will begin to morph and transform into what it will ultimately become as the director leads his collaborators to a meeting of the minds. The director fashions the final vision by integrating her ideas with her collaborators and approving all completed designs to make certain each serves that vision. The director then keeps watch that all collaborators remain consistent throughout the creative process. It may take several brainstorming sessions to arrive at something everyone feels good about, but this is necessary time spent making certain that everyone is on the same page and the entire artistic staff has enough information to move ahead.

Visualizing a Show

Andrew Lloyd Webber's *Evita* opened first in London in 1978. It was wildly successful but according to Scott Miller's analysis of Evita, "London critics complained that the show was too infatuated with Eva." He went on to explain that the following year and some months later, the production that Hal Prince directed for its American debut "went too far the other way and he took all the warmth and emotion out of the story, while also expanding and developing the character of Che from anonymous Argentine to the world-famous Marxist revolutionary" (2010, para.: "What's New, Buenos Aires?"). Miller characterizes the production as being as impenetrable and inaccessible as she was, and so it was difficult for the audience to know what they should feel about Eva Peron. In her review of a national touring production of director Michael Grandage's 2012 revival of Evita, writer Sharon Eberson states that Grandage and his choreographer Rob Ashford "have wiped away the sheen from the original version…turned down the lights to a candle's glow and infused the tango – or its attitude – into almost every move. The adoring and aggrieved masses are most often seen as shadowy figures in a literal haze on stage or as a black and white screen presence" (Eberson *Pittsburgh Post-Gazette*).

The above paragraph cites three different productions of the same musical that interpret the story in three distinct ways. If you used Frankel's element "Story" and stated the story in one sentence, it might be quite different for each of these productions, although the plot analysis and synopsis of the play would be the same. Prince stated that he felt the story was about media manipulation of public opinion (quoted in Eberson). For him, Che was a hot-headed revolutionary, but in Grandage's production he was Everyman—one of the Argentine masses. Most pertinent to our discussion is the choreographer's use of the tango, which is a choice that resonated with me and affected my overall feeling of Grandage's production. The sound and the use of the tango throughout the production, while not necessary to the telling of the story, not only infuses the production with a feeling of sexuality and seduction, which parallels Evita's seduction of men and the Argentinian people, but places the audience squarely in the lap of the proletariat. The tango originated in the lower class districts of cities such as Buenos Aires, so using this throughout the play grounds Evita as having originated there herself and reminds us constantly of her essential nature. Grandage and Ashford use this theme whenever possible, even in unlikely places, creating a powerful unity of sound and image that was deeply affecting, unlike the glossy veneer of Prince and Fuller's *Evita*.

The song "The Art of the Possible," depicts the strategies of military figures as they rise to political power. As envisioned by Prince and Fuller, the number was a game of musical chairs performed by a group of Generals who each begin sitting onstage in a rocking chair; the number ends with only Perón left onstage. Clever, well…even a brilliant approach to this moment because after each chair was removed from the stage the tempo of the music became a bit faster until at the end, it seemed like a frantic last ditch struggle for the win. The increasing tempos also kept a potentially repetitive and low energy song from going on too long. In the Grandage revival, Ashford's staging began each verse with the political figures moving around the space in military-like fashion and ended with two of the men in a tango-influenced battle, after which one was defeated and left the stage. This motif repeated in like fashion until only Perón was left. Adding to that was a reconfiguring of the orchestration from a brassy militaristic rendering of the song to a slower more eerily twisted tango. This complete rhythmic change turns the song into something more subversive and sinister—again making you feel as well as know what is happening. This concept was also a brilliant idea, and one that stayed true to and developed the creative team's overall vision for the production.

Abstracting the Visual

As director/choreographer for *Jane Eyre, the Musical* (Caird and Gordon 2000), before meeting with our creative team, my choreographer brain met first with my director brain to hash out and brainstorm my initial responses to the play. After that somewhat "schizo" session, I put my *entire* head together with scenic designer Dale Becherer before anyone else because I knew the most important problem to solve had to do with the musical's numerous locations. Not only would a realistic treatment of this play be expensive and require a great deal of man-power to accomplish, but it would also halt the flow of the show throughout. As is my custom, I was drawn to this show by its music, so by the time I sat down with the designer, I was emotionally and intellectually connected to the script and score. I instinctively knew that our production had to take place on a unit set that allowed for swift movement from one locale to the next; it had to have a number of levels to allow for an ample variety of staging possibilities to facilitate our changing environments quickly and easily. Most importantly, I saw Jane herself, though reserved on the outside, as an internally lyrical creature whose journey through life, while indirect and circuitous with mysterious and unexpected outcomes, was always traveled with a sense of freedom, purpose, and grace. Therefore, the multi-leveled unit set we decided upon to facilitate the flow of the show had to be constructed only with graceful and fluid curves. I envisioned Jane as a bird, flying in swift, circular patterns. So, when Dale asked me to take a crayon and "draw how I felt" it was indeed filled with sweeping curves and an overriding sense of lyricism—in the musical sense of being melodic, broad, emotional, and lush (see fig. 6).

Figure 6. Unit set for *Jane Eyre, the musical.* Elon University Archives, 2005.

    Finally, we decided the overall treatment would be abstract rather than realistic or representational, whereas realistic furniture pieces would be used to create the myriad places called for. These scenic elements "suggested" specific environments and lighting took on a more important role in defining place. Costume and property elements had a more realistic aesthetic than any other area and, except for one complete change, costumes were constructed to be readily modified for different looks, particularly for the ensemble. The ensemble was an ongoing and abstract unifying element in the show as each member took on a wide number of personages throughout the course of the play. They moved through songs and scenes as would a Greek Chorus, carrying out my "story theatre" aesthetic and commenting on or becoming a part of the action. They not only changed character frequently, but became the internal workings of Jane's mind in passionate musical passages. I was able to present them in a highly theatrical fashion through lighting invention and placement on our abstracted architectural set, which provided me with a variety of levels and looks. While there is no real technical dance in the show, aside from a fully staged ballroom waltz sequence, there is an abundance of musical staging, which requires a choreographer's sensibilities. I would be hard-pressed to say where the director's work ended and the choreographer's began, making it a perfect concept vehicle for a director/choreographer (see figs. 7-9).

Of course, this is not an original concept in staging a musical. Choreographer Michael Bennett is known for his innovations in regard to this kind of cinematic, thoroughly connected staging in shows such as *Dreamgirls,* which used Plexiglas towers that Bennett moved from scene to scene, forming a series of configurations throughout the show to create abstract environments for the action. Instead of only choreographing the performers in the space, he also choreographed the set. Bennett's ideas and notions regarding cinematic staging went into formulating our own abstract and lyrical concept for *Jane Eyre*. It is thought that Bennett was most influenced by Jerome Robbins, who always created movement to serve the production as a whole or as a part of the storytelling. Biographer Kevin Kelly wrote, "What Michael Bennett perceived early in Robbins' work was totality, all the sums of a given piece adding to a unified whole" (37-38). We will take a closer look at Robbins in just a bit.

Figure 7. Ensemble as narrators, characters, and symbolic aspects of main characters in *Jane Eyre, the musical.* Elon University Archives, 2005.

Figure 8. The ensemble as the tormented Bertha's damaged mind in *Jane Eyre, the musical.* Elon University Archives. 2005.

Figure 9. Close up of ensemble. *Jane Eyre, the musical.* Elon University Archives, 2005.

The understanding of concept is all important because it is the concept that will determine the style of production, and both dance and staging carry a great majority of that style. The choreographer needs to have this information the first time she or he enters a dance studio alone to improvise.

Bob Fosse's Choreographic Style

When we think of famous MT choreographers we generally associate them with a personal style of movement that becomes easier to recognize the more often we see them dance or view their dances. To some extent all dance artists retain their personal movement style in all of their work. A choreographer's *personal style vs. use of appropriate historical or musical style of movement* might be examined on a kind of continuum. How much of one's own personal style is willing to adapt and even mutate to suit the demands of a particular production, or are there styles so distinctive the choreographer would always be recognized by the movement?

Obviously, one choreographer who is an answer to this latter question is the great Bob Fosse, whose style became progressively distinctive during his career, so much so that even today, almost 60 years after choreographing his first Broadway show, his name is synonymous with the elements of his choreography. Fosse's earliest work, such as the small section of the dance "From This Moment On" he was charged to choreograph in the film *Kiss Me Kate* ("From This Moment On," 1953) and his work on the film *White Christmas*, show a strong Jack Cole influence because he was still a young dance performer who had not yet discovered a great deal about himself as a choreographer. Cole was a part of Fosse, so that influence was always there, the isolations and the powerful and earthbound modern jazz dance of the 1940s and 50s—earthbound, but with great *ballon* when airborne. As Fosse developed, however, his aesthetic developed as well, and ultimately dominated all aspects of his movement style. Even though his first few Broadway shows were not yet completely "uniquely Fosse," his style could be seen beginning to take shape in *Pajama Game* in the iconic "Steam Heat" number ("Steam Heat" 1954), and also in Gwen Verdon's quirky movements for "Whatever Lola Wants" in *Damn Yankees* ("Whatever Lola Wants" 1958).

I was in college when Fosse's choreography started to be thought of as "the Fosse style" and the filming of *Sweet Charity* telegraphed his aesthetic to the world. It was becoming more and more apparent that Gwen Verdon, his muse, was helping him discover and fully develop it. Shows like *Pippin* and *Cabaret* developed cult followings of people who could not get enough of his highly idiosyncratic movement choices. Many of the shows he did from that time on, such as *Pippin, Dancin'* and *Chicago*, are so indelibly marked by his style they become one and the same. Minimalistic, staccato movements, copious use of isolations, angularity, props, hats, pigeon-toed leg positions, and androgynous deadpan sexuality came to characterize his work and define Fosse's version of *Chicago*. After first seeing *Chicago*, I wouldn't say I thought very much about its theme or message. My mind's eye, on the other hand, was immersed with images of Fosse's movement and his treatment of the ensemble. As a director/choreographer his personal movement proclivities became his "concept," his *mise en scène*; Fosse's personal style became his way of telling the story. Fosse's choreography can be brazen and even bawdy, but utterly elegant in its absolute precision and understated (but thorough) reliance on technique and physical control. I believe it is this paradox that many find irresistible. Regarding *Chicago*, it was encouraging when Rob Marshall was chosen to choreograph the film version, if only to demonstrate that the show itself is still open to interpretation. It was still good to see Fosse's influence in the choreography, however, and difficult to imagine this show without it.

Jerome Robbins' Choreographic Style

Dissimilar to Fosse in respect to styling his choreography was Jerome Robbins. For each show that Robbins choreographed, he defined a new movement vernacular based not only on the period setting of the musical but for the various characters depicted in it. New York Times critic, Ann Kisselgoff wrote: "[His] genius for capturing the essence of an age was the Robbins' signature" (Kisselgoff 1998). But, unique to Robbins, after he dealt with the specifics of the time and place and situation, he incorporated into the form and dynamics of the movements the psychology and emotional realities of the characters performing the dance. Even in his earliest musicals, *On the Town* and *Wonderful Town,* both of which he created with composer Leonard Bernstein and lyricists Betty Comden and Adolph Green, his choreography attended to the inner life of the characters as well as the external realities of the script. But of course, all of his knowledge, the many small innovations he made along the way, and his own artistic maturity came together in *West Side Story*, which so integrated dance into the story, the same story can no longer be told without it. Just as the music is integral to telling the story of *West Side Story*, so is the dance. It outwardly describes every aspect of the characters' internal journeys. One can watch the characters dancing the number *Cool* without hearing the song, and know their state of mind and the extent of their anxiety. Robbins himself said, "The possibilities of the human body are endless. Why not use them all? Why limit ourselves to a set language which, in spite of its good qualities, is no longer fit to express the feelings and problems of today?" (Conrad 223).[1] Why not use them all….indeed?

Many of our distinguished musical theatre choreographers, like Robbins, have movement proclivities that are more malleable than Fosse and can adapt more easily to other styles of movement. Fosse was an astonishing exception who saw the world in the abstract and chose vehicles that not only work in the abstract but are more powerful because of it. It is difficult for me to envision what the classic *Fiddler on the Roof* might have been with Fosse's fully developed style, or many of the shows from the golden age for that matter. It is even possible that Fosse didn't begin coming completely into his own until after that period when the narrative in shows was sometimes more loosely structured.

---

[1] Robbins quoted by Conrad from *World Theatre,* Winter 1959-60, p. 315.

Regardless of choreographic styles, musical theatre is a popular art form that has always been both a product and a reflection of its times, good or bad. Since minstrelsy in the early 19th century through operetta and musical comedy, through the upshots of America's heavy immigration culture at the turn of the century to *Oklahoma!,* which buffered the isolating effect of WWII in the 1940s, and from *Hair's* anti-establishment statement in the '60s to *Rent's* message of inclusivity in the '90s, musical styles change with the times they are examining. Even when it tells stories about days gone by, the musical will still reflect the sensibilities of the time in which it is written. When we teach musical theatre dance, we include social and folk dances because they will show up and morph themselves time and time again in countless musicals to mark an era and often to express the authenticity of the music. In the musicals, *Rags, Ragtime,* and *Titanic,* ragtime and ragtime-inspired choreography helps to set the place and time and to tell the story, as do production numbers such as "The Farmer and the Cowman" in *Oklahoma,* "The Bottle Dance" in *Fiddler On The Roof,* "The Dance at the Gym" in *West Side Story,* and the eerily compelling atmosphere of "Come Spirit, Come Charm," from *The Secret Garden.*

So, unless you are a "Fosse," meaning that unless you are marked by the universe with a thoroughly charismatic, innovative, and distinctive style of movement that can always work in the abstract, you will need to be proficient with as many musical and dance styles as possible. But just one more note: in case you *are* the next Fosse, and you well may be, I in no way want to discourage that. So while you are gathering knowledge about more derivative movement and are developing your abilities to make your choreography reflect the inner and outer life of the character, continue always to experiment with your own movement proclivities and test them often.

Assignments – Chapter 3

In-Class Assignment

Continue to free improvise but begin to improvise to a variety of styles of music, allowing your body to take on the feeling of the music and notice how it guides your body to move. Also begin to notice if you repeat similar movements, patterns, or gestures often—or have a tendency to use levels a great deal—or not at all—or you prefer leg gestures or jumps—or are you stuck on turns? How much do you use isolations? Are your movements predominantly staccato and precise or lyrical and flowing? Jot down your observations and continue to tune into your personal proclivities when you dance.

Out of Class Assignments

1. Take your time in the studio to uncover the various aspects of your natural, preferred way of moving and write up a description, create a drawing, or make a list of descriptive words that describe your style of dancing. Develop your ideas and think things through.

2. Partner with a classmate and do the same assignment based on each other's style. Don't share your thoughts until after both phases of the assignment have been completed. You will hand these in to your instructor.

3. Based on the play assigned to them, each student will prepare for a mentoring meeting with their instructor to discuss a concept or vision for that production. Students should enter the meeting with thoughts and ideas of their own, based on their initial reactions to the material. This should be a mentoring meeting where they will collaborate on issues of concept and style, overall and, more specifically, with 2 or 3 of the musical numbers. Choreographers should be thoroughly prepared for these preliminary discussions and might also think about their own personal style and how that may enter into the production or how they may need to work against it.

Chapter 4

Gotta Find My Purpose
Why is *This* Song in *This* Musical in *This* Spot?

Analyzing musicals can and should use the same elements as straight play analysis; the same elements evolved from early methods of play analysis in ancient Greece. According to Milly S. Barranger's text, *Understanding Plays,* these elements have traditionally encompassed conventions used by playwrights to portray the human condition. They are *plot, action, character, meaning, language, spectacle, space, and time* (5). Because musicals integrate additional elements, however, Baranger's analysis must be expanded to accommodate them. Another text that devotes separate chapters to both analyzing and interpreting the musical is *Staging Musical Theatre: A complete guide for directors, choreographers, and producers* by Elaine and Deborah Novak. This book covers a great deal of the nuts and bolts of the minutia involved in directing or mounting musicals. For musicals, the Novaks delineate the same elements as Barranger but substitute the term "thoughts" for "meaning" and separate "language" into two categories: "analyzing the words of the dialogue," and "analyzing the music, songs and dances," a good call as each of these components—dialogue, music, songs and dances—are all part of the language of a musical. The Novaks also change the category "spectacle" to "spectacle and sound" but stop there and actually address space and time as part of their earlier research on the history of the musical, as mentioned above (Novak and Novak 14-27).

Writing the Broadway Musical by Aaron Frankel, which I first refer to in Chapter 1, is a text on the craft of writing musicals that has been the most beneficial to me in learning to analyze librettos. Frankel is a well-known and highly respected name in both academia and the professional theatre world and his text, originally written in the 1970s and updated in 2000, is a comprehensive and knowledgeable lesson in libretto analysis. Reading it in total, and referring back to it when working, ensures aspiring choreographers that Frankel's insights to understanding significant aspects of libretto writing will become part of their own knowledge base.

When Frankel analyzes the play elements of a musical, like the Novaks, he changes certain terms to better describe the make-up of a libretto. Frankel's categories are *action, character, situation, time and place, dance, dialogue, sum: plot*. Plot, rather than being a separate category, is what results from a playwright's unique arrangement of all the other elements. The following table lays out three different ways of considering structural elements when analyzing a musical using Baranger's play elements as a basis. My own list tweaks Frankel's a bit further, particularly to specify the "languages" present in musicals (see table 1).

BARRANGER	ACTION	TIME	CHARACTER	MEANING	LANGUAGE	SPECTACLE	SPACE	PLOT
NOVAKS	ACTION		CHARACTER	THOUGHTS	WORDS MUSIC SONGS DANCES	SPECTACLE AND SOUND		PLOT
FRANKEL	ACTION	TIME	CHARACTER	SITUATION	DIALOGUE	DANCE	PLACE	*SUM*: PLOT
SABO	ACTION/ STAGING	TIME	CHARACTER	PURPOSE/ MEANING	DIALOGUE/ SONG/ STAGING/ DANCE	DANCE	PLACE	*SUM*: PLOT

Table 1. Comparison of Elements used in Play and Libretto Analysis

Like Frankel, I see plot as being revealed through the sum of these other elements. Each of these other elements must also be studied in depth, as well, so that the choreographer enters every rehearsal with a clear understanding of the time, place, what motivates each character, what they say to each other, what they sing, and what each song and scene means.

In the integrated musical, each song has a specific purpose (or meaning) that serves the story being told. Most are fairly obvious and fall into one or more of the following categories:

- To act as exposition. (Introduce and give context to characters, situation, place, time, and purpose.)

- To establish/reveal character. (Introduce or give information about the character or characters important to plot development.)

- To establish/reveal relationship. (Introduce or give information about the characters' relationships to each other important to plot development.)

- To establish/reveal situation. (Establish and give information about situations that are relevant to the plot.)

- To establish the environment. (Create and emphasize the place, time, and other aspects of environment, establishing & giving context to the plot.)

- To create a specific mood or atmosphere/to foreshadow an important event to plot development. (Prepare the audience for, and give weight to, an upcoming event.)

- To further the plot. (The song or dance results in the plot moving forward to the next stage of its development, such as rising action, climax, falling action, denouement, or resolution.)

Be careful not to mistake the way a song is written for its purpose, such as to tell a story, add humor or comedy, add spectacle, etc., and look for it to fulfill one of the intentions listed above. Other things such as "to tell a story," are normally encompassed in one of the ideas listed above, and refer really to the *way* the song is written, not its purpose. One might tell a story, for instance, that further defines a character, and that same song might be written and delivered in a humorous manner, such as Sipos' song "Perspective" from *She Loves Me*. *West Side Story's* "America" certainly provides an entertaining song and dance interlude between "Maria" and the balcony scene, but more importantly, it gives us information about the Shark women, allows us to become more familiar and sympathetic toward Anita, which increases the pathos later in the play, and it keeps the ethnic tension fresh in our minds as we witness the unfolding of the story of forbidden love between Tony and Maria. Thus, even if the tone of a number is particularly upbeat and devised that way because it would help the pacing or likeability of the musical, it actually needs to be capable of more than that; the bottom line is that in some way, each song must continue to tell the story. Although some composers and librettists were experimenting with integration before *Oklahoma!*, (as in the Princess Musicals, *Show Boat*, *Pal Joey*), most early musicals and operettas included spectacle numbers that had nothing to do with the plot, or comic scenes added strictly to break up the evening, lighten the mood, or cover a scene change. Now, however, it is expected that within each song, every gesture or dance movement should be motivated and devised to serve the story, as well as seem natural and completely appropriate for the character executing it. In modern dance or other concert dance forms, this close attention to motivated movement is most applicable when the choreography is structured as a narrative with specific characterizations built into the work, such as in *The Nutcracker,* DeMille's *Fall River Legend,* or Graham's *Cave of the Heart*. In musical theatre, however, not only should the movement embody the emotional, psychological, and appropriate historical physicality of the character, but it should *always* contribute to the telling of the story in at least one of the ways listed above.

Deciding upon the purpose of the song

Once a choreographer begins thinking about purpose and nuance within a song, this next organizational and categorizing step is relatively easy. I find it useful to walk through the entire show notating the identifying elements of each scene, the accompanying song, the list of characters singing and /or dancing in the song, and its purpose. Excerpts from my scene/song breakdowns of the musicals *She Loves Me* (Masteroff, Bock, Harnick, 1963) and *110 In The Shade* shown below represent a continuation of the process of plot analysis begun in Chapter 1 and stress the importance of analyzing each moment of a play for specific details. Scene 1 information for *She Loves Me* includes the purpose of the song "Good Morning, Good Day" (*why*), its function as exposition (*what*), the time (*when*), place (*where*) and the introduction of the characters (*who*). Note that exposition for *She Loves Me* is given in only this one song, whereas the exposition given in Scene 1 of *110 in the Shade* occurs in a sequence of three songs and two extended dialogue sections.

SHE LOVES ME
Scene Breakdown
Act 1, Scene 1

SCENE 1:
The Shop Exterior. The front exterior of Maraczek's Parfumerie. A city in Europe. The 1930's. Early morning of a mid-summer day. We need to be able to see a storefront window display. Arpad must ride in on a bicycle, possibly circle the set, or go offstage and reenter.

OPENING SCENE/SONG (1-1-13 to 1-1-19): "Good Morning, Good Day"— ARPAD, SIPOS, KODALY, MS. RITTER, GEORG, MARACZEK.

PURPOSE: *This song provides exposition about the main characters, introducing them and providing background information on each. It also sets the lighthearted, romantic mood of the play and provides information about place and season of the year, which gives the audience a point of reference for the future move from summer to Christmas time. After the song: characters move into the shop for the beginning of a new workday.*

In my breakdown above, I include all of the information given in the libretto. It is fairly straightforward and includes a general time and place, a specific time and place, the characters, and the purpose. After production meetings and further decisions are made, specific details about city, time, year, etc., will be made that will further specify these initial givens and therefore modify my documentation.

As stated earlier, the opening sequence of *110 In the Shade* contains *three* songs that introduce the characters, give us necessary exposition, and set the plot in motion (see Ch. 1, 4-7). These songs are cushioned between two stretches of dialogue: the first facilitates the transition from the introduction of File and the townspeople and the overall conflict of the play and the next stretch of dialogue establishes the family unit and the solution to Lizzie's impending spinsterhood as the play's super objective. Below is my breakdown of that sequence. Notice that I include notes of technical elements I feel necessary to communicate to my collaborators. As rehearsals progress, precise casting of ensemble scenes and songs will be determined and communicated to the team, as well.

---

110 In the Shade
Scene Breakdown (Opening sequence of songs)
Act 1, Scene 1

The Depot before sunrise, with a jewel-blue sky silhouetting the station, the sign that says THREE POINT, and the water tank of the Texas & Redrock Railroad.

SCENE INTO SONG (1-1-1 to 1-1-2): FILE, TOBY, TOBY III, PHIL MACKEY. TOWNSPEOPLE enter during song. Toby III, the stationmaster's grandson, is sitting on a bench stage left playing the harmonica. File, the sheriff, enters from the jailhouse. PHIL MACKEY is dozing on the park type bench outside a building front stage left.

SONG: "Another Hot Day"– FILE, TOWNSPEOPLE, except six or seven of them who are on the train, including Lizzie. Also, not in the number are H.C., Noah, Jim, and Starbuck.

This song gives background information and states the Townspeople's objective for the show, to see an end to the drought. Everyone's, that is, except the Curry family's, which is to get Lizzie a husband. We meet File and most of the townspeople. It is important to introduce the sense of family and community in this song as well as to individualize the townspeople as much as possible. Adding these elements will give the town a face and increase pathos for their plight and credibility to their easy acceptance of Starbuck in the third scene. We learn that the time is in the mid-1930s and the place a small established Texas railroad town that is going through a time of impending crisis.

After song:
SCENE INTO NEXT SONG (1-1-3 to 1-1-5): FILE, JIM. Toby exits into depot and most townspeople leave except those waiting for the train, Jim runs on and begins next song as H.C. and Noah enter behind him.

> SONG: "Lizzie's Coming Home" – JIM, H.C., NOAH and 8 TOWNSPEOPLE.
>
> **PURPOSE:** *This song gives us a humorous and upbeat introduction to the Curry men, Lizzie's father and 2 brothers, and foreshadows Lizzie's entrance, giving her character weight as a main character and initiation of the plot. As part of this opening sequence, it continues to offer exposition, now more specifically about the Curry men as they each sing about how much they love and have missed Lizzie, for their various reasons. Throughout the song, I would like to highlight more of the townspeople, as well as pump up the energy and uplifting impact of this song to follow the composer's intention to counteract the somewhat gloomy message of the opening song.*
>
> **After song**:
> SCENE (pp. 1-1-5 to 1-1-9) LIZZIE, OTHER PASSENGERS, CURRY MEN. Passengers enter stage right. They and the Townspeople gradually exit, leaving the stage to the Curry's. Just before Lizzie's song, H.C., Jim, & Noah exit UPSL.
> SONG (1-1-9) "Love, Don't Turn Away": LIZZIE.
>
> **PURPOSE:** *This scene establishes the close, easy and loving relationship between the Curry family and Lizzie's place in it. We are given information about what is currently important in their lives, which is finding a husband for Lizzie; she is returning from visiting extended family and there were hopes that she would find a suitor there. The men leave and in Lizzie's song she reveals her innermost hopes for the first time, and her overriding objective. After showing how she puts up a brave front to her family, acting as though she's resigned to spinsterhood, we see how much she really wants to be a wife and a mother. Having her sing about this in private, as an inner monologue, shows the audience her genuineness and vulnerability. It establishes the super-objective of the play and so introduces the plot. The audience must bond with her now so they will pull for her throughout the story. At the end of the song, Toby enters to escort her off as set changes.*

Creating such breakdowns for the shows I work on forces me to think more deeply about each character's journey and the ultimate meaning of each scene and each song. The two opening scenes used in this chapter to illustrate writing my scene/song descriptions are two very good examples of exposition being served in the opening numbers of musicals. But while the songs and the dialogue give us a great deal of information, other important information comes to us directly from the performers (the work of the director, choreographer, and actors) in terms of what the characters do, how they act, and how they carry themselves. The old saying "actions speak louder than words" should be every choreographer's creed because in fact it is true. Like "Another Hot Day," opening numbers in musicals are replete with opportunities to not only give necessary background information to the audience, but also to reveal individual characters, create a mood or atmosphere, establish the style of presentation for the evening, tell us about time, place, and situation, or even place us in a particular frame of mind. In these ways, the choreographer is the grand manipulator because if he is masterful, he helps the audience not only to know what is going on, but to feel deeply about it, be moved by it, and empathize with the characters. He can lead an audience to have deeper insights about life, understand others on a gut level, or even take action to make changes in the real world. This sort of ability, to affect people in a meaningful way, carries with it some responsibility and so for my money, an artist's goals should always be altruistic and seek to inspire the human spirit rather than to weigh it down.

What is *your* purpose?

Your *personal* purpose as a choreographer is also important to have thought about when working on any production. In addition, as the choreographer of a musical, you should believe that not only are you important to the production, you are indispensable to it. Your role in each production will change slightly, based on the needs of the show, on how much staging the director will want you to do, and how much he/she relies on your judgment and partnership. But my question here has more to do with you as an artist. What drew you into this field? Why do you want to be a choreographer of musicals and what do you see your contributions being? I was a dancer all my life, grew up with musicals, memorized scores from listening to show albums throughout my childhood, and watched movie musicals on television whenever humanly possible. The first stage musical I remember seeing was *Peter Pan*, but it was on television. Mary Martin's *Peter Pan*, directed and choreographed by Jerome Robbins, was an annual TV event during the 1950s when I was growing up. I waited for it every year. Neverland was absolutely real in my mind and Tinkerbelle was my personal guardian angel! When we finally got a stereo in the house and bought the album, I began staging myself in these numbers, memorizing the songs and imagining myself as Peter and Tiger Lily, and even all three of the Darling children. It was my early practice. I didn't know that I wanted to be a professional director-slash-choreographer at that time. I wasn't aware that I was working on how to tell a story in my own unique way. I was just very certain that I wanted to be around song and dance for the rest of my life. Regarding my question of personal purpose or why I feel artists are important, I now better understand this than I did in my youth. Now, it has more to do with the elevating and redemptive value of the performing arts, rather than merely the blind need to perform or create. Almost half way into my adult life I stopped dancing long enough to think about why I was dancing and if I should continue to dance. Was being in the arts serving humanity in any way? Obviously, I decided that it was. However, my belief is that today's young dancers are unlike me in waiting so long to consider this question, and many have already identified their purpose for wanting to be an artist--their deeper purpose. However, if you have not yet thought about it, perhaps (like me) you tend to live life a little in reverse, and by instinct. So I'll pose the question to you now—not to solve—just to make sure you get to thinking about it before too much time slips away.

In the following chapters we will discuss useful methods for choreography and staging that will put these theories regarding song purpose, and your personal purpose, into practice.

Assignments – Chapter 4

Out of class assignment

1. Re-read my examples above that outline scene and song breakdowns for the musicals *110 in the Shade* and *She Loves Me.* Use them as a template for the following assignment: Go through your own show, choose the two songs you will be choreographing as your final class projects and work out your own scene breakdown for those numbers. This is for submission, so type it, and follow the examples given. Be sure to include all of the information given in the librettos by its creators.

2. Think back to remember the first time you were moved deeply by a musical you saw. What was the show? How old were you? What was the song that resonated with you most closely? Write a short reflection about it. After that, choose three or four songs from that musical and analyze their purpose in the show. Write this down to present to the class.

In-class assignment

You will be assigned a song from a musical to begin staging with your classmates in 1 or 2 class sessions. Begin to utilize the techniques already introduced and incorporate ideas from the readings or class discussions. These studies are intended to have you work quickly, in collaboration with others, and to integrate your growing technical knowledge with your dance instincts.

Chapter 5
What's the Buzz?
Staging Exposition To Give Important Background Information

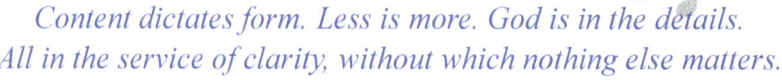

> *Content dictates form. Less is more. God is in the details.*
> *All in the service of clarity, without which nothing else matters.*
> —Stephen Sondheim, *Finishing the Hat*

The preliminary historical research I have done on the time and place and other more specific information depicted in a musical, along with the work I have asked my principle *and* ensemble actors to formulate in terms of creating their characters, will help *me* to prepare and set choreography for the opening number. The rehearsal studio is where my preparation meets the actors' homework. Normally, the opening of a musical, along with any amount of dialogue before or after the song, will give background information of the story being told. Sometimes dialogue will lead us into an opening song, such as in *Crazy for You*, but for the most part, somehow music will eventually take over to get the show off and running. The song will introduce what we need to know about the characters and often set up the major conflict for the show. A classic example of how this can be done through music, even without lyrics, is *West Side Story*.

WSS opens with an instrumental "Prologue," to which Jerome Robbins set a ballet that established the background of the gang war between the Polish-American boys and the Puerto Rican boys in Manhattan during the 1950s (Bernstein, 1957). In approximately six and a half minutes, we come to understand the era, the social climate and the environment through Bernstein's complex be-boppy urban jazz score coupled with the deliberate finger-snapping of the characters onstage, a well-conceived but minimal scenic design depicting an urban backdrop, and carefully selected movement that establishes a contextual account of circumstances leading up to where the audience will enter the story. Robbins' choreography[2] introduces the two rival gangs representing the main conflict: ethnic hatred or intolerance of difference. The movement is tailored not only to embody the emotional and psychological state of each character, but it also represents who they are as a group. "Jet" movement often travels indirectly and more freely through space than "Shark"

---

2 Descriptions of the choreography are based on the film version of West Side Story released in 1961 by MGM.

movement, which is at a lower level with more resistance; its elements are more direct and cutting. Jet images are at a higher level: soaring runs into jumps with arms spread in expansive winged positions or high traveling *chassés* into repeated *saut de basque* turns. Motif movements for each gang are established here, as well as motifs common to both gangs, tying them together as sharing a common space. We recognize the characters through their actions, particularly gang leaders, and we understand by the end of the dance that there have been ongoing battles over turf in this area of Manhattan for a long time; the tension between the gangs is mounting. The final incident depicting the slicing of Baby John's ear is ominous in that weapons are used and the fighting becomes physically harmful. There is danger ahead (Robbins and Wise, 1961).

An opening for a musical also establishes the style of the show and the conventions used by the director that the audience will be expected to adopt, and believe, for the rest of the evening. In his essay "Inside *Bare*," Scott Miller cites Sondheim's ten minute rule claiming that "a show can employ any device, any convention, any rule-breaking, as long as it happens within the first ten minutes, to establish for the audience the rules for the evening" (Miller, 2011, in para.: "Hear My Voice"). Movement can be pedestrian and natural, suggesting a tendency toward realism, or stylized, such as the opening movement for *How to Succeed in Music without Really Trying*. It can be theatrical, making use of the abstract over the representational, or suggest a conceptual storyline over one that is linear. Each show will have its own unique manner of presentation that is established in the opening number. In order to illustrate some of the contrasting concerns that choreographers might deal with, I will continue my discussion of *110 In the Shade* to contrast the more realistic treatment of that musical to the opening of *Jekyll and Hyde*, for which my choreography had to be of an abstract and highly theatrical nature.

Staging Exposition

For the opening number of *110 in the Shade,* I was most interested to look closely at the era historically because the play takes place in the mid-1930s during a particularly arduous and complex time for our country. Not only were we going through an economic depression that affected all echelons of society, but there were other events stemming from various influences that affected people in all walks of life, such as unionism, political unrest and activism (particularly within the arts), and events happening in Germany that were leading up to WWII. In the midst of all this, in the Great Plains of the American Midwest problematic farming and drought conditions led to a series of dust storms in 1933 that lasted for most of the remainder of the decade. This area, dubbed The Dust Bowl, hosted an environmental disaster that led to devastation of the agriculture, soil erosion, loss of homes and land, and a vast displacement of people, rendering the land barren and killing livestock. Playwright and librettist Nash uses this setting, a drought-ridden and potentially empty land, as a metaphor for the emptiness and barrenness felt by the heroine of *The Rainmaker*, Lizzie, who fears she might never find love or bear children. In the end Lizzie discovers that belief in herself will make her simple, yet seemingly insurmountable dreams become a reality. The show delivers a message about the power of family, community, hope, and above all faith—that believing in others so that they can believe in themselves—might just allow the impossible to happen.

The Harvey Schmidt/Tom Jones score is lyrical and evocative. The opening number, rather than delivering the expected raucous musical theatre opening, has a languid quality of people worn down by the heat. As the townsfolk enter and walk to the water tower to fill their buckets we meet them for the first time. For me, what would make this deliberately dreary, lackluster opening compelling and even more informative would be to highlight the individual, and by doing so, highlight the sense of community. The *purposes* of the opening number, as written, are to deliver exposition by: 1) introducing the audience to Three Point, Texas, 2) introducing the audience to the people who live there, 3) explaining to the audience what their problem is, and 4) establishing for the audience the ambiance for the rest of the play. The indolent quality of Schmidt's music and the disconsolate message of Jones' lyrics accomplish a great deal of this on their own. File sings:

Overhead the sun is risin'; not a cloud across the sky.
Not a sign on the horizon; and, it's gonna be another hot day;
Yes, it's gonna be another hot day.
(We learn it is very early morning—"sun is risin'"—the heat is ongoing, possible drought conditions?)

Underneath, the earth is burnin'; crops is bad, and land is dry.
(We surmise that at least some people here are farmers, but the earth is too dry to support their crops, which are dying. A drought is in progress. Listener also gets the sense that the singer has a dialect, an informality with "ing" word endings and, at times, an incorrect use of grammar.)
Still, the sun keeps on returnin'; And, it's gonna be another hot day;
Yes, it's gonna be another hot day.
(Again, the singer is reinforcing how incredibly hot it is.)

When the rain comes!
(The ensemble joins in; now everyone is singing.)
What a day that'll be; what a revelation; when the rain comes!
Such a sight, can't you see; what a celebration.
(The lyrics change from negative factual statements and take on the positivity of how they would all feel when it finally rains. They would revel in the event and celebrate. The melody also changes and becomes less conversational and more elevated—soaring—which changes the mood of the moment completely for these few wistful seconds.)

And, the whole darn town will pour into the streets
To feel it streamin' down. When the rain comes;
(A strong sense of community and collective longing.)
When the rain comes; when the rain comes; when the rain comes.
(The melody takes a downward slope and gradually decreases in volume and excitement. This musical choice transitions the characters from the joyful anticipation of rain, back to the reality of the drought.)

Overhead the sun is shinin'; not a cloud across the sky.
(We return to the weary monotony of the original melody here. Time has passed; the sun is up ("shinin'" now) and getting hotter.)
Not a sign on the horizon; And it's gonna be another hot day.
Yes, it's gonna be another hot day. It's gonna be another,
Gonna be another scorcher today.
(This song doesn't really present a dramatic arc for the actor. The characters essentially end where they begin: tired, worried, and dry. It is clear to the observer that this drought situation is serious and the town is becoming desperate, exactly what they need to know to understand the rest of the show.)

(Schmidt and Jones, "Another Hot Day," 1963)

Linguistically speaking, the lyrics suggest aspects of a casual nature, such as dropping the "g" in the "ing" endings, as well as using incorrect verb tenses such as "crops is" instead of "crops are," and colloquialisms ("the whole darn town"), which give information about the formal education level of the characters, as well as place; certainly we get a sense of rural background over urban. Because the song is sung by File the sheriff, and one of Lizzie's love interests, it will be important to show him to the audience as a sympathetic character and as part of the town. Do I want the audience to relate easily to him, find him charming, kind, masculine, and friendly? (Yes, to all of the above.) But he is also reserved, careful, and not openly emotional about the situation. He and the ensemble set up the conflict and deliver all of the background an audience needs to know about the primary plot situation in this opening song exposition. From the brief dialogue before the song, we know that File is the sheriff and Toby is the stationmaster. There's a drought and the town needs rain. These are rural folk; many are farmers who are losing their livelihoods and are probably not educated to do other things. They are weary and somewhat worn down due to the heat and lack of water; but they are also hopeful. It is early morning when the song starts and later in the morning when it ends. We can surmise all of this from the song alone.

Individualizing Your Ensemble

What the song does not give us, however, is individual background information about the ensemble. We are not told who the townspeople are except for Toby, who is the first person we see at the top of the show. One or two others have solo singing or speaking lines, which may give us a clue about them, but no more. Nothing is written into the song to personalize the ensemble or to make any of the characters distinct individuals. The message of certain shows, certainly this show, will be more compelling if the audience knows and cares about all of the characters, including each member of the ensemble. If we do not come to recognize them as individuals, we can really only care about them on a general level, and then this ensemble becomes very much part of the background, like scenery. They give us an overall feeling about what we're *supposed* to feel, but we don't become invested in anyone other than the principle characters. A bit later in this chapter we will examine when generalizing the ensemble is appropriate and effective for some shows, but for this show, knowing the townspeople moves the audience to care more about their plight, and then better understand the power that Starbuck seems to hold over them later. Therefore, besides making this a song about delivering exposition, I made it a song about revealing (or beginning to reveal) character, not just File's, but each of the townspeople's. At the time of casting I gave each member of the ensemble names and made them parts of families; ultimately they were required to write detailed character sketches and share their backgrounds with me and the cast. As the director, I would use these characters not only in the dances, but throughout the show. Even if I was only choreographing the show and the director did not require the ensemble to take on such specific characters, which sometimes happens, I would still require it for the dance numbers because doing so is the best way to create convincing and legitimate stage business for an actor.

Another thing we did to establish relationships and create a tight ensemble was to plan and engage in a town potluck picnic. Tables were set up for families, and the cast interacted with each other throughout the "picnic," in character. Although the ensemble was large for this show, because of these and other activities that became part of the rehearsal process, they became tightly bonded as both a performing group as well as people from a small town in Texas back in 1936.

Creating Realistic Business For The Characters

My choreography and staging for the opening were carefully structured to engage the members of the town with each other, not only to perform actions that revealed their present task, but which could also disclose deeper things like age range, relationship, station in life, and personality traits, among other things. In straight plays this kind of physical staging is called "stage business," but is generally referred to as "musical staging" in this instance. In this number, members of the ensemble were each engaged in specific kinds of business, often stylized, that helped tell smaller stories about who they are. When the curtain rises we hear a train whistle in the distance and see the old station attendant Toby coming out of the station. His grandson, Toby, Jr., the town cabbie, is seated on a nearby bench, waiting for the early train to arrive and drive his customers to their destination. Toby Jr. takes his harmonica out of his pocket and starts playing the first few bars of the opening number when File comes out of the sheriff's office and greets them both. After a few lines of dialogue, the song begins and the townsfolk begin to enter, carrying buckets downstage right to the water tower to fill them. Some of the people we become acquainted with are Connie and Mack McCarthy, characters I fabricated to be best friends of Lizzie. Connie is pregnant, which adds to Lizzie's angst over the possibility of her becoming a spinster. Old Toby walks right up to Connie and greets her as the three adolescent Buehler girls (also dreamed up) run in and almost knock him over. Throughout, people are moving around the street as they would realistically, greeting each other in character-specific ways, such as the irascible and man-loving Snookie Updegraff who is pulled away from flirting with the sheriff by her older sister, Betty Lou. Snookie, of course, is one of the principles in the play and girlfriend of Lizzie's youngest brother, Jimmy. She doesn't actually have a sister that was given to her by librettist Nash, but I gave her one so she could have a more natural connection to others in the ensemble. The three teenage Buehler girls are herded together by their gossipy, flirtatious Aunt Bea Buehler, an adoptive parent (and another concoction of mine). And, the list goes on. The natural movement continues until everyone is onstage (see fig. 10). It changes gradually when a small group of girls begin moving in a more stylized fashion. The men join them and the natural movement, continued by some in the background, changes to dance movement as the "boys" move toward the "girls" who are dancing and perform a unison lift when the music swells at the top of the bridge, *"When the rain comes…,"* and where the music crescendos. Following the fundamental musical theatre "rule" that we sing and we dance when we can no longer adequately represent our feelings with mere words, four boys run forward and lift four of the girls, spinning them as they lay prone, the small of their backs on the men's' shoulders and faces to the sky. This group, now established as the young people of the town, dance together for a time (see fig. 11) until the music spirals down ominously with each *"When the rain comes…When the rain comes… When the rain comes,"* to the quietest, most pensive moment in the song. There is a second or two of stillness at the end of this phrase when they all stop and hold in place for a few beats. The way they are positioned and grouped during this stillness is also an opportunity to reveal personalities, relationships, or even a collective state of mind. Images or stage pictures such as this are "worth a thousand words." During the last repeat of the refrain, begun by File, the ensemble moves naturally again, as some of the townsfolk get ready to exit and others stay waiting for the arrival of the train, which will bring Nash's heroine, Lizzie, back home.

Figure 10. Ensemble character development in opening number from *110 in the Shade,* Elon University Archives, 2010.

Figure 11. Ensemble character introduction in *110 in the Shade.* Elon University, 2010.

Figure 12. More character development in opening from *110 In the Shade.* Elon University, 2010.

Figure 13. A "crossover" of ensemble members to picnic grounds further establishes characters and relationships in *110 in the Shade*. Elon University Archives, 2010

One of the most difficult, or at least time-consuming aspects of a number like this is the devising and stylizing of very specific movement or business for each ensemble member, making certain it is all motivated, and helping them find creative ways to express their particular reasons for being where they are at that particular moment in time. It is also the most "fun" part of doing this kind of work because it involves careful crafting until all units are working together to make an effective whole. Much of the time, the majority of the cast are moving as individuals, which gives the audience a strong semblance of reality. Reality is appropriate because this show, although saturated in metaphor, is written in a realistic style. Choreographing and staging character-specific chores for each member of the ensemble heightens not only *their* involvement and potential for creative input, but also heightens the feelings held by the audience for the message of the show, simply because they begin to know, relate with, and have feelings for the characters they meet in the opening number.

"Façade," A Horse Of A Very Different Color

Inversely, the song "Façade," which is the opening of the Leslie Bricusse/Frank Wildhorn/Steve Cuden musical *Jekyll and Hyde*, does not deliver *specific* exposition. However, it does have the same purposes as the opening of *110 In The Shade*, such as to introduce the characters, give background information, and to set the proper tone for the evening ahead, only in a more abstract way (1997). The treatment here is less representational and much more abstract and theatrical. Our director, Cathy McNeela, worked with me and the musical director, Ken Lee, to divide the ensemble members into wealthy vs. poor identities that they would hold throughout the show and which would determine not only what numbers they would be in, but other things such as their costume needs, what song parts they would sing, what solo lines or harmony groupings they would be assigned, and which performers I could use to dance and when. There is less nuance in this show than in *110 In the Shade* because of the broader themes of good versus evil, so getting to know individuals in the ensemble was less important than the overall statement made by their carefully constructed presence onstage. In that sense many of the ensemble numbers were less representational and more abstract in their presentation, so I was able to stray somewhat from the "givens" present in the script to take some flights of fancy, and hopefully, creative thinking. For "Façade," I asked the costume designer about the possibility of putting some of the ensemble members in masks, but masks placed on the backs of their head so that when they turned around, we saw a different *persona*. Characters were still costumed as either poor or wealthy, but this added element cast shadows on both levels of society and added the element of mystery and confusion that surround(s) the main character(s) Dr. Jekyll and Mr. Hyde. With the use of a turntable sporting a spiral staircase, and a number of platforms of different sizes around the stage, I was able to find great variety in the use of space and levels allowing for a feeling of constant movement, the element of surprise, mystery and a little bit of excitement, all of which were intended to prepare the audience for what was to come.

Rehearsal Hall Complications

Staging "Façade" in rehearsal was very different from staging "Another Hot Day." While there was an enormous amount of movement in "Façade," there was no dance, per se, and as stated earlier, detail was prepared for group placement of characters, rather than individual characters. Even so, the amount of preparation time was certainly as significant, if not more so. Because the set was so complex, both the director and I had models that we could work with to prepare for rehearsals. Raised levels formed a walkway like structure around the sides and back of the stage, which allowed not only for levels of considerable height, but also spaces underneath which actors could move through or inhabit. The central piece was a large circular platform center stage positioned on a turntable. On the platform was a large winding staircase. Turned to face one direction the staircase served as the entrance into Jekyll's basement laboratory; turned to different angles, however, it would become the ballroom, or the bar where Hyde meets Lucy, and various other places. My idea for the opening was to utilize all of the set as much as possible, seeing different "faces" of the set, as well as the actors' facades, throughout. As the turntable moved, the ensemble moved up and down the staircase and under, around and through it. It took at least sixteen hours of sitting at my kitchen table playing with the model and my cardboard "people" to work out the patterns and the groupings, as well as the movement, all of which was immediately recorded in a notebook that became the most important part of the rehearsals for this number. This was not a piece that could tolerate improvisation or anything that looked spontaneous. Façade was a classic production number, staged precisely and specifically in a highly stylized fashion directly to the audience; there was absolutely no pretense of a fourth wall. My "authoritarian" choreographer-identity emerged as I walked into the rehearsal space and began telling everyone exactly where to go and what I wanted them to do.

Another challenge that is important to discuss here is that of working on a large production number in a rehearsal space that is not the size of the stage and that holds none of the levels or platforms on which the piece will take place. The only way that I can possibly surmise the effect of a dance and the balance of objects moving on and off the set is through the use of a model with all the scenic design elements, including set pieces and appropriately sized figures to represent at least some of the performers. Studio spaces that are used for rehearsal are most often dance studios; usually they are large enough to allow a taping out of the set in real measurements. However, gaining enough distance from the set in order to see it in a balanced way is always a problem. This number was staged in a space that allowed only about three feet of extra downstage space, so I often felt as though I was sitting onstage with the performers during large production numbers. I have often wished I could use one of those cherry picker camera towers we see Bus Berkeley positioned in when he was filming one of his many lavish precision dance numbers. Alas, standing atop a folding chair was the closest I ever came to that!

Once forty-some performers enter this space, visual and aural cacophony ensues, which is difficult enough to respond to intelligently. However, after I quiet the sea of excited people in front of me, I will need to organize them so they are ready to begin the process of creating the opening number. Regardless of the fact that the finished set will consist of several platforms of various heights plus large moving pieces, I can only see the actors perform the movement I give them on one level until we enter the stage space on which the actual set is constructed. Decisions regarding visual balance and effect will have to remain "soft" or "deferred" until I see the staging performed on the completed structure. This part of the *Jekyll and Hyde* process was frustrating for me because I had to consider the lengthy time I spent in studio rehearsals as essentially a rough draft of the staging, rather than something a bit farther along than that. In every case, I normally consider my dances "a work in progress" until technical rehearsals take place, but what I didn't know about this production was that large sections of the opening number would have to be *completely* restaged when we moved onto the set. As the choreographer, however, I know that each piece of the staging I complete is not being created by me alone. This medium is more comprehensive than that. The final product (the *pre-audience* final product) doesn't exist until the actor works with the scenic elements, in costume and microphones, under the lights, and with the orchestra in the pit. The creative team for a musical works in layers, as do other performing artists, but I believe that these layers are especially complex because there are simply more of them, and more that are on a grander scale than most singular artistic events. And to push this point a bit, the additional elements of live music and singing in combination with a fully scripted play shift musical theatre a step up in intricacy from other forms of theatre. And so, as someone who must have been very wise once advised, to get something difficult right you must "practice, practice, practice" (Anon.). However, even with hours of practice, the possibility of mishap is the theatre-makers' constant companion.

Complications On The Stage

The first "snag" that I encountered after setting and rehearsing "Façade" in the dance studio happened the first night we moved onto the set and it became apparent that the number of actors I was told the turntable could hold at any one time was far over an acceptable number. The mechanism was brand new and guesstimates given by the manufacturer were optimistic, to say the least. I instantly had to start making modifications and changes. The tech crew and designers worked along with me for at least two full evenings while I restaged what the actors did, and the production team re-rehearsed what needed to happen scenically.

At the request of our exacting and methodical director, we had a "Plan A," which would be in place as long as the mechanics of the turntable stayed intact and moved electronically and predictably. There was also a "Plan B," which would take place if the turntable broke down and had to be pushed manually—the latter of which actually happened during the number on opening night. Of course, this kind of thing happens more in academia or small regional theatres than it would on Broadway because academia does not have the budget or resources of larger venues; however, the lesson here is that no matter how well rehearsed or prepared you *think* you might be, *anything* can happen. The best advice I can give in such situations is just to take it in stride. After all, as I often remind myself, it isn't brain surgery! However, it can stop a show in its tracks and the overall effect you wish to make, so having a "Plan B" for such situations is the smart thing to do, and it saved the opening number that night when costumed deck hands appeared and began maneuvering the set as rehearsed. Before the second performance I modified the number of singers on the moving turntable even more, so the breakdown would not happen again. This was one of those situations when "being flexible" became this choreographer's most important asset (see figs. 14-15).

Figure 14. Utilizing moving pieces in "Façade" from *Dr. Jekyll and Mr. Hyde.* Elon University Archives, 2006.

Figure 15. "Façade" from *Jekyll & Hyde.* Elon University Archives, 2006.

    The differences in these two opening numbers illustrate the range of ways a musical can be launched by its creators and the ways an ensemble can function as either highly specific individualized and realistic characters, as more generalized figures that become abstractions of an idea or concept, or as symbolic of a message or theme laid out by the librettist. You—as the choreographer—must spend time perceiving the song from every angle, understanding its purpose and determining what information the staging is responsible to convey; or to decide what choices might stand out as incongruent or inconsistent with the script. You—as a member of the creative team—must make certain that you work your choices out with the rest of the team in order to preserve unity of concept, style and purpose.

Assignments – Chapter 5

Out of Class Assignments

1. Using my two examples in this chapter, create a breakdown for the opening sequence and song of the musical assigned to you. Decide what information needs to be conveyed by the movement you create for this number, the purpose of the song, the characters involved, what the audience needs to learn about them, and where it takes place. List the scenic givens, and then the overall style you will be using for the movement. Record this all in your breakdown.

2. Create some movement, including spatial patterns, groupings, etc., and an overall outline for the above opening number. Record it in your own way, which will allow you to easily convey to me the concept, main events, and style of movement you will be using when staging this sequence.

3. Decide how you would begin working on this with an ensemble and how you would structure your first rehearsal. Record this in your notes.

Chapter 6

On My Own
Staging the *Who, What, When, Where* and *Why* of the Inner Monologue and Solo Song

During Shakespeare's time and until naturalism became the predominant style of presentation in Western theatre, the soliloquy was used to allow a playwright to connect to the audience intimately and specifically with what was going on in a character's mind. Although they are usually lengthy speeches, the soliloquy shouldn't be confused with a monologue or an interior monologue. During a *soliloquy,* such as the famous "To be or not to be" speech from *Hamlet*, the speaker is in effect thinking to himself (out loud) to examine a problem, emphasize a state of mind, rejoice in something wonderful or bemoan something awful that has happened to him, or any number of things, allowing the audience to overhear his/her thoughts, as it were. A *monologue*, on the other hand, might have similar purpose but is directed to another actor onstage, or possibly to the audience. It has a target. The literary device used in novels to accomplish this is referred to as an *interior monologue*, during which a character, through stream of consciousness, reveals his/her innermost thoughts, feelings, fears, or joy to another character so that the reader can experience that character on a deep, even empathetic level of understanding. Again, it has a target. The "aside" is a dramatic device that also has a target, which is the audience, but unlike a monologue or soliloquy is only a brief comment. In an *aside* the actor turns to the audience directly, steps out of the action of the scene momentarily, and confides his/her honest reaction to someone or something out of earshot of the other characters. Before realism, audiences were more accustomed to these theatrical devices, as well as to the convention of actors being onstage during another actor's monologue (or song) but not hearing it. Such conventions require audience members to employ "a willing suspension of disbelief" in order for them to be effective. Musicals, by nature, demand their audiences to employ a willing suspension of disbelief every time the music begins. Not everyone can do this, so not everyone likes musicals. That's okay, not everyone likes Greek Theatre or Monday night wrestling. However, if you *do* like musicals, this may be one of the reasons why; you are just fine with believing the unbelievable.

Musicals are a form of theatre that still employs the use of the soliloquy, but in song form. And, because musicals are already highly theatrical and presentational by nature, the use of the solo song to reveal the inner life of the character singing it is a perfect medium. I refer to these songs as *inner monologues*. Directors Joe Deer and Rocco Dal

Vera use the term, as well, characterizing such a song as "...probably the most authentic set of ideas a character can have. Here is where the character's ideations are uncensored, filled with taboos and thoughts of the unthinkable (42). For me the *inner monologue* is simply a more modern term for the *soliloquy*; it also characterizes the dramatic action for the actor, giving them a point of view. If an actor thinks of the song as "thinking out loud" then the fourth wall can remain up while the character is still somewhat removed from the present action of the play. Unless the script intends a character to address the audience directly, the actor will need to play the truth of the situation and continue to keep the audience outside looking in.

In his soliloquy, Hamlet is tossing around the idea of whether he should somehow deal with his despicable uncle or just let the pain he is in disappear by letting go of life. We feel his anguish intensely through the high emotionality and poeticism of the words Shakespeare wrote for him. Through the soliloquy we begin to suspect his impending madness, the inability of his mind to make sense of what is happening, and how the pain he is experiencing is skewing his thoughts. Without this speech, we could not have this kind of insight nor would the ensuing events seem as compelling or inevitable.

The solo song in a musical, which acts as an inner monologue for a character, is used profusely in musical theatre writing to allow us to better understand a character's state of mind. Listen to or observe any musical, and you will find at least one such song, and sometimes they are not even solo moments, but several individuals singing their own inner monologue within the same musical sequence. The beauty of the song, as with Shakespeare's poetry, is that we also are able to tap more deeply into the character's emotionality as well as their psychology, and we don't just *know* what is going on with them, we also *feel* it with a like intensity.

A Song About *Who?*

In the song "Maria" from *West Side Story (WSS)*, we are swept into Tony's euphoria over a girl he met at the dance earlier that night (Laurents, Bernstein, and Sondheim, 1957). Despite the title of the song, this is really a song about Tony. It doesn't matter that he *just* met this girl. The intensity of his feelings, conveyed so powerfully through the music and lyrics, overrides the implausibility of the situation and allows us to believe that he is already deeply in love. This point is crucial because our belief in their love for each other is the reality the rest of the play rides on until things go tragically awry. The main action of *WSS* all takes place in just over 24 hours, but because we believe in Tony and Maria's love for each other, we can accept as credible each of the ensuing events, and since we also develop an affection for and a stake in many of the other characters, we care deeply about the outcome. We mourn the loss of each of them and are deeply affected by the play overall. Tony's death at the end of the play is devastating to us because it is devastating to Maria, but also because he is the show's symbol of love in the presence of hate and of hope in the face of despair. The outcome of the bigotry these characters feel for each other was shattering and confounding, but for at least a few hours Tony and Maria counteracted it through their love for each other and their tolerance of difference. *WSS* is a love story, in the broadest sense of the term. The song "Maria," Tony's sudden and overwhelming understanding of the beauty in difference, propels the play forward, off the runway, and to its inevitable end.

What Is the Character's State of Mind?

When staging such inner monologue songs, the choreographer must first consider the character and his present state of mind and allow only credible movement that emphasizes and authenticates those things.

Tony's state of mind is determined by what has just happened to him; he has experienced love at first sight! Bernstein and Sondheim went to great lengths to assure we feel what Tony is feeling when we hear him sing this song, so it is useful for the choreographer to notice some of the devices present, particularly in the music. For instance, Tony's repetition of the word "*Maria*" during the verse of the song (notated in B flat) follows two lines that give us the beginning of his thought process, or perhaps we are just tuning into his mind in the middle of its wonderment. He chants, "*The most beautiful sound I ever heard*," and then repeats the tritone "*Maria*" four times, suggesting his growing obsession with this word (Bernstein and Sondheim, M. 1-4). This verse, like most, is conversational and loosely constructed—like recitative in opera. But what has always struck me about it is its similarity to Gregorian chant. So, I researched Gregorian theory and discovered that this similarity is not accidental. Bernstein employed the Lydian mode in the writing of his song, and the Lydian mode is associated with Gregorian chant, as well as with the tritone. According to musicologist Harold Powers,

> Because of the importance of the major scale in modern music, the Lydian mode is often described as the scale that begins on the fourth scale degree of the major scale, or alternatively, as the major scale with the fourth scale degree raised half a step. This sequence of pitches roughly describes the scale underlying the fifth of the eight Gregorian (church) modes, known as Mode V...theoretically using B♮ but in practice more commonly featuring B♭. (Powers 2001)

Tony's repeating of the word "*Maria*" is followed by a second line of chanting "*All the beautiful sounds of the world in a single word,*" after which he repeats "*Maria*" six times, followed by one more repetition that builds in intensity as the key modulates to D major (M. 5-8). That last "*Maria*" resolves the tritone and launches the song from its verse into the refrain. (I do not use the word "launch" lightly—this "jet" is in the air!) The hint of a Latin rhythm we hear in the orchestration not only keeps the cha-cha at the gym fresh in Tony's mind, and ours, but also continues to remind him, and us, of Maria's "difference," which is at the heart of his astonishment (M. 9).

The use of the tritone throughout Bernstein's score symbolizes the discord and conflict that threaten the happiness of all the characters in the show. In her blog, *From Score To Stage*, music theatre performer and scholar Kerry Fergus describes the tritone as "…the interval that sits right between the perfect fourth and the perfect fifth. The tritone has a jarring, unnatural sound, and thus is used carefully in Western tonal music" (Fergus, 2017). Bernstein's use of the tritone in "Maria" keeps us rooted in the story, reminding us of Tony's longing and the tensions associated with that. His desire now has a definite direction, however, and his overriding optimism allows Tony to resolve the tritone as he did earlier in "Something's Coming," and as he and Maria do throughout the play:

> Bernstein makes great use of the tritone throughout the *West Side Story* score, most famously as the first two notes in the refrain of "Maria" [where] Tony again finds a way to resolve the tritone. Here the ascending tritone resolves up to a perfect fifth. And indeed, the rest of the piece is filled with perfect fourths and fifths. The aurally pleasing quality of fourths and fifths stands in stark contrast to the jarring nature of the tritone. As we shall see, Bernstein will continue to use these fourths and fifths throughout the show in contrast to the harsh quality of the tritone and as indicators of the power of love. (Fergus, 2017)

Sondheim did not want to "overwrite" the lyrics for this song, or have them compete with Bernstein's emotionally rich music for attention. He also hated the idea of writing "poetic" lyrics, which Bernstein loved. Sondheim felt that street kids in New York would never speak in such lofty ways, which is true, but he does concede that some of the lyrics he hates that are in the show because his collaborators liked them, may indeed be why the songs were so successful (Sondheim, 2010). Regardless of his misgivings, the combination of Bernstein's music and Sondheim's lyrics is, for many, an extraordinary experience. For instance, during the first two sections of the refrain, Tony's discoveries seem charmingly naive. First, he met a girl whose name is Maria and instantly that word took on new meaning for him. Second, he kissed her, which made even just the sound of her name *"wonderful."* In the bridge of the song, he analyzes those feelings singing, *"Maria, say it loud and there's music playing, say it soft and it's almost like praying. Maria, I'll never stop saying..."* and then he again runs out of words to express the depth of his feelings, so instead of going back to repeat the A-section after the bridge, the melody gives way to an ecstatic frenzy of repeating *"Maria"*—ten times! Around the fifth repeat he sustains the second syllable of the name way up in the tenor stratosphere taking the listener with him on his beautiful flight...this Jet (Bernstein and Sondheim, M. 34-39). During this section, I imagine him as a plane in an aircraft demonstration performing loops, spins, and rolls--swooping around in free flight! The last two *"Marias"* bring him, not back to earth but into a holding pattern just long enough for him to reinforce how good it feels no matter how he says her name (M. 28-45). He becomes pensive after this and returns quietly to the reverent chant he sang at the top of the song: *"The most beautiful sound I ever heard,"* then from the name's first syllable he swoops back up into the stratosphere on the second and last syllables, which he sustains throughout the long beautiful ride out of the song *"ri a..."* (M. 49-53). The end of this song is like a beautiful aircraft that glides off into the sunset. I like to think it never lands.

Tony repeats the name "Maria" twenty-nine times during the song! "Maria" is a brilliant musical interpretation of a young boy discovering love for the first time. His inability to wrap his brain around how a word he has heard a thousand times before suddenly changes his perception of the world is truly moving. He keeps saying it because it feels so good!

Researching the composer and lyricist to learn how they structured various technical elements of the song informs my analysis and therefore deepens my understanding of what they have already established in the score. I am more connected to the character and his emotional state of mind *moment to moment* during the song. Creating for myself the image of him as a jet plane is not only consistent with his history as a member of the Jets but also gives me a concrete movement concept to work with—one I have already established for the Jets. I can use verbs such as launching, flying, gliding, floating, soaring, etc. as a basis for how Tony expresses his euphoria physically. Not dancing, of course, but what he projects through the pedestrian movement we establish. It is important for the choreographer to ensure that what the audience hears Tony say jives perfectly with what they see Tony do.

In this scene, Tony is physically and psychically super-charged. His body, even when still, must always indicate this. He is ecstatic, optimistic about the future, and blissfully in love. The body must be true to how he tells us he is feeling. (Now, what I am about to suggest may seem minor, or inconsequential, but I see these physical qualities in singers all the time, often because actors feel it makes them more "real." OR, they are concentrating only on singing the song correctly. OR, they feel awkward in their own skin.) However, if *Tony* is feeling euphoric but the *actor* is slumped in the torso, predominantly immobile, stiff and detached from his physical self, the song may still work if it is sung well—it's a great song—but Tony himself will not ring as true. He will not create as credible an experience for the audience because the actor is not completely committed to his character's state of mind. But what *is* logical for Tony to "do" in this state of mind? Based on the givens outlined in the next section and the virtuosity required of the song, you and he should work through the lyrics, moment to moment, making choices together based on the subtext he has created for himself. If you have the actor improvise movement before setting it, take notice of how his body is integrating into his emotional state and call him on it if it seems even slightly out-of-character. Ultimately, what the audience "sees" during Tony's singing of this song makes as much an impression as hearing the song itself, even if these impressions are primarily subliminal.

Where and *When* Is the Character Singing?

What are the givens inherent in this scene? In addition to his inner reality discussed above, Tony is walking home from the dance, but the script also indicates that he is "looking for" where Maria lives; he is traveling (I will wager flying, if he could) through the streets of his neighborhood in Manhattan, thinking about this beautiful girl and the instant connection he felt with her. "Traveling" on stage can be a difficult illusion for choreographers to create because actors are confined to a 30'-40' square space, filled most often with settings and set pieces. Audiences may be required to take on that "willing suspension of disbelief" previously mentioned. Depending upon how you interpret the designer's space, you can choose to see it abstractly, ignoring the fact that the scenery doesn't change as Tony travels, or you can imagine he has simply stopped in one area of the neighborhood where he will complete most of the song. It is important to decide upon a specific environment, I believe, so that the performer can feel grounded in a place he can make "real" in his mind. His spatial patterns and intent should depict, for him, the reality of *where* he is and where he is going. His overall intent is to find her. While he is looking, however, he cannot get her out of his mind and wallows in the sound of her name. His body language and movement choices, places of stopping, turning, gesturing, etc., must personify his inner life. For instance, because he is "daydreaming" about her, his walk might be vaguely disoriented and meandering at times, maybe he needs to lean against a building for momentary support or even stop at a park bench to sit down and think. Any number of things could work for this song, but important givens to guide choreographers and performers are the time of day, the location, the character's intent, and his state of mind. What the audience "sees" is the domain of the choreographer, or the director if she is staging the song. Although his actions must stay minimal and pedestrian, of course, every movement on the stage is like every brush stroke on a canvas. It is there for a reason. Each movement sends a message and these messages join forces to create impressions, which elicit feelings from an observer. The performer can collaborate with you to come up with the most effective staging, but ultimately the final choices, particularly the broad strokes, are (and should be) approved and set by you, the choreographer, and they should be repeatable by the actor or actors who will play Tony in that production. Keep in mind that the lighting and sound designs will remain the same for each performance. Nuance or gradations are in the actor's domain and can change slightly from performance to performance, but the overall placement of the actor during the song must be finalized by who is staging it. Helping the actor make these placements work, to make sense of transitions, and to help with gestures or power in stillness, are all techniques the director and choreographer can supply for the actor who is not yet ready to bring them to the table on his own.

Why Does The Character Sing?

The song "Is Anybody There" from *1776* is another excellent example of the soliloquy song (Edwards, 1969). John Adams' ability to unite the Congress in favor of Revolution is at its lowest point in the play. Because of his refusal to remove the slavery clause from the Declaration of Independence, the three southern states have walked out on him, followed by Pennsylvania who cannot obtain a majority vote in favor from their three delegates. They are followed out by most of the other delegates because uniting against England now seems like a futile cause. After this scene John reads one of Abigail's letters—which he does regularly throughout the play for solace and advice. She appears on stage with him and they interact, and even though these interactions are not in "real" time with the rest of the play and occur only in his mind, they allow the audience to know the depth of their relationship and of his strong connection to her. He is at his lowest ebb when he speaks to her now, thinking that he may be wanting independence for selfish reasons or that he may be wrong to feel so strongly about it. He is losing resolve. She reminds him of his own words regarding "commitment," and he is re-energized to keep fighting. Back inside the Chamber he sends the remaining two delegates (Franklin and Jefferson) out on missions to sway delegates back to the fold and says good night to Hancock and Thomson, who leave for the day.

Left in the chamber alone (*place*), Adams is feeling exhausted, depressed, unheard, and ineffectual (*state of mind*). Despondent, he speaks aloud, asking if anyone is there. He continues, "Does anybody care?" and then, "Does anybody see what I see?" (Stone and Edwards, 7-106). The questions are rhetorical. There isn't anyone in the chamber, but it is the same kind of question we have all asked ourselves at different points in our own lives. We can instantly relate. His spirit is in deep distress and we are privy to the inner musings of his mind. His wife Abigail's recent reminder of his early resolve and strong commitment to the cause of revolution re-energizes him to continue fighting, but it is his own inner journey during this song that convinces him to go on. In the song, he reviews all he has done to this point and likens his journey to Caesar's crossing the Rubicon, beyond which there is no going back; and he states clearly those things he sees for America that seem to elude his colleagues. Recapping his vision so passionately fires him up and by the end of the song he has moved past his fatigue and despair to renew himself for his final battle. Edwards' music is somewhat militaristic, even nationalistic, which is appropriate in view of the war John is asking Congress to wage. The melody is formal and matter of fact, but the lyrics are passionate and remind me of an inspiring speech at a political rally.

The song functions in two ways. In one way it moves John to push through the next day's battle with the senators he has yet to convince. This has bearing on plot movement. In another way, it reminds us of the magnitude of what the founding fathers were voting for and of the sacrifices they made to accomplish it. The composer gives this cause the weight it deserves… in this song…in this moment. John Adams unravels himself from all the conflict he has faced and describes how he sees America in the future—down to the fireworks! Freedom! It is his 11:00 number. The *denouement*. As John thinks of the future and visualizes what America can be, he emotionally moves away from his confusion and back to a place of resolve, "come what may." Again, there is no going back and so he vows that whatever happens he will stay committed, come what may. He resolutely states, "Commitment!" (Edwards, "Is Anybody There?").

Figure. 16. John Adams alone in the empty chamber, "Is Anybody There?" from *1776*. Elon University Archives, 2014.

In a sense, he is talking himself into a state of mind he knows he needs to be in for the next scene when the delegates return to vote on the resolution. Alone in the chamber, he begins the song among the desks and spaces the audience is now familiar with. We need to see him there, a lone figure disconnected from the rest of his immediate world. As the song builds, however, I believe it is imperative to pull him downstage to be close to the audience. Bringing a solo song forward and out of its environment emphasizes its presentational character, yes, but also renders the work more immediate and infinitely more compelling. This is an example of Frankel's description of the "platform stage" and how a musical opens up and expands the action. The character moves downstage just forward of the play's environment, lessening the distance between him and the audience; his emotionality is directed squarely toward the audience even while he remains in character. His nearness to them deepens the impact of his intent (see fig. 17).

Figure 17. John leaves the chamber and advances on the audience. "Is Anybody There?" from *1776.* Elon University Archives, 2014.

Adams throws the song out beyond the fourth wall, allowing the audience to be pulled into the power of what this all means not only to him and those people of his time, but to ongoing generations, as well. Although he never speaks directly to the audience during the song, they must commiserate with him and share his passion for this cause. Even though everyone knows the outcome of play, the audience suspends that knowledge in order to savor the suspense and continue to engage with the material. What they may not know is how Congress managed to finally agree after its recent deadlock and are curious as to how their differences resolve. During this song, the audience should pick up on John's passion and ride with it until the end of the play. John's exhilarating projection into the future, his prediction, is for me the most galvanizing lyric of this song. He actually describes how we celebrate our July 4th holiday citing the parades, fireworks, bells and cannons—and finally his vision of "all Americans free forever more" (M.100-114).

Again, as with "Maria," it is imperative that the choreographer maintain use of pedestrian movement for Adams, but it should assume the mood of the song and the energy and state of mind of the singer. Adams begins the song inside the chamber worn out and unsure of how to proceed. During the song he talks himself into an energized state and becomes almost exultant as he envisions a future free from tyranny. As his spirits rise, he moves downstage—close to the audience—and "outside" of the chamber. He does not break the fourth wall there, but his close proximity to the audience heightens their enthusiasm and is, hopefully, infectious.

The song resolves with John back upstage in the chamber proper. The audience is returned to reality and the quiet uncertainty of the present as John once again asks "Is anybody there"? (M.129-130). His mood at the end, however, is lighter and more hopeful. John feels energized and recommitted to his mission. By bringing him back upstage into the chamber for the end, the choreographer also brings the audience back to the present, exactly to where John was when he began his musings, indicating that the entirety of the song took place in his mind. What is different at the end of the song, however, is that John's uncertainty no longer lies with his personal sense of resolve, but only with how the vote will turn out. Remember, however, that the song has prepared both John AND the audience for victory, which is, of course, what happens.

Juggling The Focus When The Stage Is Shared.

Staging a song with two or more people singing, not together or to each other but who are going through their own private inner monologues, requires a strong sense of what the choreographer wants the audience to take from the song in the way of character intention and state of mind. The choreographer must have a strong sense of focus—who is *in* focus and what makes focus shift—and understand how to manipulate the actors' movement to control what the audience watches and when they see it. Learn to become keenly observant of your own work. Notice what you notice because if *you* notice it, so will the audience. The slightest movement on stage can shift focus from one character to another in the blink of an eye.

The song "Anything for Him" from *Kiss of the Spider Woman*, (book by Terrence McNally, music by John Kander and lyrics by Fred Ebb, 1993), is an inner monologue song sung simultaneously by three characters, Valentin, Molina and the Spiderwoman (Kander and Ebb, "Anything For Him"). Each singer has a different objective. The song itself is very simply written. Both its melody and lyrics are uncomplicated, straightforward, and somewhat repetitive. As the audience, we become privy to what each of them are thinking and what each of them want. The song takes place the night before protagonist Molina is released from prison. He is in love with his cell-mate, Valentin, and states frankly, *"I'd do anything for him he must know. I'd do anything for him I want him so"* (M. 8-12). Meanwhile, Valentin needs Molina to do his bidding outside of prison by calling his friend when he is released. He reasons that, *"He'd do anything for me I can tell. He'd do anything for me I know him well. If we touch before he goes he'll make that call, He'd do anything for me, anything at all"* (M. 17-26). The third character, the Spider Woman, is a figment of Molina's imagination, which he envisions as a glamorous movie star from the 1930s. The Spider Woman signifies Molina's impending mortality. Her only lyric in the song repeats several times: *"Soon I feel it, soon somehow. I will have him any minute now"* (M. 5-7, 27-34, 45-56).

So, they all want something from each other. They are all thinking about these things while confined together in a small prison cell. Initially, they sing at different times, stating to the audience what their objective is. When one sings, the characters not singing need to be seen in a thought process that will lead them naturally into their solo part of the song. The characters also sing together, but again not directly *to* each other. Staging for this song should remain uncomplicated and pedestrian. It is essentially blocking, but the movement of each character is precisely decided to coincide with musical and dramatic beats, emphasis, and rhythms, as well as clearly show that at no time, except during the dialogue at the end of the song, are the two men talking directly to each other, nor do they hear what each other is singing. They are, after all, *thinking* these lyrics…out loud…but not really. At the same time, the presence of the Spider Woman suggests to us that Molina is also considering the danger of what he is about to commit to. At the end of the song, the two men do come together physically, the implication now being that Molina will do whatever Valentin asks him to do when he leaves the prison.

The simplistic nature of the song itself, both lyrics and music, are offset by the complexity of the situation and of the inner workings of Molina's mind, in particular. Some thoughts I might jot down as I prepare to stage this song are: The characters are apart at the top of the song. Where is the Spider Woman? How does the scene move into the song? Use the beds and chairs in the room for level changes, to facilitate focus, and to create power structures during the song. Does Molina see the SW, acknowledge her, touch her? Clarify how he feels about her at this point. Clarify his point of view throughout. The two male characters never look directly at each other until the end of the song. They should never give the impression they are listening to each other. Where can the SW go? Is she in the cell with them or somewhere else? She is Molina's cypher and only relates to him. How aggressive is she during this song? I encourage choreographers to answer all such questions in extended conversations with their directors before making any specific choices on their own. It is more difficult and time consuming for your actors to unlearn things they could have learned correctly the first time around.

As the choreographer it is your job to manipulate the focus during this song, to be attentive to what each character says to move the story forward, and to elicit sympathy for Molina, who is falling into a trap set not only by Valentin, but by his own self-destructive nature. Also, the choreographer should keep in mind that this song serves to foreshadow Molina's demise as it may affect choices made. The choices made, both large and small, clarify and emphasize the lyrics and bring the audience to that inevitable turning point at the end of the scene. This song drives the plot forward; it is what changes the status quo and moves the final action into place. Every moment is telling. Perhaps in one instance the focus is on Valentin singing, but Molina does something that you want the audience notice. At that point you would keep Valentin's movement at a minimum with nothing new or important to see, and allow Molina's to be large enough that it is still natural, but will pull focus, such as rising from a sitting position, turning abruptly, or gesturing broadly. Remember that anything a character does that is specific, well seen, committed, intentional, abrupt, or large will always pull focus. If it causes *you* to look at it, it will cause the audience to look at it. After the audience has seen what you want them to see, bring that character back to secondary focus, and allow the singer to take back the stage by again doing something slightly broad in scope to pull the focus back, such as he steps forward, changes body direction, sits down, picks up a bottle, or lays back on the bed. Any such movement will affect focus.

The choreographer must always consider the solo song or two person ballad as important and as complex as any larger group dance number or production number in a play. The changes that take place in the principle characters ultimately carry the theme of the play and most deeply affect the plot. Take the time necessary to understand your actors and the characters they are portraying, as well as doing what you can do to adequately and appropriately tell the story incorporating natural and authentic movement. In the next chapter we will begin by talking about the stage space itself, assessing its places of power and weakness and how to utilize that to your strongest benefit.

ADDITIONAL TECHNIQUES FOR STAGING A SOLO SONG

1. *Employ the actor's natural tendencies as a starting point.* Not every musical theatre performer needs to be a technical dancer, but the ability to project the body into a variety of periods and performance styles is a welcome commodity in this field. In the meantime, if you are observant when auditioning the principle actors, and begin to notice the physicality rather than just their emotionality, then you will be more aware of what will be needed when working with the actors once the show is cast. Often, early on in your career, you will have less say about casting and be relegated to working with the directors' choices. Pray they see the same things you see. Often, you will work with actors who take direction flawlessly, bring themselves to your staging so it looks completely natural, and make every choice organically. However, when you are working with someone who cannot bring these qualities to the table, be ready to make all, or many, of an actor's choices for them and to set every moment of staging with great specificity. Be ready also to work tirelessly with an actor who needs more time to combine the elements of performance well.

2. *"Perform" the song yourself.* When you are preparing a song for a principle actor, it can help to imagine yourself as that character and improvise through the song several times, making choices as if you were going to act the role yourself. If you are about to work with someone you have worked with before, you will know what to expect and that will streamline your preparation somewhat. If you are working with someone you do not know at all, you will need to be prepared for every situation. Call upon the script and score analysis you have done and improvise movement for the character(s) involved. Choose what feels natural and "right" and take those choices into rehearsal with you, even as just a starting point. Collaborate with your performer. Be open, but be ready. Trust your knowledge of each

character you create movement for...but only because you have also done your actor's homework.

3. *Collaborate with your musical director to integrate techniques.* When staging a solo song or duet, I like to start rehearsals by hearing the actors sing through it once with the musical director and accompanist. I will also listen to the notes the musical director gives to the singer afterwards so I can be privy to what is important to him or her in terms of what the performer accomplishes while singing the song. It is most often a benefit to have the musical director with me when I first stage a number, particular a production number, for the obvious reasons of working through the score as I create staging, answering questions, making modifications or adjustments, and inserting their expertise in any number of ways. This kind of integrated collaboration is the most fun for me. Performers love to join the collaboration, as well, because it helps them integrate techniques for a seamless performance. If your rapport with your musical director is free and easy, having that person present for those initial staging rehearsals can be a tremendous time-saving and artistic boon to a choreographer. I cannot stress enough the delight of working with a musical director who is a knowledgeable, willing, and patient collaborator, particularly if he or she is also the show's conductor.

4. *Work with rehearsal props and scenic elements from the beginning of the staging process.* Make certain that your stage manager simulates the scenic design, in scale, in the rehearsal room, as well as makes available rehearsal pieces for the furniture, props, and other scenic elements that will be onstage during the song. As the choreographer, you will not want to stage any song for your show, large or small, in a vacuum and removed from what will ultimately create the stage environment during performance. Rehearsal props and furniture are particularly important because they affect motivation, physical business, timing, and more. If you work without them, not only are you missing important aspects of the song that can authenticate and strengthen it, but you are simply putting off the inevitable. At some point, the elements will all come together and the choreographer will have to continue to modify the song or add rehearsals to deal with those elements. When you create staging for a song with all of the elements present, you are sure to save time and know immediately that the actors can accomplish what you are asking of them. The actual props can also be used to inspire creative ideas and add to the credibility of the characters and the situations they are in.

5. *Maximize the purpose of others on stage.*

    If a character launches into her song and begins a thoughtful self-analysis while, at the author's direction, other characters are still onstage, consider carefully why those other characters are there and whether you should keep them onstage or have them exit. I confess that many times I will add ensemble members to the stage during solo songs if I believe their presence is appropriate and gives the song setting a more natural air. If the song is an inner monologue those other actors are obviously not there to listen to it or respond in any way, but you can employ them physically to intensify the moment, normalize it, or somehow enhance or emphasize what the character is going through. Maybe you want to create or maintain a mood or atmosphere, such as people sitting at tables in an outdoor cafe in Firenze, strolling through Central Park, or sitting in a train car on their way to Gary, Indiana. Remember, also, to carefully communicate to ensemble members what their purpose is each time you incorporate them into a scene or song. When an actor steps onstage, she must know *why* so she has something to act. Help your actors make specific choices for their character's purpose onstage and you can better create authentic movement for them. Finally, be sure to employ your eye for focus and balance and consider these "extra" actors when creating the overall image or aesthetic.

Assignments – Chapter 6

Out-of-Class Assignment

Find and list ten soliloquy songs from musicals. At least one should be from the show you are assigned to research. Choose **one** of these songs and analyze it through the following elements:

- What is the author's intention—what do the author and songwriters want the audience to know or understand by the end of the song?

- What is the environment? Where is the character? Where is she going? Are there physical obstacles or other things there that can affect her? Is there anyone else on stage?

- What is the character's state of mind?

- Is the character working something out in his mind?

- What does the character decide, realize, or believe by the end of the song? (Describe the arc of the song.)

- In broad strokes, describe some staging choices you might make for this song.

In-class Assignment

Instructor should find two inner monologue songs from well-known musicals, one with one character, and the other with more than one. Assign the choreographers to work with the performers during the class period to create staging for each song.

Chapter 7
Were Thine That Special Face?
Staging Character Development and Relationship

Relationship: the way in which two or more concepts, objects, or people are connected, or the state of being connected, associated or involved; the way in which two or more people or organizations regard and behave toward each other; an emotional or other connection between people; a sexual involvement; affair (various Dictionary definitions).

If living is about anything, it is about connecting with another living creature or at least something other than ourselves that we are invested in, be it a work of art, a vocation, or a passion. Works of art are either created about people or are about ideas or things that affect or are affected by people; vocations bond us with our society, ideas, or a deity on a deep level; and passions consume our thinking and activities because we relate so deeply with them. Artists put their passions on display in order to influence how another person feels about something. Right now, I am writing this book about how to do just that (to influence feelings) effectively through a particular discipline, by a very specific kind of artist. But, even if we hide our art in a remote garret somewhere, we have a relationship with the art itself that happens when we create it. Our minds, or who we are, connect with ideas that affect others constantly. Society even makes being alone without outside stimulation a punishment by putting criminals in solitary confinement when they really want to make an impact on them. Being alone on a desert island seems like heaven to a beleaguered housewife, but truly, only a short time would pass before that housewife would start padding around the island looking for adventure or someone else to talk to and engage with. Even pirates have parrot sidekicks on their shoulders; Peter Pan had Tinkerbelle, Don Quixote had Sancho Panza, and the Lone Ranger had Tonto. Why, Geppetto *made* himself a puppet so he would have a little boy to love!

Would musical theatre, or any drama for that matter, exist if it were not about people and their relationships with other people or at least in what they imagine those relationships to be? In the musical *Sunday In the Park With George* (Lapine & Sondheim, 1984), post-impressionist painter George Seurat was consumed by his art, but Sondheim and Lapine created Dot, Seurat's model, as a double metaphor to point out the artist's detached and conflicted nature. Seurat is passionate about *making* dots (or his brush strokes that become his personal and innovative technique), and he is also passionate *about* Dot (his model). The irony is that he can neither connect intimately with his art, nor with Dot. While he may have forged a psychological need, his emotionality eludes him. He lives outside of his art and he lives without Dot. The musical is about the *inability* to connect and, ultimately, how an artist must learn to do so to move toward being content and fully realized. Audiences watch the struggles of characters in a play or film, but unless they come to believe in and care about the characters through the actors who are portraying them, they certainly will not care about the established or ensuing relationships depicted, nor do I believe will they be *emotionally* affected by the message of the story. When we *read* a well-written play, or novel, we care about the characters as we imagine them to be in our minds. In a musical, however, even if the libretto and score are as brilliantly constructed as *Sunday in the Park with George,* we rely on the directors and the actors to make us invest in and *care* about people essentially pretending to live in front of us. And we need to care within the first ten minutes of the play because during the exposition relative strangers must begin to matter deeply to us. It is the nature of live theatre.

Using The Stage To Make A Statement

In my Doris Humphrey "bible" of dance composition, Humphrey spends all of Chapter 9 on the importance of understanding stage values. This chapter is required reading for my choreography classes because of its interesting and useful analysis of the proscenium stage. Please note that in thrust or in-the-round spaces the specs will change. While there is no effective way to adequately summarize all of her analysis, I will direct my readers to those pages in her text, which she titles The Stage Space (72-90). Putting aside her personal opinions, which I know can be vexing to some of today's young choreographers, we can focus on what is pertinent. Humphrey approaches the space itself with both a sense of wonder and an understanding of its structure, writing "...a stage is a highly specialized kind of space—not, like a studio, bounded by four walls, windows, mirrors, chairs, and whatnot; nor is it wide open like a meadow or a beach" (72). She goes on to quote Ruth St. Denis who said, "I never in my life set my feet on a stage without thinking of its magic and my destiny" (73). Her analysis of the strong and weak areas of the stage, the power of the diagonals, and the impact of body lines and placement can seem rigid, but truly work if applied. By "work," I mean that the director and choreographer can influence, and even direct, a viewer's emotional response—moment to moment—by where they place performers on the stage. Any proscenium staging or blocking could be considered through the Humphrey lens to create meaning, such as to emphasize a power structure or equality between performers, to increase pathos or victory, to play down, or play up, theatricality, and to use distance and nearness effectively—among a host of other script-serving techniques.

If you consider the proscenium architecture, most prominent are its four corners, each supported by powerful verticals. Humphrey suggests standing a dancer in any of the four corners and to note the result. "The upper two," she states, "make the figure seem important with a remoteness which suggests, if there is no other specific mood, a heroic beginning. The powerful verticals energize the body; it seems to be upheld by walls of both physical and spiritual strength" (74). Regarding center stage, she considers up center through dead center to down center as a particularly potent area. When a dancer walks that path slowly, he or she begins as remote and mysterious and, way up there, has great potential for symbolism and the power of the abstract. Then,

> …as he advances, the electrically charged center takes over and he increases in stature and in power. Now note that as he moves to the apron, although he looms larger physically, the power diminishes rapidly, and on the footlights—or where the footlights used to be—we see this is a fellow student…in short, a real, non-magical and non- potent young lady. (80)

Albeit a line of seventeen dancers rather than only one "young lady," remember that Michael Bennett had his line of dancers walk just this path after the cut dancers exit the stage in the opening number of *A Chorus Line (ACL)*. Those dancers not asked to leave are standing upstage in that iconic line, remote and blurred. From there, in military unison, they step downstage through Humphrey's "electrically charged" dead center where, momentarily, the audience is jolted to attention by the dancers' combined intensity. The lights suddenly blackout as they walk, coming up, as suddenly, a moment later when we see them standing dead still on the line holding their resume pictures in front of their faces. They are now downstage of the proscenium where their "power diminishes rapidly." Here we can see them, not as a generalized group of Broadway gypsies, but as individual and vulnerable people. I use this particular show to talk about relationship because, although it was created expressly to de-marginalize Broadway chorus dancers and even to glorify them, (i.e. Michael Bennett's "valentine" to Broadway gypsies), it also, paradoxically, highlights their commonality with the rest of the world. Through the dancers' monologues we discover how, like everyone else, they were shaped and, for some, marginalized by their early relationships. To examine this point a bit further, I will state my observance that professional dancers were and are indeed marginalized, not just as back-ups to the stars but to society as a whole where they are set apart and exoticized by non-theatre people. Classical and modern dancers who work in companies, in particular, are marginalized in the workplace in the way of lower salaries, lack of job security, and lack of support for their work. America does not support its artists so dance companies and private artists must constantly rely upon grants, donations and subscriptions to survive. Dancing is not a "real job," but more of a hobby. In addition, people still tend to have poor opinions of performers, a stubborn puritanical hold-over since our country's beginnings and early opinions of female performers. The women were thought of to be generally weak and complicit fodder for "stage door Johnnies," and the men were considered devoid of any morals at all. These opinions have improved to some extent, or at least have become more covertly expressed, but in these ways, and others, professional dancers represent the "Other." My point regarding *A Chorus Line*, however, is that in this musical, the marginalization of dancers exists alongside their commonality with everybody else in the world, and this commonality has to do with the importance of the other people in our lives.

Most people are not dancers. People in *ACL* audiences are initially intrigued by this difference, but are ultimately drawn into the magic of *ACL* through the dancers' stories. The magic of this show lies in the sameness of the dancers' concerns to those of almost everyone else in the world. Through the highly specific and unusual world of the Broadway dance audition, Kirkwood, Dante, Hamlisch, Kleban, and Bennett render the everyday ordinary shared concerns of humanity. Like *West Side Story*, dance helps to tell the story of *ACL*, but the heart of these shows are in the stories being told. *WSS* retained its heart when it was made into a film because it retained the authenticity of the original story and its characters. *ACL* did not, so it had no power as a film. We must remember that the book is paramount unless we are making dances strictly for entertainment purposes. Even (especially) the dances in *A Chorus Line*.

The Commonality of *A Chorus Line*

The individuals in *ACL* are all professional dancers (both the characters and therefore the actors), which I will wager is a very specialized and relatively small percentage of the world's demographic.[3] For the most part, the characters' stories, while about themselves, all have to do with other people in their lives. The dancers reveal their individuality through stories about how they were/are affected by these other people. When audiences watch *ACL,* these stories are what most people relate to—not the fact that the performers are dancers. However, the excellent side-perk

---

3   I estimate that only .00004 % of people filing income tax in America are professional dancers and this includes dance performers *and* choreographers, or around 15,200 professional dancers and choreographers (U.S. Bureau of Labor Statistics, *Choreographers & Dancers,* 2017) in 327,850,000 people (U.S. Census Bureau, June 4, 2018).

of this production is that audiences become fascinated with the fact that they are watching dancers reveal themselves as people, rather than the faceless bodies that audiences normally see when they watch a musical on the stage. Each of the dancers talks about other people and how they were led to this place in their lives because of how much they loved, followed, needed, were hurt by, were changed by, challenged, or disappointed by *other people.* Maggie, Sheila, and Bebe had cold and distant parents who they felt did not value them. In the absence of that parental nurturing, they escaped to ballet class and into their imaginations. There, "everything was beautiful" (Hamlisch and Kleban, "At the Ballet"). Many can relate, maybe not to the ballet class but to a place to escape and to the distant parents. Paul talks about the pain and humiliation he suffered when his parents first saw him dressed as a drag queen, and although most of us haven't had that exact experience, many of us have been caught unawares by our parents in a compromising situation or had the feeling of being a disappointment to them…and so we relate. Mike talks about watching his sister in dance class, and Bobby talks about rebelling against a provincial upbringing around people who viewed him as "strange" during his formative years…and we can relate. Diana overcame the humiliation leveled on her by her acting teacher and Cassie is trying to get over her failure to appeal to film and television audiences and to work again with Zach. Because failing at a profession we are passionate about or having a skill that no one wants and with nowhere to use it are universal experiences, audiences are able to relate, and they feel vulnerable. *ACL* is a musical about relationships and how life-forming and life-changing they can be. It will be instructive to look at how the director and designers staged this show to bring its message across so profoundly.

To begin, where are the actors while they are telling their characters' stories? They are far downstage standing alone in that very vulnerable part of the stage that shows the actor for the ordinary person he or she is, and a place of intimacy with the audience. When you think about all of the places on stage the actors could be and of all the different characters in the play they could be speaking to, or how else the play could have been structured to focus on the lives of Broadway dancers, it is interesting that Bennett and his collaborators chose the premise and structure they did, given the difficulties inherent in writing real life people and situations into a theatrical work. He chose the absolute "real-life" premise for a Broadway dancer, which is on a Broadway stage auditioning for the next big musical, the next well-paying and artistically validating experience to which each character onstage aspires. No, dancers are not normally asked to step out of a line-up and told they need to share their life-stories, at least I never was. This liberty was taken by the creators and was effective, probably because it points up the vulnerability factor like nothing else can and it is much more interesting than the normal play-out of an audition experience. Except for a few instances that will require a larger use of space, this line formed downstage is where the actors will be for a large part of Act 1. As stated earlier, from a horizontal line across the upstage area, with their resume pictures hiding their faces, the entire line of called-back dancers walk in precision, powerfully and directly *en masse* toward the audience, like brave lambs to the slaughter. They stop near the proscenium line, a few feet upstage from the orchestra pit. From an in-one position, which is forward several steps in *front* of the proscenium line, or between the line of dancers and the footlights, the characters speak to Zach and reminisce about their lives as dancers.

Note: *An "in-one" position is normally a scene played in front of the act curtain. There is an exit wing there on both sides of the stage, which is between the act curtain and the proscenium wall. That would be counted as the first wing, or number one. Hence, a scene played forward of the curtain is known as a "scene-in-one." In* ACL, *instead of the curtain, a white line is painted horizontally across the stage just forward of the proscenium arch.*

Much of the first act of ACL is played from this "in-one" position, or very close to the audience. In a sense, the fourth wall is gone (they talk to Zach in the audience) but in a sense, it is not. Except for Zach and his assistants, the characters must still believe the theatre is empty so the actors' fourth wall is still up... in a way. Interesting actor's problem.

Though rarely seen, Zach, the hiring choreographer and the person everyone on the line is addressing, has the most power in this production. He lives in the back of the audience where no one can see him except for the times he comes onto the stage to teach the audition material or to comfort an emotional dancer. He is the "God-voice" coming from the audience, calling each dancer in turn to answer his questions. He is safely hidden in the darkness, unrevealed. His vulnerability factor is quite low. When called, a dancer steps even more forward of the line to speak to Zach and reminisce about how he or she became a dancer. From that position, the dancer's vulnerability factor is quite high. When there, the dancers tell Zach how they connected with and were formed by other people in their lives. Why? Because they want desperately to connect with *him* in any way they can, enough so that he sees their uniqueness and gives them a job. As they speak they are also relating to *each other* for support and acceptance. They are forming new relationships or relying on old ones to help them emotionally through the audition. When called to speak alone, they stand in that section of the stage that slips them into a one-on-one relationship with the audience. Wedged as they are between the "Line" behind them and the orchestra in front of them, they are alone in no-man's land, the most unguarded part of the stage where the audience can see them most clearly. Theron Musser's innovative lighting design enhanced the actors' feelings, as well as their vulnerability, by giving each of them two lights when they were standing on the line: a "thought light" and a "face light." When they were standing alone speaking directly to Zach, Musser used a less color-saturated and harsher front light, (light that is focused onto the stage from in front of it), to illuminate them. This is opposed to when they were watching or "thinking," for which she used softer warmer colors and angled focus (Jeffries 6). She also placed each of them in specially positioned 55 degree angled follow spots to further isolate each dancer without picking up environment or other characters (4). Even the character Sheila talks about the harshness of the light on her and asks for a warmer colored gel to soften it. Her defense to feeling so vulnerable is to use sexy sarcasm because that is familiar and comforting for her. Bobby exudes a kind of edgy, caustic sense of humor, and Morales becomes tough and shielded. In contrast, some just go with the flow and react as they would in any circumstance. Essentially, the way they react to being put in this position reveals a great deal about each of their characters. The collaboration of the lighting designer and the director/choreographer in *ACL* was complete and effective.

Epic Theatre—With A Twist?

...as the performer 'observes himself,' his objective is to appear strange...to the audience. Making obvious the manipulative contrivances and 'fictive' qualities of the medium, the actors alienate the viewer from any passive acceptance and enjoyment of the play as mere 'entertainment.' Instead, the viewer is forced into a critical, analytical frame of mind...This effect of making the familiar strange...teaches the viewer not to take the style and content for granted, since the medium itself is highly constructed and contingent upon many cultural and economic conditions. (Willet, 1964, "Distancing Effect")

The use of stage mirrors during selected times of *ACL* is obviously pulled from the dance studio/rehearsal hall look of the traditional dance space and is not something auditioners would see on a Broadway stage, although they would see it if they were auditioning in a dance studio, which is also done. Bennett conflated these spaces, most likely in order to show the audience how professional dancers learn and perfect movement. How much he knew about Brechtian theatre devices I do not know, but by using the mirrors on the stage space, with particular awareness of their scope and size, along with a number of other conventions that make up the show's script and production concept, places *A Chorus Line* in the territory of Epic Theatre. Epic Theatre is a term and a mode of presentation that Bertolt Brecht borrowed from director/producer Erwin Piscator and then developed and popularized. Brecht described his theatre-making as the *Verfremdungseffekt* (estrangement effect), a distancing or alienation effect. Brecht believed theatre should have an agenda, be instructive, particularly socially and politically. His aim was to distance his actors from the audience emotionally so that playgoers would develop intellectual empathy rather than emotional empathy, engage their critical skills and try to right the problems presented by the play. He wanted audiences to retain awareness of being in a theatre and of the show being an illusionary experience rather than to engage them emotionally or have them believe in the illusion. Brecht was developing his philosophy and artistic techniques during the 1920s and 30s in Germany. Ironically, his alienation effect was in direct contrast to the realistic acting and naturalistic staging of Stanislavski's method acting techniques, which were spreading and taking root around the world during this same time. Stanislavski's "art of experiencing" vs. the "art of representation" (Stanislavsky, 1938), was in direct contrast to Brecht's desire to intellectually engage his audiences by distancing them emotionally. While I certainly do not believe the creative team of *ACL* was trying to distance their audiences emotionally, I find it interesting that so many Brechtian influences are present in their show and wonder if the way these influences bump into and interact with the "art of experiencing" is what makes the show so powerful. See Table 5 below, which enumerates instances where Brechtian techniques appear in *A Chorus Line*.

EPIC THEATRE TECHNIQUES	**A CHORUS LINE**
1. Transposition into the past	*Dancers' histories are the material.*
2. Speaking the stage directions out loud	*Dance steps are lyrics. Zach, & assistant, are constantly giving stage directions.*
3. Actors "break the fourth wall" by speaking into the audience	*Actors speak to Zach in the audience, breaking the fourth wall.*
4. Stage "purged from anything magical"	*Realistic, minimal setting; realistic costumes.*
5. Use of multi-media (acting, dance, music, mask, chorus, signs, film)	*An empty, undressed stage is primary set. No use of media but performance genres all used.*
6. Use of *comedy, satire*, grotesque stereotypes. The audience is invited to laugh at them and ultimately condemn what they stand for	*Dancers speak satirically of people in their past, condemning their actions. (Bobby's story, Val's story, Sheila, Maggie, etc.).*
7. Gestures used to indicate inner feelings- stage pictures used for effect	*Common in dance, common in musicals.*
8. Use of ensemble	*Check.*
9. No 'fourth wall'	*Check.*
10. Minimal props	*Dance Bags, Hats.*
11. Playwright structures episodically	*Yes, but within a linear framework.*
12. Awareness of events in the past	*Check!*
13. Socialist message prevailed	*Yes—i.e., "Don't forget about the faceless gypsies who support the stars!"*
14. Anti-illusive techniques, flash backs	*At the Ballet, Montage, Bobby's monologue, etc.*
15. Lighting Designer abandons idea of hiding sources of light to achieve mysterious effect and pull audience into the action.	*Discrepancies here in real versus abstract, which is used often during monologues or songs. We often see sources of light, at times we do not.*

Table 2. Brechtian Influences in *ACL*

Still with me? Deep breath. Going on. Using some of these techniques in his design, *ACL* scenic designer Robin Wagner created an empty stage, no illusion there. No curtains, legs, or wings, just the space and one width-long white line and a row of mirrors upstage, *some* of the time. Lighting instruments were also in full view. The show opens on a Broadway stage during a dance audition—what used to be termed a "cattle call." (Horrible, right?) This environment lays down a real-life, documentary-like foundation for the play. The dancers face upstage looking into the mirrors with the audience behind them. This is what the audience sees as the lights come up at the top of the show. Everyone in the theatre is facing those mirrors, which mirror the reality of being in a theatre performing or being performed to, reminding the audience they are watching a show. Seeing the reflection of their own faces in the mirrors causes audience members to remain rooted in a theatrical space, but also places them in a symbiotic relationship with the performers indicating to them a shared vulnerability. The audience is also "on the line," as are most people in the world every day of their lives, dependent upon other people for acceptance and validation. (An important point about the show should be inserted here. The show, as conceived and created by Bennett, *et al.*, is a show about Broadway gypsies, seasoned dancers who have been making their living dancing. The film on the other hand, re-conceived and directed by Richard Attenborough, was about young dancers trying to break into show business. A vast difference in content, tone, point of view, and…well everything.) Back to Brecht…

Having the dancers tell stories about themselves that are based on taped biographical accounts seems almost like a documentary as they are in a teacher/learner discourse with the audience; they are informing the audience (through Zach) of the challenging pasts and the uphill climbs of a Broadway dancer. Here is the "working class" of Broadway performers; the blue collar *hoi polloi*. This is another Brechtian characteristic, a populist statement pointing out and emphasizing inequities within society. As the audience observes the dancers, the dancers also watch each other as they are telling their stories. Throughout the play, there are almost always observers on stage—another Brechtian device. The dancers' shared need for a job is also their need to be good enough to be accepted, a need certainly felt often by members of the audience, and that is what is actually on the line. This shared need creates an emotional connection, and maybe herein lies its departure from true epic theatre. That need, that vulnerable spot in each of these characters, must remain apparent in every song they sing and every dance they perform throughout the course of the play. It must remain apparent in Sheila's jaded and callous approach to herself and her life, which is the legacy of unloving parents. It must remain present in Val's matter of fact, "no-big-deal" approach to life, covering an obviously strong need to be the perfect Broadway chorus girl. So, despite all of the Brechtian or distancing factors conceptualizing the show, we still develop feelings for these characters and are swept into their memories and their immediate desire to get the job. A detailed examination of how this happens is material for another book, but as suggested earlier, it may be a combination of the performers acting in a naturalistic style (*pathos*) rather than using Brecht's overly theatrical acting devices, the shared need to be accepted (*ethos*), and the obviously theatrical pseudo-portrayal of reality, and other epic theatre techniques, (*logos*) that makes this show such a powerful experience.

So, as per Stanislavski, the choreographer should don the director's cap to ensure that the creation and performance of the staging include consideration of state of mind, intention and relationship, and to craft stage movement around what is most natural for these dancers in this situation. Truly, if there ever were the quintessential director/ choreographer musical, *A Chorus Line* is it.

Tangent. *A Chorus Line is a show that is hardly, if ever, produced without the original staging and choreography, which is pretty darn unusual. Of course, there* **are** *directors and choreographers who are hired to recreate original Broadway staging for National Tours, which must be as close to the New York experience as possible. There are choreographers who borrow liberally from original productions of musicals, and some are hired because they were in the original and know that choreography. Sometimes, the original choreography is written down and rented along with the other show materials, such as with* Carnival, *which sends Gower Champion's choreography accompanying the libretto. Generally, however, choreographers like to create their own version of a show and when possible, start from scratch with their own choreography allowing for the vision of the director and the specific givens of the venue, scenic design and the dancers cast in their production. However, whether deliberate or not, Michael Bennett and the creators of* ACL *locked in almost every aspect of their show so that it would be difficult—if not impossible—for subsequent productions to put their own spin on the show or interpret it differently. Song lyrics, of course, are tied into dances and the teaching of dance combinations, e.g. "I Hope I Get It" and "One." Creating new choreography for those numbers, while done for the film, is virtually unheard of for the stage and, because of this, Bennett's' dances have become iconic and expected.*

Bennett entrusted the authenticity of future productions of the show to his long-time friend, Baayork Lee. Lee, the original Connie Wong and assistant choreographer and dance captain for the original production, has since re-staged productions of it around the world, as well as for the 2006 Broadway revival (Viagas et al, 341-42).

Relationship—No Matter Who Is In The Spotlight

If a character is onstage, they are important whether they are singing, speaking, dancing, or not doing much at all. Whoever is onstage is telling the story. No one should be taken for granted because another actor is in stronger focus. Nothing goes unnoticed. Every movement or expression has an impact. There are no small actions, but there may be inattentive choreographers.

Several years ago, I was teaching a pilot Musical Theatre (MT) Choreography class to undergraduate musical theatre majors. All of my students taking the course were strong singer/dancer/actors (in any order) who wanted to try their hand at creating movement. I had them work in pairs analyzing a musical and then choosing two songs from it to work on: one song had to use predominantly musical staging and the other could be a number that employed technical dance choreography and a group of technical dancers. Two of these students chose "If I Were a Bell," and "Luck Be a Lady Tonight" from *Guys and Dolls* (Loesser, 1950). Each song would have its own choreographer with the partner acting as an assistant choreographer. The student in charge of "If I Were a Bell," brought it in for its first showing with a fair understanding of the script and who the characters were in this scene but, as I find a great deal with first time choreographers, was more focused on the music and movement than on the characters and situation. I have chosen this assignment to discuss because the early pitfalls of these choreographers are indicative of how most young choreographers approach such a number—I know I did—and also because their final showing of the song was beautiful and triumphant. Reminder: tell the story. In an integrated musical, a star turn is never ONLY a star turn…

The characters who perform this song in *Guys and Dolls*, Sky and Sarah, are from different worlds. Sky is an uneducated gambler who has no sense of responsibility for anyone or anything; Sarah is an educated Salvation Army missionary worker who has made herself responsible for the saving of souls. She is concerned about any and all souls and at this moment is desperate to find some so that she can keep the mission going. Set in a "mythical" New York City, the Damon Runyon stories that inspired this musical are set in the 1920s and 30s (Burrows & Swerling, 1950). The precise time of the musical is somewhat "fluid," but authenticity would set it during Prohibition. Sky has made a $1000.00 bet with Nathan, a fellow gambler. Sky says that he can get Sarah, the missionary "doll," to go to Havana with him for dinner, and she does agree to go because he promises her 100 bona fide "sinners" for her prayer meeting the following night. Sarah naively gets herself drunk during dinner and on the street afterwards tells Sky how great she is feeling. *In a tipsy state* she sings the song "If I Were a Bell." As I previously wrote, my students choreographing this song were gifted dancers and singers and good critical thinkers, and I was sure they would have solid answers to my questions.

Some of the first questions I usually ask after seeing a piece are: "What is happening in this scene"? Why is this song in the show? What is each character thinking/feeling before/as/after the number takes place? What compels her or him to sing here? And, maybe most importantly, what changes happen from the beginning to the end of the song, (i.e. what is the arc of the song?). After seeing their staging for the first time I believe one of my initial questions was, "Why is Sky in this scene?" Sarah sang the song and danced throughout. She performed well and it was entertaining. Regarding the storyline, however, I knew that was not being addressed because she related very little to Sky, who mostly stood or sat nearby, watching her and smiling. I hadn't learned anything specific about why the song was important to the plot or about changes happening between them. I heard her words, so I could surmise certain things, but the psychology and emotionality was "general." When acting or directing choices are "general," the audience will get a general idea about what is going on and can assume things one way or another...or just observe and not participate in a personal way. In an integrated show, this number would not just be a star turn for the actress playing Sarah, but a moment that will affect the plot and how the story turns out. When I brought this up, I believe the choreographers--and many in the class—seemed taken aback and even a bit disconcerted that I was not asking questions about the dance they had created for Sarah. Even in light of our reading and writing assignments and class discussions, I believe they were still primarily focused on the "dance" they choreographed or, at least, that I would look at that before asking theoretical questions about the characters. We talked more, and it was clear they did understand that Sky starts having strong feelings for Sarah *during* this number. Without him engaging with her throughout, however, the audience could only guess at that. The focus would be only on Sarah being a little drunk and loosening up rather than on Sky's journey, as well. Now I will admit that the premise of the main story in *Guys and Dolls* is definitely a stretch. Even if Sarah and Sky get together at the end of the show, which they do, who is to say that either of them would ever change enough to get along in a marriage in real life terms? Highly unlikely. But, that's the stuff that "romance" is made of. The best of all possible worlds. The trick for the directors and performers, therefore, is to convince the audience that this relationship is viable, and because these characters love each other so much, this unlikely match is entirely possible. The audience needs to see these feelings of genuine caring begin to emerge, rather specifically, during this number. By the end of it Sky decides not to take advantage of Sarah's condition and keep her overnight in Havana, but instead, *against* her wishes, he takes her back to New York. In real life, is this a feasible scenario? Would a lifelong cad suddenly change colors so quickly and completely, put lust aside and become a nice guy who loves this buttoned-up woman enough to respect her? Well, maybe I am the world's most cynical cynic, but I think probably not, which would make me work pretty hard to build this "unfeasible" blossoming of mature and unselfish love clearly into the staging of their song. With precise, unambiguous staging events, the actors will have well-defined progressive action that gives them opportunities to share their emerging feelings with an audience.

Also, Sarah's movement cannot be just dance for dance's sake. The fact that she is drunk is motivating her actions. She doesn't normally act like this. She is someone who holds her feelings in and most likely denies them more often than she admits them, even to herself. Her *everyday* movements are more bound than free, more on a straight and narrow path than random, and more measured and deliberate than she is being now. Knowing this, the choreographer immediately has clues to how Sarah is approaching movement. It might be dancelike because it is working *against* her natural tendencies. Very much so. But the real Sarah is still inside this new emerging Sarah, so care must be taken to make her journey gradual and so also make the audience's journey gradual, and more feasible.

For Sarah to be executing technically precise dance steps as a strong performer and to be relating to her audience as a performer, (even if the audience is just Sky), would take us out of the reality of the scene. In the given scenario, she is *not* self-conscious. She is not self-censoring, and the audience should be aware of these differences in her. This is the Sarah he is falling in love with, most likely. She is flawed and is showing him aspects of her real self, something she does not show to many people. He is amused, yes, but he is also engaged with her because she is engaging. He is having as much fun watching her as she is having just being herself. We should see these qualities in them both emotionally *and* physically. His catching her as she's about to fall, his saving her from a misstep, or her engaging him to dance with her a little allows them both to find times to let the chemistry flow between them. Another thing to remember, by the way, is that physically, drunks normally try to appear sober rather than "drunk." Being drunk is someone trying to walk a straight line who cannot. Having Sarah work against her diminished capacities adds variety and realism to the moment. While Sarah is predominant in this song, Sky is still on the stage—on purpose. As a choreographer, you are not *just* the person who makes up the dance steps to fit with the music. You must have the analytical skills of a director to understand the story's moment to moment needs and each character's "befores, durings, and afters" in order to make specific and believable movement choices. Know where the characters are coming from and where they are going, so you will understand where they logically should be during this scene. You cannot just listen to the music and know what to do. Well you can, but then you may create a good number for a revue, not one that is in-context with the show. Doing careful background work sets you up with the "givens" of the scene. These givens are your tools.

Choreography in musical theatre is rarely dance for its own sake but exists in order to serve the story. You know you have to get Sarah from here to there psychologically; you know you have to get Sky from there to here emotionally. You have to do both accompanied by what the composer has written. The choreographer is responsible to give the actors staging that allows them to sing the song well, keeps the characters in their moment to moment realities, fulfills the song's purpose, and appropriately fuses the music and movement stylistically. Choreographers must bring their own sensibilities into play. The choices made from their private improvisations, the clues heard in the orchestration and arrangement of the song, the scenic elements making up the environment are all in the toolbox. Are they on a street corner? Is there anything to sit on nearby? Is there a lamppost or a bench? USE these items. Are they walking from one place to another? Are there passersby? USE THEM. Remember that in a musical, the dealio (Urban Dictionary, 2005), is that there are clues and tools everywhere, from inside and outside of the script and from all the collaborators working on *that* particular production. Don't let any of it slip your notice or your consideration as you problem-solve getting Sarah from here to there and Sky from there to here.

SUMMARY: POINTS WHEN STAGING

1. *Do your homework.* Research the characters as though you were acting them yourself; understand their background, psychology, motivations, and objectives for the scene. If you have not yet, discuss the scene with your director to be sure you have come to the same conclusions before you work with the actors. What you do not want to happen is a disagreement on these foundational ideas *after* you stage the number.

2. *Study the progression of the song*. Do a close reading of the dialogue before and after the song, as well as of the lyrics. Understand where each character begins and where they end. Understand its purpose and what we need to know/feel by the end of the scene. When in doubt, always go back to the script.

3. *Try getting into each character's body.* With or without music, move through the song as the character. Understand what would be appropriate and logical for these people. This is not to say that all the movement is always strictly pedestrian—you are still working with music and we are still a step above the real world because of that—but the movement still must come logically out of moment and be performed in a way singular to the characters performing it

4. *Draft it*. Try getting something up on its feet—your first ideas. Something. Anything. Then play with it. Get ideas from your actors. Improvise. Watch them together and find movement they instinctively go to and craft that into the piece. Don't expect the first go-around to be the last. Writers compose many drafts before the final draft.

5. *Collaborate*. Your musical director may also have some great ideas to point out or add musically while you are mounting a number. It never hurts to ask if a musical idea you have is possible or amenable to work in. All they can say is "no" or "I'd rather not." Also, be sure you talk over the characters with your director beforehand to learn if there are specific ideas she or he already has to incorporate. Also, where will the blocking leave the characters on the set just before and after the number, or will it be your job to have them begin or end in a specific place? These things are important to know before starting, or you may have to go back to the drawing board after the blocking is completed to re-do the top or the end of the song.

6. *Heed the bottom line*. What is the relationship of the people who are onstage together in this song? Whether two characters or twenty, how are relationships affected during the number? If one person is observing, when appropriate, find active ways for him to participate in telling the story. Remember that a response doesn't always need to be physically active as long as it is specific and moves the story along.

Short Tangent. *I was prompted to add my last statement above after watching a television broadcast of a two-person number where only one of the characters was singing. This is a less physically active example and it may have been more noticeable on television that it is from a distance, but worth bringing up here. In a scene from the musical* The Band's Visit, *actors Katrina Lenk (Dina) and Tony Shalhoub (Tewfiq) performed the song "Omar Sharif." Only Dina sings, telling Tewfiq about her experiences listening to music on Egyptian radio and seeing Omar Sharif in the movies as she was growing up. As he listens, he is getting to know someone he just met a few hours earlier. Sitting at a café table after dinner, as the song progresses, Dina's physicality amps up as her body expresses how she is feeling about it. Her minimal physicality tells us a great deal about who she is and seems to create a kind of sexual tension between them. Tewfiq only enters the song as someone reacting to her, enjoying her, and probably feeling closer to her because of this interaction, but I found Shalhoub's reactions specific, compelling, and an integral part of the song. We see his experience reflected mainly by his countenance, not in his overall physicality. His body retained the essential character of someone who is quiet, reserved, and proper, but very warm. A perfect "less is more" illustration.*

7. *Play the mood.* Find the temperament or outlook of the number and, as you watch it, be sure it comes across consistently and as you intend it to be. Should humor be a part of how the story is most effectively told? Humor, while completely appropriate in "If I Were a Bell," would not be, for instance, in "The Proposal" from *Jane Eyre, the Musical*, nor in "Not While I'm Around" from *Sweeney Todd*. While there may be a humorous moment in a serious song, or vice versa, the overall intended tone of the song should be maintained. Sometimes it comes down to common sense, and to taste.

Assignment - Chapter 7

In-class assignment

The instructor should choose two-person songs from a variety of musicals and assign one to each pair of choreographers to prepare a first-draft staging of it. Having the same song staged by more than one team is also fine to show different treatments of the same piece. Two performers are assigned to each of the teams. If the material is new to the students, they should conduct some basic research on their own before the next class meeting, which they will use as a rehearsal period to stage the song they were assigned. Also, before that class, the performers can set a common time to meet with the accompanist in order to learn the music and tape it for the choreographers to use in rehearsal. The instructor may act as the "director" and answer any questions choreographers have regarding the scene or the characters. Choreographers may also choose any scenic elements they feel are necessary for the song to play appropriately. Some song possibilities are: "If I'm Not Near the Girl I Love, I Love the Girl I'm Near" (Finian's Rainbow), "If I Were a Bell" (Guys and Dolls), "People Will Say We're In Love" or "All Er Nuthin'" (Oklahoma), "Fit as a Fiddle" (Singin' In The Rain), "Perfect for You" (Next to Normal), "Small Umbrella In the Rain" (Little Women), "Embraceable You" (Crazy for You), etc. Note that I chose more active numbers. One of the reasons for this assignment is to learn to prepare and make choices quickly and allow the choreographer's instinct to enter the work.

The choreographers must know **who** the characters are, understand **what** situation they are in, and **when** and **where** it is happening. Also, what do each of the characters want, what is the purpose of the song to the musical, and finally, how do things change by the end of the song? This assignment is done in-context. During the talk-backs, center discussions around how well the choreographers achieved the above elements.

Note: I usually allow 2 or 3 in-class sessions for choreographers to work on this assignment with their performers. Yes, it is difficult to find a place with enough space to have students work during class times. I have used this assignment, however, in both a small studio space and in a very large studio. Small spaces may require splitting time between choreographers, but with good planning, this work can be accomplished.

Chapter 8
Muddy Water
Choreography or Staging? Or Both?

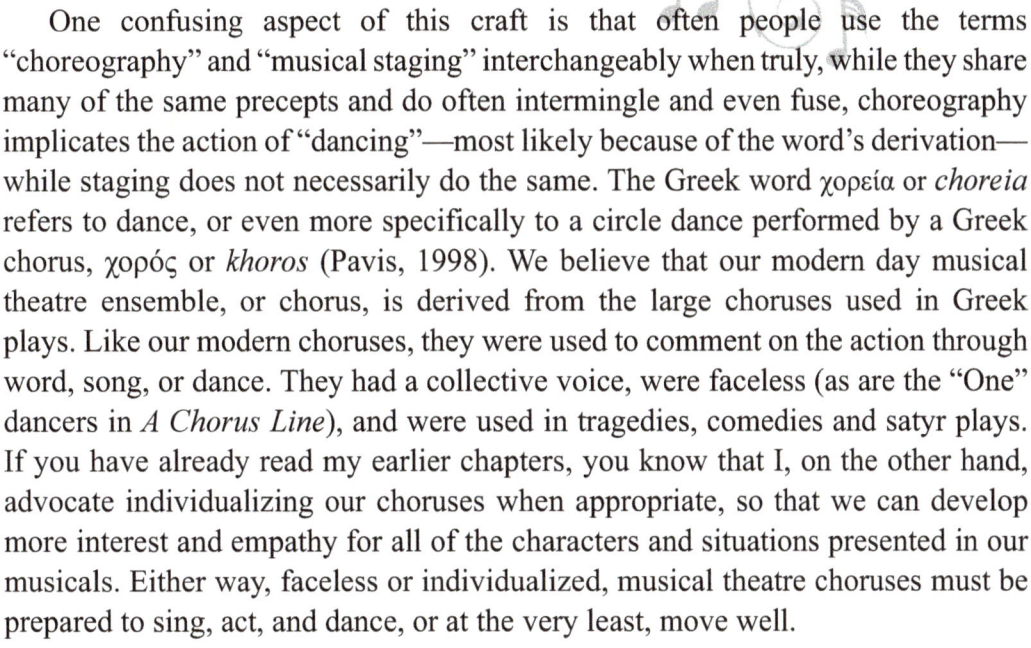

One confusing aspect of this craft is that often people use the terms "choreography" and "musical staging" interchangeably when truly, while they share many of the same precepts and do often intermingle and even fuse, choreography implicates the action of "dancing"—most likely because of the word's derivation—while staging does not necessarily do the same. The Greek word χορεία or *choreia* refers to dance, or even more specifically to a circle dance performed by a Greek chorus, χορός or *khoros* (Pavis, 1998). We believe that our modern day musical theatre ensemble, or chorus, is derived from the large choruses used in Greek plays. Like our modern choruses, they were used to comment on the action through word, song, or dance. They had a collective voice, were faceless (as are the "One" dancers in *A Chorus Line*), and were used in tragedies, comedies and satyr plays. If you have already read my earlier chapters, you know that I, on the other hand, advocate individualizing our choruses when appropriate, so that we can develop more interest and empathy for all of the characters and situations presented in our musicals. Either way, faceless or individualized, musical theatre choruses must be prepared to sing, act, and dance, or at the very least, move well.

An English derivation of the Greek *choreia* (dance) is chorea and refers to a neurological disease in which the body is subject to rapid, jerky and involuntary movements of the limbs and face, comparable to dance movements (Chorea, 2017). So, the first part of the word *choreography* historically does have to do with "dancing," the second part with writing. This derivation being known, the proclivity for people to associate the word choreography with dance steps and movements makes sense, and one of its meanings *is* the arrangement of dance steps and movements into a particular structure that makes a "dance." However, choreography also implies the use of spatial patterns, directions, and the mover's relationship to space that the dance employs. The word has also come to include the *way* movements or steps are performed, the amount of energy placed into movements that give them meaning, and how we can situate meaning into the kinds of designs these movements create in space. So in a way, the term "choreography" is all inclusive and can refer not only to technical dancing but to any kind of structured or specific movement created for the stage. The term "musical staging" is perhaps less inclusive because it does not necessarily suggest the use of dance or dance movements. Musical staging can often employ "stylized" movements, but I use the term predominantly to refer to any organized movement that exists simultaneously with music during a musical. Musical staging does not necessarily need technical dancers, but some degree of dance training gives stylized movement a more polished and professional outcome, to be sure. Nor, does it always need a choreographer since directors of musicals can be adept at musical staging, as well. Also, very often the director wants to handle the ballads or dramatic songs between the principle characters so they can direct them at the same time. The goal is to organize highly specific movement that looks spontaneous and that also expresses and enhances a character's inner life.

What kind of song is indicative of musical staging? Here is a list of examples:

- Two-person love ballads, such as "People Will Say We're In Love" from *Oklahoma!*

- The 2 to 3-person comedy/character songs "Sadder but Wiser Girl" from *The Music Man* and "Friendship" from *Anything Goes*

- The 2-person dramatic relationship/ situation songs "You're Not Foolin' Me" from *110 In the Shade* or "A Boy Like That" from *West Side Story*

- Ensemble numbers such as "Where will You Be When the Flood Comes," from *Parade*, or "Sit Down, John" from *1776*.

All of the above, and very many more, I would categorize as numbers that require musical staging. None of the songs mentioned require technical dance, and only two of them might utilize traditional dance steps and/or a more stylized way of moving. I would also categorize certain production numbers, such as "Sit Down, John," as either musical staging or choreography, not because the performers are dancing, but because of the size of the ensemble, the detailed precision involved, the stylized groupings of the characters, and the highly coordinated musical/movement relationship. What these songs all require is a knowledge of dramatic stage blocking and stage values, a director's understanding of the characters, and strong musicality.

If musical staging requires no dance, then it should be easy, right? Then, why do I think that accomplishing musical staging effectively can be even more complex and intricate than a large choreographed production number such as "America" or "42nd Street"? Because of my experiences with them all—some of which I will share with you here.

Sometimes A Walk Is Just A Walk...Or Is It?

A song in Adam Guettel's *The Light in the Piazza* entitled "Let's Walk," traces Signor Nacarelli and Margaret Johnson waxing philosophical as they walk the streets of Florence, Italy during the summer of 1953 (Guettel, Vocal score 53-56). Their walk allows Nacarelli the time to agree to a marriage between his son Fabrizio and Margaret's mentally challenged daughter. Signor has recently become aware that Clara is six years older than Fabrizio but does not seem to be aware of her disability. In the previous scene he is angry with Margaret and very concerned about the appropriateness of their children's age difference. Margaret, who is very aware of her daughter's disability, ups the ante, raising her dowry offer by $10,000, (almost $100,000 in today's terms). Signor initially refuses it, but she knows immediately that he has softened. She asks him to take a walk with her. The money makes the difference, but he doesn't want to readily admit to that. Nor do the words of the song "Let's Walk" give us clues about the deeper reasons for why he eventually changes his mind; he just seems to be making small talk while rationalizing a way to put aside his objections to the marriage. At the end of the song, Nacarelli kisses Margaret on the lips, which surprises her, and the audience, for that matter. The song leaves the audience with a strange taste in their mouths for Signor, and a bit unclear as to his part in this friendly mutual manipulation. The following paragraph illustrates some of my early thoughts about the song's meaning.

As the choreographer of this piece, I began to look at the song for its purpose in the play. The song is there to advance the plot, but I know that only because at the beginning of the song the marriage was off and at the end of the song the marriage is on. The song itself does not actually execute that progression—but it does facilitate it. The song provides a space for the walk to occur and creates an ambience that gives the characters time for a significant change to happen. They eventually come to a tacit agreement about the future of their children's lives; for Margaret it is regardless of her husband's protests and even her own qualms about the situation.

Regardless of what the characters project, it seems to me that each of them has already arrived at the decision that alters the plot *before* the song begins. She has made him an offer he cannot refuse, and he has agreed to "consider" it. Signor is persuaded by the generous dowry, I believe, and agrees to further discussion to make his change of heart seem less abrupt. The walk allows him to save face but, more importantly, it allows Margaret time to set her own convictions in stone and own her decision. By its nebulous and repetitious nature, the music leads us aptly through this change and gives the actors the necessary space to make a discreet and "polite" leap to a new reality. Although the song does not give us this information explicitly, we do feel it implicitly because of the way Guettel so expertly structured the music.

Dialogue and lyrics will help us to understand things intellectually. In musicals, however, the deeper emotional, psychological, and even spiritual meanings are almost always found in the music. When in doubt, study the music, and since Guettel thinks out of the box it will be important to jump out of the box with him to find the bottom line. Musical director Peter Hilliard points out,

> Guettel's harmonies are tonal, but they often move in unexpected ways, led by the most subtle ear for harmony active in musicals today. A careful listen to nearly every Guettel song reveals a bassline or interior moving part of the harmony that leads the chords in unusual directions. The bassline is often leading the charge into exotic harmonic territory. (Point 2: An obsession with moving interior chromatic lines, 2014)

The baseline in "Let's Walk" is repetitive and unvaried, which is appropriate as the characters are strolling casually through the city. Hilliard characterizes it as "The… familiar Guettellian offbeat pulsing rhythm, the chromatic bassline are all in play here, but this time in the introduction, the bassline is moving back and forth tracing a half step like two feet walking in place, until the singers enter and it finally moves" (Hilliard, 18. "Let's Walk," 2014). Underlying that and the main melody is a third melody that is lovely, just like someone would feel strolling through Florence on a beautiful summer day; it is pleasant but with a worrisome or disquieting quality that is so slight, it may just be something you imagine. This (very slight) dissonance creates an ambiguity in the music that "un-grounds" the walk and parallels the reality that they are discussing important issues (their children) in a trivial way. Their conversation has an awkward quality, like they are avoiding the 800-pound gorilla in the room by making casual comments. In a 2001 interview with Guettel, columnist Ryan DeFoe asked him about the dissonance found in his music and he responded by saying that he sees harmony in music as being an emotional tool that he thinks of as being on a continuum. I love this explanation, so I will share here:

> As far as dissonance in my work, to me harmony is a continuum from Gregorian stricture to atonal chaos. And my music obviously lands somewhere in between there and occasionally accesses either pole. To me harmony is just a way of creating emotional syntax in songwriting or in music making, or in storytelling with music. Emotional syntax for me comes

through harmony. Harmony as an emotional tool, I think, is predominately a tonal thing, as far as how it effects the listener. And dissonance is another color, it's another thing that is emotionally useful. So, when people call my work dissonant, I think they're really just describing some section of a piece I've written where I was trying to create a certain kind of emotional syntax and those were the tools I was using. (Guettel, "Talkin' Broadway, 2001)

I am not a trained musician and my music theory chops are limited, so it is important to me to find out as much as I can about a song before I stage it. Learning the theory behind the music broadens its meanings for me, but I do not rule out my own instincts and how it makes me feel. The way I feel about this music is that it characterizes the uncertainties and reservations both characters have about the marriage, particularly Margaret. Besides the subtle dissonance and the use of simultaneous contrasting musical lines, Guettel uses other devices, such as substituting lyrics for the syllable "Ah," as he does in other places in the show. Either he is giving the characters time to consider subtext in those places, or perhaps they have run out of words to say—or are searching for the *right* words to say. Or, as in the love ballad "Say It Somehow," there *are* no words to convey the powerful emotions the characters are feeling. The cautious, almost precarious feeling I sensed in the music and lyrics of "Let's Walk" did not define its purpose to me, but it defined the way to arrive at the purpose. Finally, the song also provides the audience time to sense an understanding or negotiation taking place, even if the words do not definitively take them there. Both characters are profoundly changed by the end of the song, not because of the song or the kiss, but because of the walk itself; but, while *his* change is essentially external, *hers* is unquestionably internal and life-altering. And so, because I believed the "un-grounded" quality I sensed in the song *was* Guettel's intended direction, I decided to follow it, and 1) use the ambiguity in the music as the overall intention for action, and 2) continue to look beyond the dialogue and the lyrics—to the music—for the deeper meaning of the song.

All this being examined, I still had a song to stage and I knew that however I decided to wrestle with the purpose of the song, the staging would have to keep the audience rooted in the story, keep their primary focus on the actors, and keep them interested and engaged without pulling focus away from either of those things.

Looking beyond the music and the script now, I had scenic designer Natalie Hart's open and movable set and my ensemble. The scenic design was modular in the sense that there were three major moving pieces that were independent of each other but could be in assembled in a variety of ways to create different settings. Each piece was large, portable, and three dimensional. Two of the structures were tall representations of Florentine architecture that looked like buildings; the remaining piece was a large panel unit of three arches that could fan in from off right and stop at any position along the way (see figures 18 & 19). There were a great many "places" the characters could appear with different configurations of the set, so I decided to share the focus in this scene between the streets of Florence and the walk itself, trusting the actors to keep the primary focus on their shared conflict. The random, circuitous, and indirect quality of the buildings changing position throughout the song echoes the random quality of the walk and the conversation. Uprooting, or "un-grounding" the buildings mirrors what I hear in the music and intensifies the insecurity underlying the characters' convictions. My ensemble are those townspeople we see previously in the play who fill the streets of Florence. Timed precisely with the music, these characters walk through the city, moving and stopping in a natural pedestrian manner. Having them move and freeze rhythmically with the music not only ties the movement to the music, but also gives the proceedings a heightened and slightly stylized look. Small groups alternate moving the buildings as Signor and Margaret move past, through and around them, as though they are negotiating buildings on the street. The technique of "freezing" the ensemble during production numbers is highly effective in such a piece because, used carefully and intentionally, the abrupt physical changes facilitate appropriate emphasis and focus, as well as create meaningful stage pictures. This kind of number is indicative of "musical staging" to me because, although the movement is heightened (or stylized) and timed to complement the music, there is no actual dance movement involved and the traveling and stationary movements of the ensemble are selected and arranged to achieve specific meaning and purpose. This type of staging can be as complex a process as a technical dance production number because rather than time being put into learning and polishing steps and spacing, it is put into precise timing of individuals and small groups moving independently of each other.

My goal was to create the overall effect of two people walking through Florence at night in casual conversation but, at the same time, acknowledge the reticence and caution behind each characters' motivations. Moreover, I hoped to achieve this while keeping the audience engaged and entertained. While the audience focuses on an authentic, yet stylized, situation and environment, Margaret and Signor arrive, gradually and feasibly, to a place of more stability. The portability and ease of moving the set structures and the effective use of both sound and lighting design are all crucial to the success of such staging. Lighting and sound not only establish the appropriate ambience, they ensure proper focus by keeping the viewers' eyes and ears where the director would like them to be (see fig. 19).

Figure 18. Overall scenic structure in *The Light in the Piazza.* Elon University Archives, 2016.

Figure 19. Ensemble as people on the street and building movers in "Let's Walk" from *The Light in the Piazza.* Elon University Archives, 2016.

Akin to the kind of set/actor-staging Michael Bennett used in *Dreamgirls* (see Chapter 3 p. 42), working large scenic elements into choreography is a balancing act, to be sure, but one that can work with creative designers and strong performers who command the stage no matter what happens around them. When incorporating the set into your choreography to such a large extent, be very sure that your actors can remain in charge of the space.

Do Ballads Really Need Specific Staging?

YES! Even quiet low-movement songs like "If I Loved You" from *Carousel* or "Not While I'm Around" from *Sweeney Todd* rely upon precise choices in staging. Remember that choreographers create moving works of art that, contrived knowledgeably, will have an effect on the audience. Questions to discuss with actors in the beginning might be "Who has power when?" "Why?" "How does your body language affect each other and what can it clarify for the audience?" As the number progresses, choreographers should note the moment to moment effect the dialogue and lyrics have on the actors and try to incorporate effective spontaneous responses of theirs into the staging. They should also notice technical elements in the music that need closer attention, such as which musical accents or rhythmic elements demand to be noticed or which words and phrases are important to emphasize. Also, familiarity with the orchestration makes a world of difference than working only with the piano score. Talking through each number in the score with your musical director before preparing it saves time later on modifying your work. *Craft* a ballad collaboratively with your actors and music director rather than authoritatively assign movement for it, but *do* end up with a piece that is a repeatable real-life moment in the lives of the characters being depicted. Then, as the choreographer, you will make the final choices. Improvising a musical number in performance or leaving it to chance works only in very specific cases and with highly skilled performers. Now, by making these suggestions regarding the staging of a ballad I do not mean to imply that songs are incapable of being entertaining and moving if performed in stillness. Theatre songs can (and do) work beautifully in stillness, and as cabaret pieces or recordings, for that matter. However, I believe that when performed in context of a play by specific characters we have become familiar with, songs can have more emotional power, credibility, and a sense of realism when analyzed deeply and staged expertly by the director or choreographer of the show.

Tangent. *Concert versions of plays can work without movement because we accept beforehand that we will not see the musical fully acted out, although to be honest,* *even concert versions of many works are now staged to some degree. Physical staging offers a more complete experience. The reason to do concert versions of musicals varies, but economically this avenue makes production more feasible for revivals, reunion performances, benefits and anniversary performances. As with concert versions of opera, audiences can place their attention on the music and the dialogue, arguably experiencing the musical in a purer form. Stage movement and stage business can be present in varying degrees, but the primary focus and expectations should have to do less with those things and more on the material itself. Even the orchestra is set up directly behind the singers, constantly reminding us that we are watching a concert. Like listening to the radio or reading a book, this mode of delivery can be equally as satisfying because we bring to it our own imaginations and realities, and it is not incumbent upon the creative team to recreate reality as it is in a fully realized production.*

At the beginning of "the bench scene" in *Carousel*, (with the enchanting song "If I Loved You"), there is a sharp contrast between Carrie's stillness and Billy's physical taking-over of the space; his showmanship versus her candor and control (Rodgers and Hammerstein II, 1945). Going meticulously through the scene allows the two actors and the artist staging it to find each character's moment to moment reality and those places of *transition*, where I (for one) most intensely appreciate the experience and skill of the actors, or most intensely lament their lack of it. When is Billy compelled to drop his façade and confide in Carrie and why? Does this cause him to move away from her, to face her, or to sit pensively and quietly next to her? When does he reveal himself to her and when does he catch himself and retreat back behind his public machismo persona? This is one of Rodgers' and Hammerstein's' early *long form scenes* in which the scene and song are intermeshed, allowing the dialogue and song to work together in a complementary fashion to form a dramatic arc. Why does the song ebb, and why does the dialogue take over when it does? The use of underscoring keeps us in the life of the song—that heightened place—even *during* the dialogue, which enables the audience to retain the daydream of this encounter. The music keeps us in that space where historian Richard Kislan believes musical theatre resides: within the theatre of romance. "Life is the stuff of all drama," states Kislan, "but while the theatre of realism presents life unadorned, the theater of romance presents life as it should be" (2). Also, the underscoring often contains the actors' subtext. Listen to it without the dialogue. It should speak worlds to you.

Also at work powerfully and subliminally are the subtleties of body language, stage values (also discussed in an earlier chapter), and the use of stage levels built into the scenic design. Body language choices will give the audience clues about each character by revealing who they are from the inside out. Stage positions used skillfully are not obvious to an audience and, as stated, work on a sub-conscious level. Awareness of this can help you to establish the nuances of a relationship and give weight to a character's psychological state at any given moment. Billy Bigalow's initial restlessness can magnify his insecurities and confusion; a simple glance at him when he isn't looking can subtly divulge Carrie's intense feelings for him. The skill to create this kind of staging effectively takes creative choices from all three artists involved in creating this scene, the choreographer (or the director) and the two performers. In such a scene, you may only need to say when a movement or stance seems anachronistic and an intelligent actor will become aware of their physicality right away. Some actors have an innate sense of it, which gives the choreographer more authentic possibilities to choose from. An instinctive understanding of human nature and skills in reading body language are valuable tools for directors and choreographers. In authentic movement lies not only subtle truth, but also great beauty. Finally, making use of the set to intensify power structures brings characters into strong focus and underlines their emotional lives in effectual but strictly understated ways. Awareness of these tools expands the range of choreographic choices considerably.

So just who *are* the authentic Carrie and Billy? What is it that pulls them together but ultimately tears them apart? What about this scene foreshadows and makes inevitable where the plot takes us next? The answers to these questions, and others, give clues for producing methodically applied, theatrically supercharged, evocative, and eloquent ordinary movement for the characters who perform this song. Answer the many questions that will help you effectively analyze your song and bring out its obvious and hidden meanings. Then use your knowledge of stagecraft to bring those meanings to life.

Staging Empathy

The musical *Titanic (1997)* is emotionally moving, not because a boat is sinking but because we become intimate with the passengers on that boat: who they are, their relationships, and for many, what they dream their futures to be. If the *Titanic* was vacant at the time it sank (by some strange twist of fate) I guarantee that a musical would not have been written about it a hundred years later. (Who would sing?) But seriously, we might be temporarily saddened about the loss of this big beautiful boat, but we would have to connect to that sadness through the loss felt by at least one other individual affected by it. It might have been a one-man musical about the passion felt by architect Thomas Andrews for his creation and the hell he went through knowing that the ship he designed would be responsible for hundreds of deaths. In this musical version of the famous story, however, librettist Peter Stone and composer/lyricist Maury Yeston included the stories of many of the actual passengers who were aboard the *Titanic* when it sank. (Remember from Chapter 1 what Aaron Frankel said about musicals opening up the story while straight drama reaches inward.) Although not all of the passengers' stories were historically accurate, the authors masterfully presented a compilation of actual people with whom we become familiar and about whom we grow to care during the course of the play. We begin meeting them in an extended part of the Overture, which is listed as song "No. 1" followed by "1a" when we first meet Andrews, the Architect, in a heartfelt and extended song about his relationship to the ship (Yeston and Stone, piano/conductor score pp. 5-12). The authors were then meticulous in writing an opening number that would painstakingly introduce each of the characters (including ensemble members) and even highlight those who would become more prominent in the story later on. In its entirety, the opening sequence is a series of songs about a brand new, beautiful, and gigantic sailing vessel named "Titanic" and the fact that it is going to depart that morning. In each of the eleven parts of "The Launching"—No's 2 through 2j—the people who will be departing as passengers or crew aboard the ship are presented to the audience (Yeston & Stone, *Titanic* Piano Score, 13-63). Obviously, the creators felt that familiarizing the audience with all of the characters, right out of the starting gate, was of great significance because they devoted fifty pages in the score to this sequence. Hence, during this next section, I would like to walk the reader through "The Launching," discussing how I attempted not only to highlight the characters as individuals, but to also point out and underline class difference and societal privilege, which both come into play throughout the voyage and during the ship's demise.

Throughout the eleven songs in the opening there is absolutely NO technical dance or even stylized movement, but it is a complex production number assigned to the choreographer to create. To do this, she or he must be just as familiar with the characters in the play as the director is.

Before I begin my analysis, below is a brief overview of each musical section that makes up the opening of *Titanic*.

In **<u>No's. 2-2a "How Did They Build Titanic," *measures 1-32* and "Fare— thee—well" *measures 1-30*</u>**, we first meet Mr. Barrett, the stoker, who is saying goodbye to his beautiful young fiancé (Yeston and Stone pp. 13-17). After Barrett's lady leaves him, Fleet the lookout and Bride, the wireless telegraph operator, join him for **2b "There She Is"** *measures 1-74.* They quickly pull our attention to the ship, which the audience only sees through the characters' eyes, building it up as the great "Ship of Dreams" and preparing us for this long-awaited launching. These three tenors are joined by several Officers and in between singing they introduce themselves to each other, and therefore to the audience, as well (17-22). During the next section, **No. 2c "Loading Inventory"** *measures 1-114,* we meet more of the seamen as well as the Maids, the Bellboy, the Steward, and the Bandmaster Mr. Hartley, who is the legendary musician who kept playing his violin to calm the passengers even as the ship was sinking (22-30). **No's. 2d & 2e "The Largest Moving Object and Pitman's Announcement #1"** *measures 1-36,* brings in The Captain, the Architect, and Mr. Ismay, the director of the White Star Line. Thus far, I have boarded most of the crew including the Captain and other key characters, leaving onstage only a few sailors to maneuver the set pieces and Officer Pitman to see to the boarding of the passengers (31-35). In **No's. 2f and 2g "I Must Get on That Ship"** *measures 1-22,* **and Pitman's Announcement #2"** *measures 1-30,* we first meet the Third Class passengers (36-40), then the Second Class passengers during **No. 2h "I Must Get On That Ship #2"** *measures 1-52* (41-43), highlighting prominent members of those groups who will help to carry the storyline forward. Alice Beane, a woman among the Second Class passengers is beside herself because she hopes to be hob-knobbing with the First Class passengers during the sailing. She knows so much about them that she excitedly sings a patter song containing a ton of information about each of them during their entrances. Alice outlines (presumably for her husband, but really for the audience) the gossip surrounding each of the families in the next to final section called **No. 2i "Mrs. Beane" ["The First-Class Roster"]** *measures 1-138.* By the end of this section (45-54), we will have met everyone written into this musical and, hopefully, begin to develop feelings about them.

In order to fashion staging that can effectively stand beside Stone's story and Yeston's songs, the "chaos" structured by the choreographer must be minutely organized throughout. Again, no actor is merely set dressing, or a vocal type needed in the ensemble. These characters are all individuals with distinct personalities. I encouraged the ensemble actors, as well as the principles, to find nuances and small ways to reveal themselves, and then was certain to organize their contributions with an aesthetic eye. The following describes some of my choices during a short section in **Part 2c "Loading Inventory**," which takes place after the officers sing and move up left, up the gangplank and exit, presumably, onto the ship.

There are 7 sailors down right of center interacting as they sing about the ship, 3 others are moving cargo from off right to the up left gangplank and off, another 3 are working with the stanchions right of center, and the staff is about to enter from above them, farther up right.

The bandmaster appears first, crossing diagonally from up right to down left, pausing center momentarily to look behind him and wait for the steward. His pause center calls attention to both him and the steward amid the bustle happening onstage and prepares the audience for a new group of people. The bandmaster and the steward, who are characters who figure prominently in the play, continue down left as the sailors are completing their vocal passage down right. Behind them, from off right, the bellboy leads on the maids who line up downstage center as the singing sailors disperse and cross behind them, heading up the gangplank and off stage left.

Each of these characters knows precisely when to move, when to stop, where to stand, and to whom to relate. Every moment is like a painting or photograph where balance, focus, and perspective matter, not just for aesthetic reasons, but also for specificity and clarity of character and relationship.

As the staff turns to head up the gangplank, Officer Pitman has the sailors move the stanchions into their next position for the entrance of the third-class passengers. I keep the balance of the stage in check as Pitman and a younger officer deal with the passengers crowding into the (just placed) third-class entrance.

During each of the three passenger entrances, my job was to make it look as if we were loading passengers up gangplanks on different areas of the dock. Inspired by a simple but highly efficient idea of the scenic designer, I was able to manipulate moveable parts of the set to make that happen. We had four 6-foot lengths of metal stanchions, like those used for crowd control. These structures were very similar to stand-alone ballet barres. I staged four sailors to swiftly reposition them for the boarding of each class of passengers, creating three visually distinct entrances. These configurations gave me the opportunity to highlight class differences and the various ways the ships' personnel related to each level of society.

The third-class passengers enter first. They are an over-crowded unformed bunch of people trying to get the best place in line as the ship's personnel herd them like cattle (see fig. 20). The second-class passengers enter in a civilized queue and are greeted by the officers with a bit more deference (see figs. 21 & 22). The first-class passengers parade onstage in family units through a symmetrically structured entry way while Officer Pitman announces each family by name (see fig. 23).

Social structure played heavily into the drama of the sinking of the Titanic; the third-class passengers' lives were devalued in comparison to how those with money were treated. Many of Stone's characters were individualized in this opening by he and the composer, streamlining my own task by guiding me through my preparation. If the song had been structured generically, offering arbitrary entrances and random groupings, rather than the specific givens it establishes, I would have had to organize and structure the broad layout of the number myself, adding hours onto my preparation time.

Even with its excellent structure, preparing this number took several extended sittings to plot out traffic patterns and timing for both people and set. I was also concerned with pointing out relationships significant to plot movement, and with introducing each actor as distinctively as possible. Regardless of how prepared one is, putting a number like this on its feet is always time consuming because of the number of people involved and the amount of expository ground to be covered. Despite the fact that there is no "dancing," an aesthetic eye, musical timing, knowledge of the characters, selected use of space, and organizational skills are the tools I put into play to keep my work both specific and informative in the manner of Mr. Yeston and Mr. Stone. The beauty of the script and song structure guiding the staging so specifically is that it can encourage the audience to develop *pathos* for many of the characters in the first few minutes of the musical. For instance, of the many stories we hear during the evening, the stoker Barrett's story is particularly poignant because we know that at the end of this journey he planned to return to England to marry his sweetheart—the beautiful young lady we meet briefly at the beginning of the show. Later, when he offers his seat on a lifeboat to another person, we care for him even more and so mourn for him and his *fiancé*. Each of the principal and supporting characters is highlighted in this opening through song *and* staging, giving the audience a quick—but distinct—introduction to them from the get-go.

Figure 20. Entrance of the 3rd Class Passengers in *Titanic* at Elon. Tony Spielberg ©, 2014.

Figure 21. Entrance of 2nd Class Passengers in *Titanic* at Elon. Tony Spielberg©, 2014.

Figure 22. Entrance of 2nd Class Passengers, full stage view from *Titanic*. Tony Spielberg©, 2014.

Figure 23. Set placement for entrance of 1st Class Passengers in *Titanic*. Tony Spielberg©, 2014

Further differentiating the classes are their dances and their social events (figs. 24-26):

Figure 24. Dinner with the 1st class passengers in *Titanic*. Tony Spielberg©, 2014.

Figure 25. Entertainment for 1st class passengers on deck in *Titanic*. Tony Spielberg©, 2014.

Figure 26. After dinner dancing below deck—3rd class passengers in *Titanic*. Tony Spielberg©, 2014.

No. 2j Opening Finale ["Godspeed Titanic"] *measures 1-121).* The climactic challenge in this extended opening number lies at the end, immediately before the final chorus when the classes blend together. As the last group of passengers (the first-class) exit up the gangplank and off stage left, there is only a very short exchange downstage between the Captain and Officer Pitman to conceal or cover the following: 1) a scrim that descends center stage, 2) the removal of the gangplank and ramp offleft, 3) the arrival of all of the officers up on the bridge, 4) the entrance of the ensemble far upstage under the bridge behind the scrim, and 5) the positioning of the 4 stanchions along the apron of the stage by the 4 onstage sailors. Then, as the passengers move downstage en masse singing "Farewell...," they will appear to end up along a side of the ship waving goodbye to those on shore.

Cramming a 2 or 3 minute event into 30 seconds, will take some expert collaborators, such as you, the director, music director, technical director, scenic designer, lighting designer, crew and cast. The tech and design staff will usually take over at such times to supervise the difficult transition because they know better how to incorporate all the elements. After the transition sequence is set, the cast and crew practice until it can happen in those 30 seconds, or less, tweaking elements along the way. Everything above must take place during a short 8-line dialogue exchange performed far down right by Officer Pitman and the Captain. This is the climax of the song, as well, because the ship is about to sail; we cannot allow the excitement to diminish by waiting and we actually need to "explode" into the finale. The "choreography" for this transition went something like this:

1. The first class passengers move up the gangplank then descend the gangplank offstage left.

2. Stagehands are in place to pull the gangplank off stage as soon as the last actor descends. (The exit of the gangplank is rehearsed several times so it takes 6 seconds to accomplish instead of 60.)

3. The scrim lowers and there is a blackout, leaving a small lit area down right in front of the scrim for the dialogue scene. During this, the gangplank continues off and all of the passengers enter upstage in the darkness behind the scrim.

4. As the scrim rises, the Captain and Pitman exit down right. We see all of the passengers in a large cluster stretched across the the very up-most part of

the stage, and the officers are all high on the bridge. The Captain and Pitman are already off stage climbing to the bridge to reenter during the song.

5. The 4 sailors are moving the 4 stanchions to stretch along the front of the stage as the passengers move forward, stopping in carefully positioned pairs and family units to sing the next to final refrain (M. 40-71).

6. The key changes (oh, yes!) and they begin the final triumphant refrain "*Sail on! Sail on! Great ship Titanic!*" as this sizable ensemble moves toward the audience to stand behind the rails of the stanchions, which depict the side of the ship (see fig. 27) (M. 72-76).

Thirty passengers and sailors are now positioned asymmetrically behind the railing along the apron of the stage; they are as close to the audience as they can be. Six officers in naval uniforms are upstage on the bridge high above them. Everyone is waving goodbye and singing Yeston's glorious finale of the song. The music continues to swell, and the size and nearness of the cast create a powerful end, which is appropriate to the long build created in this extended opening number. The Titanic has been launched.

At this instant all the classes of passengers are completely integrated. They are totally unaware of that, however, thinking only of the glory of the moment. In the final positioning along the railing, I will rely partially upon the actors' improvisatory skills to help create specificity in storytelling about people of different class levels who conduct themselves in diverse ways as they excitedly embark on their journeys, bid farewell to their loved ones, and meet and interact with new people from different walks of life. There are opportunities for actors to react to each other throughout this number in distinct ways that continue to define their characters. Rather than relying only upon these acting moments, however, choreographic techniques are useful, such as the effective use of levels and placement of the actors in the space. The simple use of levels gives a more random and authentic look to a moment, besides creating an aesthetically more interesting design. The actors will improvise their way into their final positions the first few times we rehearse it. I will adjust specific moments, make suggestions, put someone on a low level and another on a high level, etc. When I feel ready, I ask them to begin setting what they do. I will tweak their final positions to create the exact look I like, and ask them to freeze their waving on the last beat of the music, which allows for a brief glimpse at a varied and integrated tableaux before moving on to the next scene. If all of the actors are doing their jobs, this tableaux should tell many individual stories on its own (See fig. 27).

Figure 27. End of opening sequence as the boat leaves shore in *Titanic*. Tony Spielberg©, 2014.

However a number ends, the final moment in a piece like this calls for several things. For the most part, the last position the actors take should synchronize with the music so the ending is specific and clear. The audience must be sure it is the end and time to applaud. This moment is also the last cap on the number, creating a satisfying and complete experience. There are times when one song segués into the next. Musically the composers and librettists typically make that choice for a specific reason and those moments are clearly defined by the continuation of the music and/or the coming in of dialogue after a song is over. Predominantly, however, songs have endings and audiences will take their cues through the actors… who get their cues from the director. These conventions form a kind of partnership between the audience and the performers as co-creators of their theatre experience each evening.

I consider it my responsibility as the choreographer to make certain the audience becomes familiar with and relates to the ensemble characters through large and small movement choices that create meaning and tell individual stories throughout ensemble moments. I am careful of how I group people, of course, but in these large scenes I also include clues about budding and developing relationships, personality traits, actions particular to a certain person, or any small moment that foreshadows something more important coming up. If caught by audience members, these small stories deepen their experience of the play. Notice places in the script that you can highlight or underline with your own ideas. By specifying characters so carefully during *Titanic's* opening sequence, Peter Stone and Maury Yeston made sure to set up pathos for these characters sailing to America aboard this gigantic new ship. Continue to tell these stories through *where, why, when* and *how* your performers move (or do not move) during every song and musical moment. Hence, when characters we've come to know and care about meet their demise in the second act, we will mourn for them. We already know the ship sinks at the end of the story, but still we pull for all on board and hope that somehow the ending might change and they can all be saved. We do not mourn long or deeply the sinking of this great ship but we do mourn for the architect who realizes errors that went unchallenged in the building and outfitting of the ship. Throughout the musical, we are intellectually caught up with the details of the event itself, like Mr. Andrews' description of the Titanic as "the perfection of physical engineering," to the reasons why the ship is sinking (Yeston 12, meas. 80-84). This is coherent and rational *logos;* but the musical is emotionally stirring because with effective artists on and offstage telling this story, potent *pathos* is produced allowing the audience to connect emotionally to the people we meet during the journey of this musical. We *care* about them and that is what keeps us invested in this already familiar story. The director's job, and so also the choreographer's job, is to keep the audience invested in these characters using the choreographer's medium—movement.

Assignment - Chapter 8

In-class assignment

1. Choreographers: you may work alone or in pairs. Several performers will be assigned to you, as well as an already established fairy tale or story written for children. Become familiar with the story and choose to either condense it or select a section or scene from it to work with. Choreographers should then create a 9 to10 minute movement-only presentation of the material with your performers (who you are free to double or triple cast, if necessary). Choose music to accompany your piece, but only after you have come up with the story. Use stylized movement and elements of staging to describe character, relationship, and situation. Move between pantomime, pedestrian movement, heightened stylized movement, and technical dance to reveal character and tell the story.

   Instructors: Two class periods may be necessary for this assignment, after which one class will be needed for performance and discussion. Assess the work for creativity as well as for facility with these different movement styles.

Chapter 9

Aftershocks
Additional Useful Tips for Teachers of Undergraduate Choreographers

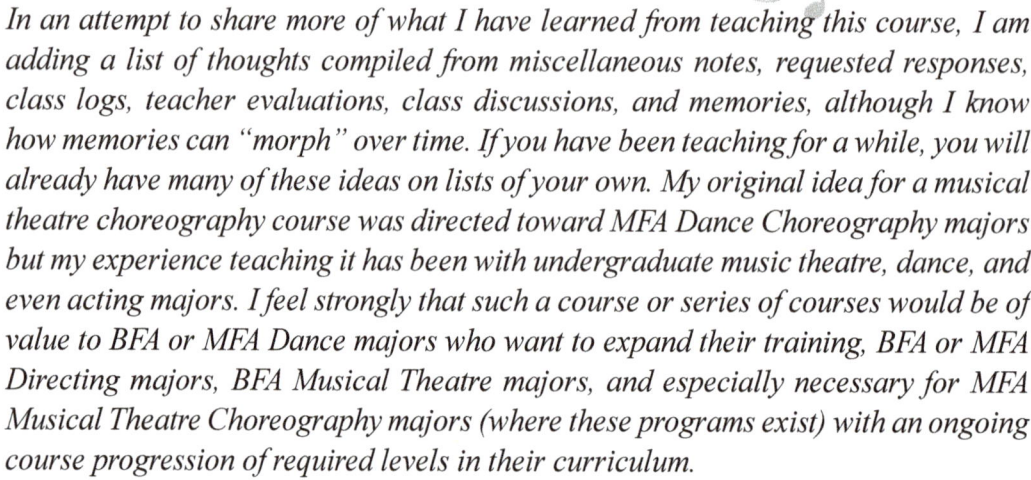

In an attempt to share more of what I have learned from teaching this course, I am adding a list of thoughts compiled from miscellaneous notes, requested responses, class logs, teacher evaluations, class discussions, and memories, although I know how memories can "morph" over time. If you have been teaching for a while, you will already have many of these ideas on lists of your own. My original idea for a musical theatre choreography course was directed toward MFA Dance Choreography majors but my experience teaching it has been with undergraduate music theatre, dance, and even acting majors. I feel strongly that such a course or series of courses would be of value to BFA or MFA Dance majors who want to expand their training, BFA or MFA Directing majors, BFA Musical Theatre majors, and especially necessary for MFA Musical Theatre Choreography majors (where these programs exist) with an ongoing course progression of required levels in their curriculum.

1. No matter how clearly it is shown or explained, only a small number of my students will follow my precise guidelines for a plot analysis of the play and a scene and song breakdown (See Appendix K) for the material they are working on. It is important to emphasize to them that eventually they will develop their own way, but right now they need to adhere to your guidelines for analyzing the work. Perhaps a template would make the task more palatable? I have seen some fine analyses submitted by students over the years, so I am certain it is possible to accomplish well. Insist on thoughtful and complete written work.

2. Teachers should find an effective way to assess students' understanding of assigned readings and be ready to help them apply ideas discussed to their work. As stated above, their written *analyses* of the scenes and songs they are working on is paramount because their attention must always come back to the *story*, what the characters are working through, the purpose of the song or scene, etc. Helping them apply this analysis might come through a question such as, "What is this character's point of view"? This was a question I felt compelled to ask quite often, because very often that wasn't clear. Or, "What is the purpose of this song in the show" is another question that will lead them back to their original analysis, which they should compare to what happens in their choreography. Does it fulfill

that purpose, or not? More focused on the movement, young choreographers may not always reflect these necessities in their dances.

3. This course needs a painstaking and meticulous balance of in-class practice with theoretical reading and discussion so that the theory is more *interesting* to the students. *Talking* about choreographing is less interesting to undergraduates than creating it, but if they can experience something and *then* talk about it (or vice versa) more of an impact will be had. At this stage of their careers they want to dance, and should, and so the theory AND the practice need to go hand in hand whenever possible and given equal time (See Appendices E-I).

4. Choreographers cannot continually grapple with rehearsal-problems like performers' lateness, absenteeism, etc. They need access to performers who also have a stake in being at each rehearsal. Having a companion class of performers who are available in class and during out-of-class rehearsals solved this problem. I created a 4-credit course for choreographers (See Appendix B) and a 1-credit course, which is the same as a technique class at our school, for performers. Having our own performers also allowed us to have in-class showings of our dances since all performers were there during class time (See Appendix A, Course Descriptions).

5. This course will need an accompanist for small cast songs that are performed by principal performers in a musical. Ensemble dance/production numbers can be better served by working with cast recordings complete with orchestration, but duets or small group numbers are better shown with live singing to accurately assess the effectiveness of movement. Things change for performers when they are singing, and the quality of the singing will affect and be affected by the choreography. This is just how it is. Also, the singing, movement and acting create a single unit, each part interdependent upon the other. Isolating the movement apart from the singing and acting is not actually possible in my mind. Accompanists should be available to work with the choreographers early on to help teach the material and again later during the class showings

6. Improvisations that focus on the tenets of modern dance choreography techniques are important to introduce or review at the beginning of the term. Several class sessions should be given over to dealing with the basic dance elements of *time, space, force,* and *shape*. The amount of time needed for this is dependent upon who is taking the class. Adding a modern dance choreography course in your department for non-dance majors would be a way to better ready

musical theatre majors for this course, or at least a dance improvisation class for non-dance majors. My classes were composed predominantly of musical theatre undergraduates. Our department does not offer choreography courses for non-dance majors so none of them had studied choreography before this. Taking some time to improvise around dance elements and create longer studies from those improvisations opened doors for uninitiated students regarding movement invention, diversity within their choreography, effective use of space and movement dynamics, and so on. Undergraduate or graduate dance majors will not require remedial sessions in these skills but may have other areas of inexperience. Prepare different strategies for different needs (See Appendix E).

7. Specific and clear rubrics are needed for each of the choreography showings. The rubrics will change somewhat as showings progress to accommodate slightly different goals. Also, specific points or grades should be assigned for in-class assignments or any reading or written work that is asked of them. Some level of objectivity must be met to facilitate grading, which is the most hideous aspect of teaching artists in higher education (See Appendices L and M).

8. As much as time allows, emphasis should be put on the historical research component of this kind of choreography and it should be discussed with choreographers in their mentoring sessions. Research narrows the field of choices to those most specific to the show and the music they are serving. With all the technological help now, there is simply no excuse to work unprepared. The days of reading about social dance or working from diagrams are long gone. There are literally tons of videos for everything you can think of and this technology can make your study time shorter, quicker, and visually explicit.

9. Initial work in "blocking" might be taught alongside "musical staging" to better understand how they intersect, and to how they differ. Discussions about stage values, upstaging, and using blocking psychologically to effectively emphasize and facilitate the emotional life of characters and influence an audience is important information for choreographers. When in doubt, students should be reminded to always come back to the story, which often gets lost in the search for movement and creating a "dance." It is important to remind students to approach their work not only as choreographers, but also as directors. The emotional life of characters, as they are singing and dancing, must be the choreographer's priority.

10. The above point also encompasses effective use of the stage space (understanding its power places)—and creating and maintaining effective focus whether in a

two-person piece or a production number. Surprisingly, I found focus particularly problematic for students, or something many did not instinctively consider.

11. Building from a scene into a song is a skill to address in class. It is important to notice the rise of overall energy *into* a song, and it is equally important that choreographers learn how to coax that from their performers. And, regarding all transitions, I learned that finessing transitions within a dance/production number is also cause for class and individual mentoring sessions. Transitions can be easy to overlook.

12. Mentor your choreographers on appropriate and most beneficial uses of the mirror. Choreographers need the mirror, not for improvising, but for setting movement and creating precise style with their dancers. We all know this about the mirror, but I think it is important enough to touch on here. Young choreographers tend to gravitate toward the mirror, so they must first be initiated into working without one so that they know it is not only possible to dance without a mirror, it is liberating and inspiring. The mirror can be inhibiting, particularly during the creative phase, but mirrors facilitate infinitely faster, easier and more successful rehearsals than trying to work without one. When is it good to use and when not? Teaching dances on a stage or in a black box theatre is sometimes necessary, but it shouldn't be the norm. A mirror is an important tool for teachers and choreographers.

13. Give choreographers a logical and consistent way of analyzing a song and finding the arc in songs and production numbers. What has changed from the beginning to the end of the song to affect the plot? Why is that song in the show? What purpose does it fulfill? The Song Analysis Form (see Appendix J) is an important tool for a deeper understanding of the music and lyrics.

14. Some space in my next text, or whoever writes the next one, should be given to building intensity within a dance production number. In "The Conga" from *Wonderful Town*, for instance, building to a peak at the end of the number is paramount. The song resolves on a high note and should bring the audience to its feet. However, because the song is musically so repetitive, building is tricky. It is written in a verse/chorus structure. Bernstein wrote the music for the verses to accommodate Ruth's pattered questioning of the sailors. Essentially, in the verses she spits out a fast-paced series of questions that sound more like talking than singing. She seems more like a lawyer cross-examining a witness without waiting for answers than a reporter interviewing her source, so the emphasis during each verse is on Comden

and Green's brilliant lyrics. The chorus pulls us out of her monotone questioning when, at the end of each verse, the sailors shout "Conga!" and they begin dancing the Conga with Ruth. The choruses are raucous, but she drops back into her droning interrogation again each time the verse resumes. My two choreographers working on this number initially did not achieve a build...only because they did not think of it, I believe. After one showing and a mentoring session, those choreographers were able to address this aspect of the work and, on their own, achieved an effective and appropriate build for the number.

15. Creating motif movements and learning how to use them is a skill that musical theatre choreographers should develop during this class. Through smaller assignments they can begin to understand how to develop successful phrases into a dance. A useful assignment would be to have them find existing choreography from classic musicals that incorporates this skill and study it, such as in *West Side Story* ("The Prologue" and "The Jet Song"), *The Music Man* ("Marion the Librarian")*,* and *Seven Brides for Seven Brothers* ("The Barn Raising Dance"). These dances can teach them to recognize motifs in theatre dance and how to develop them. One of the best examples of this was preserved by the original American Dance Machine. Joe Layton's choreography for the number "Popularity" from *George M.* is nothing short of a brilliant study of playing with motif in dance (See Appendix E).

16. Improvisation around certain conventions of musicals and technique practice to become more proficient with them is always a good idea to include in such a course. For instance, that "magical" use of time that stops characters in mid-action, or has them move in slow motion, are conventions used in musicals that make creative moments of specifying focus, emphasizing or deemphasizing an action or a character, giving the impression of a passage of time, revisiting a past time, or abruptly jumping into a future time. Nurturing our students' awareness of the *time* component of dance, as heavily as we emphasize *space and force*, will give them confidence to examine ways of manipulating time in their own choreography as an effective storytelling device. Skills, such as getting your performers to effectively execute an action freeze, freezing with life energy, breaking a freeze with energy, and using slow motion movement in primary focus or in the background, are examples of skills and techniques that are useful to MT choreographers.

17. Using props, costumes, and scenic elements should be addressed with in-class assignments so that choreographers have some background in using them

effectively. In musicals these elements are inherent in scenes and the more that dancers engage with their environment, the more authentic the work will seem. Student choreographers will ask to use props and set pieces, and if there are available items that students can borrow or find on their own, teachers should be prepared to critique and guide students to work with them effectively.

18. Consideration of the singers and actors is something that should be discussed during mentoring and critique sessions. Does the movement compromise the performers' work in any way, or does it facilitate it? If the former, choreographers are charged to be flexible and find more effective solutions to make their choreography a more appropriate vehicle for each individual performer.

19. Working in pairs is useful for some of the assignments and for in-class work. Working alone is also an important component of this class and should be required, not just allowed. Students should have separate practical assignments that contrast with their collaborative projects so they can test their own skills in their own ways. This approach seems achievable providing class sizes are not too large.

20. Finally, and most importantly, I learned that the most difficult skill for a teacher of musical theatre choreography to develop is how to effectively critique their students' work; it is the chief area of how this course differs from a modern dance composition course. Part of the difficulty lies in the many conventions and traditions of theatre dance, the ghost of the original choreographers' work looming over all subsequent choreography of those same musicals, and the sense that a choice in the choreography "works," meaning that the comedy elicits a response or the emotions are coming across as desired or intended. None of these issues would normally be discussed in a modern dance composition class because they are contrivances. The choreographer is engineering movement to affect the audience in particular ways. Concert dance traditionally allows the audience to form their own point of entry into a work. Musical theatre dance meanings are more precise. Here, I find myself giving, (or wanting to give), criticism that is ultra-specific, or even to give possible alternative ideas for how something might better serve the script. I believe what I learned during the first two years of teaching this course is that land mines suddenly appear all over the dance space as soon as the critique session begins. Some of the choreographers like that sort of hands on "right or wrong," "works or doesn't work," kind of input while others said I wanted them to do something like I would do it. While that was not true, I can see how it could be perceived that way. I did make every attempt to state a problem clearly and I also assured them that they

were not bound to use any of my examples but come up with solutions of their own. Some students may not hear everything said, however, because their focus tends to gravitate toward the negative part of the critique. Being an artist is soul-baring and I know how difficult it is to hear negative feedback on something you made that you love. Often, subsequent class discussions and peer critique inevitably covered those difficult areas and I found that peers can be even tougher and more candid to each other than I would ever be. Their classmates' criticism, however, seems to be much easier for young artists to accept. Consequently, over the years, I became more fastidious about praising the effective aspects of their work and to simplify any negative critiques to 1) stating the problem areas, 2) explaining why a character's intention may not be coming across, and 3) allowing them to work on the solutions without more input from me. After all, the "trial and error" method is the truest path to each artist's creative process. Pointing out weak areas of their work is useful, yes, but praising the small and large triumphs gives them the confidence to journey on, and so it is the greatest gift you can give to the young artists in your care.

A Postscript to Part One
A Glimpse of the Weave

There is more I would like to say about the craft of musical theatre choreography. This was simply a "glimpse of the weave" (Bucchino, 2006). There is always more to talk about, but I would like to wait and see if what I have already written is useful to my readers. If I were to write more, there is much I would open for discussion, such as

- more examination of stylized movement and learning how that has been used in the past,

- the art of physical comedy, choreographing comedy, or bringing your particular sense of humor into your work,

- psychological staging to emphasize the drama and facilitate actors' work was touched on throughout this text, but more can be said about that, particularly its use in contemporary musicals,

- the large production dance number…so much to talk about,

- the significance of "making the hat" or merging your dances with your collaborators' work,

- the importance of technical rehearsals and production week, how incorporating the settings, cyclorama, costumes, orchestra, and lights are the elements that enhance the meaning of and complete *your* work,

- parody, and

- the inclusion of reflections from other working musical theatre choreographers on how they approach some of these issues themselves.

In the meantime,

Teachers, feel free to try out any of my suggestions or methods to guide you and your students if this genre of choreography is somewhat new to you, and keep up your incredible work passing on the art of dance. Also, if it will help, please feel free to use or get ideas from any of the documents I have listed as Appendices at the end of this book. You will develop many wonderful ideas of your own that I hope *you* will publish so that I and others can learn from them.

Students, study the tenets of modern dance composition in choreography classes as soon as you can (if you have not done that yet) and watch the work of successful choreographers of musicals. Keep finding and viewing those old movie musicals and continue to choreograph whenever possible. There is nothing like experience to hone your skills. Bless you all for sharing yourselves with the world.

PART TWO

The Development of Choreographic Theory and Teaching Practice

A Chronology of the Development of Modern Dance and Theatre Dance

and

A Review of Prominent Literature in Modern and Musical Theatre Choreographic Pedagogy

Overture for Part 2

In Part 2... of this text, you will find strictly historical information about the teaching and codification of choreography, the evolution of the theatre choreographer, and the acceptance of musical theatre performing into the Academy. Musical Theatre directing and choreography are just beginning to be accepted as separate art forms from non-musical dramatic forms and it is clear that very little has been written down or technically developed by artists working in these disciplines. This delay in acknowledgement by academics and dance scholars is partially because musical theatre choreographers rarely write about what they do, but I believe it is also because of a remaining elitist bias toward popular dance forms. My purpose in offering this overview of literature on the teaching of choreography is not to share a comprehensive history of these topics, but rather to offer a brief synopsis of how the pedagogy of theatre dance choreography evolved alongside that of concert and classical dance forms, and to show how direly needed are more musical theatre choreographers to codify and document their methods.

The Development of Choreographic Theory and Teaching Practice

I. CHOREOGRAPHERS TEACHING CHOREOGRAPHY

Training artists in the performing arts is often a precarious business. Recognizing and guiding the emergence of a student's *artistry* in choreography while teaching tenets of the *craft* require a teacher with an innate sense of balance —one who knows when and how to emphasize craft without stifling creativity. My own circuitous route to artistic discovery has shown me that artists are not "made" but become who they are artistically throughout their lifetimes. Ideally, that identity will continue to change as they change, mature, and accumulate new knowledge. As this section will review, the art of modern dance choreography as set down by the modernists introduced tools and methodologies to guide and focus new artists as well as to create a particular aesthetic in that genre. Beginning a little before mid-twentieth century, as modern dance was making its place in higher education, we see the earliest documentation of how to approach dance composition. At the same time, professional dance directors and choreographers of musicals were creating dances in a popular theatre genre and, as they did so, were developing standards, techniques, and traditions exclusive to *that* arena. In 1926, prolific turn of the century Broadway dance director Ned Wayburn documented his teaching and choreography methods for show dancing, but nothing since had been documented in the area of musical theatre dance until 1989, although, like modern dancers, musical theatre choreographers had been working to establish compositional traditions in this field since the turn of the century. In fusing the choreographic pedagogical history of these two genres, I will attempt to account for what was happening *in practice* in Broadway musical choreography, in relation to the choreographic theory developing outside that discipline. All the arts are inextricably linked to the timbre of their time. As times change, so does the artist, and so any established technique must be open to new and sometimes revolutionary ideas, contradictory aesthetics, and the personal natures of those being trained. Teachers should welcome and encourage intuition and divergent thinking in all artistic arenas. That being stated, we should recognize that musical theatre methods of dance presentation have not strayed too far afield from modernity in that there is still a reliance on the deep structure of theatre dance. If the aesthetic of theatre dance has these things at its core: entertainment, spectacle, musical expression, social expression, and performance proficiency, then I think of those things as the deep structure of theatre dance, while dance as a storytelling device is a derivation of that or a surface structure. In this case, however, the deep structure is not abstract or hidden, but co-exists openly, side-by-side, and even conflates with surface structure in the book musical. While modern and contemporary dance artists, and even librettists and composers of musicals often do call into question conventional standards and long-held beliefs in their disciplines, theatre dance stands apart from current dance or theatrical trends that problematize and resist traditional forms. In the concert dance world even *how* choreographers work with dancers has deviated from the traditional identity of choreographer as "dictator" and maker of all movement. Jo Butterworth, whose inclusive pedagogical ideas regarding the dancers' input into the choreography they are learning are now commonplace, only fifteen years ago wrote that the practice of a choreographer creating all of the movement and teaching it to the dancers is traditional and usually found in a theatre context. She states:

> The interaction between choreographer and dancer(s) [in the traditional way] is one of transference: the dancer is required to observe, imitate, reproduce, and replicate the dance material and its style precisely, and to work with other dancers to ensure that the reproduction/replication of the dance is precise. (2004, 54)

And, this statement is still predominantly true regarding the creation of theatre dance. However, newer methods and pedagogical trends should consistently be investigated and examined, particularly as pedagogical tools for every genre. Regardless of where musical theatre is presently on the evolutionary timeline, all choreographers should have access to current training methods and a forward-looking education. While the literature and theory discussed in this section focuses primarily on traditional and conventional methods and ideas, particularly regarding the teaching of form, a great deal more scholarship exists that proposes new approaches to guiding the creative process in postmodernity.

Existing Texts on Traditional Choreographic Pedagogy

Ballet choreography can be traced back as early as 1581 when Catherine de Medici commissioned musician and dance master Balthazar de Beaujoyeux to stage the first fully scored and lavish ballet for a court entertainment. From the mid-17th Century, Pierre Beauchamp's efforts as dancer in the court of Louis XIV "resulted in numerous advancements in the creation and the production of ballet" (Lee 76). The Academie Royale de Danse was established in 1661 to train dancers and dance masters, and to produce ballets. By 1700 a text on ballet steps and technique, as well as choreographic technique, was written by French ballet master

Raoul Feuillet (80). From that time, ballet progressed through periods that allowed it to evolve, but it remains formulaic and predominantly derivative of traditional models. In the late 1800s and around the turn of the century underground rumblings were being felt in the world of concert dance, instigated by the work of European movement gurus Françoise Delsarte and Émile Jaques- Dalcroze. Those rumblings became a roar when one revolutionary American woman called Isadora rebelled against the conventions of ballet. She introduced freedom of expression into the art of dance and a non-conformist attitude toward form that eventually became known as modern dance (Beckman 26-27).

Most of the existing texts on teaching modern dance composition, and even the few on musical theatre choreography, show reliance on traditional methods of teaching craft (Wayburn, 1926; H'Doubler, 1940; Humphrey, 1959; La Meri, 1965; Ellfeldt, 1967; Blom and Chaplin, 1982; Sunderland and Pickering, 1989; Berkson, 1990; Hawkins, 1991; Hayes, 1993; Novak and Novak, 1996; Stratyner, 1996; White, 1999; Nagrin, 2001; Van Dyke, 2005; Minton, 2007; Smith-Autard, 2008); and there are several that encourage teachers to expand their methodology to acknowledge the postmodern and contemporary dance aesthetics even as they continue to make use of traditional models of choreography (Turner, 1971; Sofras, 1976 and 2006, Nagrin, 2001; Smith-Autard, 2008, 2015). Much of the current information regarding divergent theories of exploring creative process in dance composition are typically not available in such classroom texts. It is extensively examined, however, in journal articles and chapters in book compilations that introduce new choreographic theory and other dance scholarship (Lavender, 1996a, 1996b, 1997; Haworth, 1997; Banes, 2001; Butterworth, 2004; Barry, 2005; Rosenthal, 2005; Lavender & Sullivan, 2008; Butterworth & Wildschut, 2009). New and innovative thought regarding the teaching of choreographic process and the analyses of teaching styles help teachers find more effective ways to relate to their student choreographers (Buckroyd, 2000; Silén & Uhlin, 2008; Smith, 2008; Värlander, 2008; Pomer, 2009). Texts that examine creativity theory and the artistic process can be found in sections of those sources already cited, in the vast array of biographical sketches and philosophies of prominent choreographers (Rogosin, 1980; Stratyner, 1989; Mandelbaum, 1990; Grody and Lister, 1996; Tune, 1997; Payne-Carter, 1999; Conrad, 2000; Wasson, 2014), and in texts that expressly address the creative process (Dewar, 2015; Lavender, 1996; Bayles and Orland, 2001; Tharp, 2005; Gilvey, 2005; Gallwey, 2008; Jeffreys, 2008; Nachmanovitch, 1991). In addition, although not examined in this overview, other current scholarship introduces the use of technology in teaching dance composition (Davis, 2006; Doughty, Fransksen, Huxley & Leach, 2008; Leijen, Admiraal, Wildschut & Simons, 2008).

In order to effectively survey the choreographic approaches to dance in *musicals,* my primary focus, I must acknowledge first the eclectic nature of theatre dance and then briefly trace the development of dance composition and choreographic pedagogy in social, modern, and musical theatre dance forms.

II. EARLY MUSICAL ENTERTAINMENT IN THE COLONIES

Theatre Dance in American Minstrelsy

The discipline of staging movement to popular music itself began to evolve in America during the 1800s with the first truly American musical theatre form, minstrelsy. For all the sins committed by this despicable entertainment, it made some small recompense in the fact that because it was so popular, when black entertainers finally broke into minstrelsy after the Civil War, some believe that it became a catalyst through which African culture was able to truly begin to merge with mainstream (white European) cultural forms. Escaped slave and early leader of the abolitionist movement Frederick Douglass despised the use of blackface but wrote: "It is something to be gained when the colored man in any form can appear before a white audience" (Douglass, 1849). Black performers developed their skills and became known and admired on a national and even international level because minstrel shows were such popular touring entertainments.

While some subscribe to the concept that minstrelsy brought Negro culture into the mainstream, others claim it did so but then distorted it. This distortion of black culture through the caricaturizing of individuals in stereotypical and derogatory ways, which black performers tended to carry on even in all-black minstrel shows, rendered it meaningless as a means of unification because it reinforced black Americans' positioning as Other. Still, I would like to believe that aspects of the Africans' deep culture were preserved in such things as Negro Spirituals, an earthbound, rhythmic and abandoned style of moving, and an intimate connection to drumming and percussive beating, stamping and calling, all of which became aspects of popular theatrical song and dance forms from the mid-18th to mid-19th centuries. It will never be possible to find strict lines of demarcation regarding what is culturally "authentic," particularly during that time in America when cultural displacement through migration and colonization was so active. The minstrel show, adding as it did to the cultural confusion that was (and still is) part of the American experience, intermingled with a thousand and one other cultural rebounds and ricochets transpiring in America during the mid-1800s well through the turn of the century. As such, it was destined to make up a part of the ethnic stew that eventually came to be seen as "authentic" *American* culture, or one that is constantly evolving. John Strausbaugh in his text *Black Like You: Blackface, Whiteface, Insult & Imitation in American Popular Culture* wrote:

> Our mutt culture, bless its shaggy, unruly heart. A culture in which Whites, Black and all manner of Others have been influencing, imitating, insulting, irritating, mocking, mimicking and ripping one another off from the very start. (Strausbaugh 34)

Another way that minstrelsy added to this cultural chaos was that minstrel songs were largely written by white Northern bred composers like Stephen Foster, Dan Emmet and Henry Clay Work, and so in that way could not be accurate representations of the black plantation experience or African cultural roots. These caricatures depicted the dutiful darkie nostalgic for a highly sentimentalized life on the plantation. And so, although there remains a great deal of scholarly controversy over how much *authentic* Negro culture was garnered from this form, some surface aspects of the culture were definitely exploited as whites took on and attempted to imitate the African aesthetic in their use of shuffling, stamping, and sliding steps, slapping, clapping, imitating animals, patting juba, and finally by invoking the African spirit in their wild, "uncultured" and abandoned manner of performance. With the advent of ragtime and then jazz, animal dances such as the Turkey Trot, the Buzzard Lope, and the Fox Trot were embraced by all Americans as was Juba dancing and, later on, tap. The "walkaround," the finale dance of a minstrel show and a forerunner of the present day production number, was also of West African origin and included exuberant, somewhat competitive movements as performers moved around the stage in an improvised or at least loosely constructed way. As described by *New York Herald* feature writer Marion Hannah Winter in 1948, "A most amusing feature of the entertainment was the comic 'walk-around,' given in true darky style, with the lean, the fat, the tall, the short, the hunchbacked, and the wooden-legged, all mixed in and hard at it" (Winter quoted in Magriel 43). In the same article from editor Paul Magriel's *Chronicles of American Dance: From the Shakers to Martha Graham*, Winter recounts a minstrel show review from the *Illustrated London News* of May 8, 1848, in which William Henry Lane (aka Master Juba, considered by many to be the greatest dancer of his day) was praised for the novelty and eccentricity of his soft-sole tap dancing:

> ...the Nigger Dance is a reality. The "Virginny Breakdown," or the "Alabama Kick-up," the "Tennessee Double-shuffle," or the "Louisiana Toe-and-Heel," we know to exist. If they did not, how could Juba enter into their wonderful complications so naturally? How could he tie his legs into such

knots, and fling them about so recklessly, or make his feet twinkle until you lose sight of them altogether in his energy? (*Illustrated London News* quoted in Magriel, 50).

Lane passed away at a relatively young age, but not before he became the first black performer to tour with white minstrels and to receive top billing (43). Scholarship is varied on how authentically African his dancing was, but Winter claims he was the most influential dancer of the nineteenth century and that he "invented" tap by "imposing Negro tradition on tap dancing" (63). Regardless of the ethnic authenticity, his performing was so spectacular that it defied traditions and habits of bigotry; doors opened to him and cultural divisions disappeared as he performed wherever, whenever, and with whomever he pleased, a tremendous accomplishment during this era of unbridled and unconcealed racism.

Since the early days of slavery, Negro ritual dances like the Ring Shout were performed in secret on plantations where the native culture of slaves was stifled, lest it provoke them to rise up and rebel against their white masters. However, slaves *were* permitted to perform European forms of ballroom and country dances. From those dances evolved the Cakewalk, a black couples' processional dance during which Negroes would imitate and parody Western dance forms. The irony involved in this ritual is complex for although the slaves were making fun of their white masters, it seems that instead of being offended, the white families would find that kind of proper and genteel behavior in their slaves amusing, most likely laughing at *them* rather than at the parody itself. The term "hokum" was coined (around 1917) to refer to the kind of punster, satirical and outrageous comedy/parody used in minstrel shows, such as the acting out of inept stereotypes, or insulting humor targeting race or sex. Eventually, it became a way to identify a type of blues music that poked fun at sexual practices and specialized in innuendo. Regardless of its bite, hokem was acceptable because this travesty/burlesque humor was really just "all in fun." This type of comedy still exists today, of course, along with other vaudeville traditions of physical comedy, such as slapstick, impersonation, and sight gags, all of which are necessary tools in the musical theatre choreographer's toolbox (Sotiropoulos 38-40).

Concert Dance Entertainments

Other dance entertainments that were popular in America simultaneous with the advent of minstrelsy were European ballet companies. Not only did European classical ballerinas such as Fanny Elssler and Marie Taglioni come across the ocean to entertain Americans, but the states were also growing their own premier classical dancers, like teenage ballerinas Mary Ann Lee, Augusta Maywood, and male dancers George Washington Smith and John Durang; the latter two were true men of the theatre who did it all while also siring and supporting large broods of children. They were primarily known as dancers but were also choreographers, teachers, actors, designers, technicians, writers—precursors of the great twentieth century musical theatre man George Abbott. Editor Paul Magriel's excellent text *Chronicles of the American Dance (1948),* which I have already cited, is a rich source of research for choreographers and dance historians, meticulously covering these and other prominent dancers and dance traditions from the mid-1700s to the mid-1900s. The articles in that text are taken from issues of *Dance Index* and contain topical reviews from the time periods covered, as well as reproductions of original photographs, posters and other pertinent materials.

Along with ballet, other European forms such as ballad opera, the circus, pantomime shows, puppet shows, and touring theatre companies (from mid-18th century), as well as opera, comic opera, operetta, burlesque and vaudeville (from about mid-19th century), were all part of a patchwork quilt of musical performance genres that ultimately became potential ingredients for use by American musical theatre choreographers.

Social Dance

Still to be mentioned, two vital "dance genre ingredients" I have used more than any other when creating dances for musicals are folk and social dance. Because of the topical nature of musical comedy, social dance is often a choreographer's most essential means for establishing time, place, character, and mood, and should never be underestimated. Because of the central place of social dance in musical theatre, a brief mention of Rosetta O'Neill's article covering the teachings of dance master Allen Dodworth, as well as related references from other dance scholars, seem pertinent to this study.

In her summary of dance education in American schools, dance scholar Ann Dils cites dance professor and historian Lee Chalfa Ruyter who explains that social dancing was important to the way of life in all of the colonies during the 1700s and remained so through the 19th century. It was of particular attraction to southern planters who utilized it in the upbringing of their children. According to Dils, "Strict dancing masters and the precise, patterned dances of the period instilled an appreciation for order and good manners in young people, both necessary to function in society" (Dils 104). During the 1800s, dance masters from Europe, many from France who came after the Revolution, moved throughout the eastern states. For the most part they were employed by wealthy families to teach ballroom dance in their homes or to prepare a community for an upcoming event. The teaching of dance was traditionally paired with the teaching of etiquette, an elegant carriage, and a cultured demeanor, and certain private schools also existed that specialized in this highly structured and rigid training. Dodworth's Dancing Academy in New York, run by the Dodworth family, was such a place. The director Allen Dodworth's text *Dancing and Its Relation to Education and Social Life, with a New Method of Instruction, Including a Complete Guide to the Cotillion (German) with 250 Figures* was really the first textbook of its kind (Dodworth, 1900). Though others had written books on current dances and good manners before him, according to O'Neill, Dodworth's book is "based on a system of teaching, containing details of method, diagrams, and musical phrases with movements clearly marked" (81-2). Dodworth's textbook was written at the end of his career, the late 1890s, but between the years of 1850-1879 he issued tiny booklets that "contained much valuable advice about manners, toilette, and dancing" (96). A musical theatre choreographer would find such research useful, not necessarily to gain the ability to replicate authentic dances onstage, although there might arise a need for such knowledge, but to learn and understand the form, structure, traditions and demands of authentic dances. This research could then inform one's original stage choreography by using a particular dance or dance form as a base, or even to provide motifs around which a theatre dance could be built. Each of Dodworth's documents are excellent points of research for choreographers creating dances from these eras, and O'Neill's article includes excerpts pertaining to specific directions, tenets, and information contained in them, as well as figures illustrating body positioning and carriage of arms and hands while couple dancing (O'Neill 85-100).

O'Neill claims that the Dancing Academy was critical to the social development of Manhattan from about 1842 to about 1920. Throughout the latter part of the nineteenth century, however, Americans began to move away from this sort of elitism, and more and more dancing schools were opened by dance teachers who abandoned the teaching of etiquette and taught only dance. Beyond the ballroom, artists like Isadora Duncan were dancing barefoot and free, and the influx of dances beginning in 1911 brought with it animal dances, the one-step, the Texas Tommy and other dances "which George Dodworth [then owner] and all the old teachers violently opposed" (O'Neill 99). Some of the dances even originated in slums and dives, bringing with them people of questionable morals and *mores*. In the popular art form of musicals, however, the sleazy stands alongside the elite in its mission to tell the story.

Dance Directors and Early Musical Comedy

All the information given up to this point is intended to lead the reader to an understanding of the hybrid nature of musical theatre dance and of the importance of the oral tradition through which it was passed down. Until Minstrelsy showed up in America in the 1840's, our musical entertainments were those we inherited from Europe. Because of the Revolutionary War, government laws forbidding the presenting of stage shows halted theatre from 1774 to 1780 (and into the 90s for some states), but by the 1790s, theatre was beginning to thrive in New York City and Broadway was a popular location for that to happen (Kenrick, 2014b). We begin to see glimmers of our European traditions merging with new forms to facilitate the shaping of theatre dance into an art form during the mid-1800s, most notably in the 1866 musical extravaganza, *The Black Crook* (*TBC*). Historian John Kenrick claims that *TBC* was not exactly the first entertainment of its kind, even though it is generally thought of as the first musical comedy (2010, 50-52). However, *TBC* is certainly the most influential because of the combination of unique elements it brought together to create this extraordinary theatrical phenomenon (62-68). There were many years of musicals on Broadway before *TBC* so I looked back five years to see how those musicals compare to it, particularly as to who was staging the dances. Interesting is that before *The Black Crook*, none of the shows listed by the *Internet Broadway Database* (ibdb.com) from 1860-1865 even mention a choreographer, dance director, or anyone billed for movement direction. The term "stage direction by" is used at times instead of "director," and the producer, director, and musical director are almost always identified. All shows with music are identified by one genre or more. For instance, *Aladdin (1864)* is called a Musical, *Blondette (1862)* was billed as Musical & Spectacle, and *Love Among the Bonnets (1865)* was a Musical, Ballet, and Pantomime, etc. (ibdb.com, "Shows..."). Rarely are casts from this period listed as larger than seven or eight performers, however, which leads me to believe that either the terms "extravaganza" and "spectacle" were used loosely, or perhaps the ensemble was simply not recorded. For our purposes, 1866 and *TBC* is a fine place to start as we think about the evolution of musical theatre choreography as an art form, particularly because we have a link to the book musical, legitimate dance, and someone credited with creating the dances or directing the ballets.

There are texts, internet sites and videos through which one can find out factual and historical information about early dance directors and their work on Broadway. Well-known musical theatre historian Stanley Green, in his chronology *Broadway Musicals: Show by Show* (3) begins his list of Broadway musicals with *The Black Crook* naming David Costa as "Choreographer." The *Internet Broadway Database* lists every show produced on Broadway, including *The Black Crook* in 1866, characterizing it as the first American musical, but lists Costa as "Ballets Directed by...," not as "Choreographer." This statement makes sense in that *ibdb.com* uses opening night programs as one of its sources and the program did bill Costa as "Ballets Directed By....," more specifically, "Ballets under the direction of the renowned Master de Ballet, Signor David Costa" (Kenrick, 2014a). He was, after all, the ballet master of the French ballet troupe that wound up in the musical. The women of the dancing ensemble, who eventually became America's first "chorines," were from a French ballet troupe hired to dance at New York's Academy of Music, and Costa was the Italian ballet choreographer who came over with that company. When the Academy burned down, the producer of Niblo's Garden hired these now out-of-work ballet dancers to help breathe new life into a play at the Garden that was in the process of "laying an egg," to use theatrical vocabulary. Playwright Charles Barras rewrote the script of that play, which was loosely based on the story of Faust, turning it into a knee-slapping burlesque comedy. He added extravagant settings and costumes, pastiche music, a hybrid of theatrical and ballet choreography, and the clincher...girls in tights. Girls, gags, and songs! Its disparate accidental components, its massive popularity brought on by touring, and its financial success morphed this doctored production into a form that became the paradigm for early American musical comedies; it was decidedly distinct from other forms of musical entertainment popular in the States during the mid-1800s. This new kind of theatre peopled by gypsies, gentlemen, tramps, working men, immigrants, slaves and thieves, was destined to become, like America, a mixed salad of diverse art forms, artists, and styles. The combination of scantily clad women, comedy, and songs, as well as the groundbreaking popularity of *TBC*, assured its place as America's first truly indigenous book musical (Kenrick 2010, 53-68).

Green's text does not list a dance director or choreographer or a "staged by" person for the rest of the shows during the 19th Century, and the next time it does mention one, it is Julian Mitchell's name we see as "director/ choreographer" of *The Wizard of Oz* in 1903. This production is not to be confused with the 1939 film for which Busby Berkeley is credited for the Scarecrow dance along with "Dances Staged by Bobby Connelly" (Internet Movie Database [imdb.com], *Wizard of Oz*). Mitchell, who left his career as a chorus dancer when he lost his hearing, had a prolific Broadway career from 1887-1926, and historian John Kenrick names him "Broadway's first important director and choreographer" (2010, 106).

Another source that chronicles who was choreographing on Broadway in the early 1900s is Thomas Hischak's 140 page encyclopedic listing of directors and choreographers entitled *Enter the Playmakers: Directors and Choreographers on the New York Stage*. Unless you decide to read it through like a novel noting each choreographer as they come up, with Hischak's text you need to know the name you are searching for first. Each listing gives 1) a brief paragraph describing the artist's overall contribution, 2) a listing of all New York shows staged or choreographed by him or her (including Broadway, Off-Broadway, and Off-Off-Broadway), and 3) a statement of whether it was a revival.

You can use *ibdb.com* when searching for who choreographed a specific show, or you can key in a choreographer's name and a listing of all the Broadway shows choreographed by that individual will show in a window. Green's chronology, however, allows you to find shows and artists by time period, since it moves in a chronological progression. In all cases, some names (like Mitchell's) that always come up between the 1870's-1910 in terms of being early, important, and prolific dance directors include: Ned Wayburn, John Tiller, Sammy Lee, Albertina Rasch, James Gorman, Julian Alfred and of course George M. Cohan, but only for his own shows. Surprisingly, Alfred was not included in Hischak's book, although he directed or choreographed at least thirty-one shows between 1907 and 1926. By the beginning of the 1900s, popular Broadway and touring shows included musical comedies, operettas, comic operas, (particularly Gilbert and Sullivan), vaudeville, and the spectacular revue, the first of which was *The Passing Show* in 1894 (Kenrick 123). A remarkable amount of work for entertainment artists existed during the turn of the century and a significant amount of musical staging and choreography was being created.

Concurrent to the growth of dance on the American musical theatre stage, also appearing in the early 1900s was the development of modern dance, a form based predominantly on an internal rather than external aesthetic. Literature cited in the following section traces the development of choreographic pedagogy in modern dance alongside the kind of choreography that was developing on the Broadway musical stage, and contrasts modern dance's predominantly improvisatory right-brained foundation to the more structured, planned, well-organized and even regimented left-brained popularity of show dancing and musical comedy's beloved chorus line.

III. EARLY DOCUMENTATION OF MODERN DANCE CHOREOGRAPHY TECHNIQUE

The Art of Making Dances (Humphrey, 1959) was at one time considered by many as the most important text written regarding the teaching of modern dance choreography, but as early as several decades before its publication, work was being done by teachers of creative movement in and outside of academia who guided students through movement improvisations designed to uncover their own movement propensities. In 1904 the American dancer Isadora Duncan, whose life was dedicated to rebelling against the unnatural physical rigors of ballet (and all forms of repression of expression) established her first school in Germany where she taught creative movement and established a company of women who toured and performed with her (Conner & Gillis, 1996a; Ch. 4). Loie Fuller, who danced in yards of silk fabric and pioneered stage lighting effects, was actually Duncan's predecessor as a performance artist, but followed suit as a teacher in 1908 by opening a dance school in Paris where she taught "natural movement and improvisational techniques" (Conner and Gillis, 1996b; Ch. 3). Dancer Ruth St. Denis was also dancing at this time, and all of these women were influenced by the work of French music and drama teacher Francois Delsarte and Swiss music teacher Emile Jacque-Dalcroze. Their expressive and natural movement techniques were permeating both the professional dance world, as well as the development of dance in education. In an article tracing the relationship between professional dance and dance in education during the 1930s, dance educator Cathy Beckman stresses the powerful influence of these two teachers on our modern dance pioneers. The mothers of both Duncan and St. Denis studied with Delsarte and Dalcroze, and dancer/choreographer Ted Shawn was actually a student of Delsarte for forty-five years (Beckman, 1981). Delsarte's attitude toward freedom of expression and his concepts of opposition, succession, and parallelism can be seen as precursors of movement theories in modern dance. Similarly, Dalcroze developed eurhythmics as a method of getting his students to physicalize music to develop in them expressiveness and awareness of rhythm. The philosophies of both of these men "accelerated the development of dance in physical education," claims Beckman, "and it was the physical education teachers who brought modern dance into the schools" (26). German pedagogue Fredrick Froebel, whose concept of kindergarten encouraged movement for children to develop both the body and mind, had a direct effect on young Isadora Duncan who, as an adult, came to develop her ideas of "natural rhythm, moving from an inner impulse to first movements (coming from life) with a flexible back" (27). Documentation of Duncan's theories and methods exists, and her dancing style is still taught in a school in Manhattan, which also houses a company of dancers (Lori Belilove and the Isadora Duncan Dance Company) who re-create and perform her dances. Likewise, a resurgence of interest in Fuller's work has spurred historical reproductions of her physically demanding and highly technical dances (Conner and Gillis, 1996b). The confluence of these theories, these artists, and the time began a movement toward dance as an individual expression that would be profoundly meaningful.

Dance as an art form and dance in education experienced a concurrent evolution. Beckman states that "it is impossible to separate the influence of [professional dance and educational dance] because their development is so closely related and interdependent" (26). In 1913 early dance educator Gertrude Colby developed a curriculum for dance in higher education at Columbia University in New York at the Speyer School. The curriculum was based on "storytelling and musical interpretation through movement." Taking this curriculum forward, Colby's student Bird Larson, for the first time, focused on training goals for the professional rather than recreational dancer. Her system of training was three-pronged in that it developed in dancers the ability to create and perform "natural body movement, designed body movement, and controlled movement with music to express an idea" (Hagood 35). Both of these educators, and others, were influenced by educational reformer John Dewey who was a proponent of an experiential and democratic learning environment. The importance of this growing attention toward natural expression played a significant role in the development of both modern dance and musical theatre choreographic theory.

Although Ruth St. Denis was a successful performer, her direct and lasting effect on modern dance came from her union with dancer Ted Shawn. Performers Ted Shawn and Ruth St. Denis married and began touring together in 1914 and by 1915 opened the Denishawn School of Dance in Los Angeles where they trained the Denishawn Dancers who toured the world with them. Their school was progressive and had "an eclectic program, open to experiments such as dancing to poetry or silence or music composed specifically for them," and most importantly they "stressed the individual" in all of their teaching (Beckman 27). This aspect of their training seems key to me because it went against the authoritative training methods of ballet since its inception, and later of the modernists who insisted on replicating their personal movement aesthetic in all of their dancers. But Denishawn honored the individual in their school, and among the Denishawn dancers were Charles Weidman, Martha Graham and Doris Humphrey who later went on to create their own theories of movement and dance composition and to establish modern dance in America. Philosophically Shawn and St. Denis both believed:

> The art of dance is too big to be encompassed by any one system. On the contrary, the dance includes all systems or schools of dance. Every way

that any human being of any race or nationality, at any period of human history, has moved rhythmically to express himself belongs to the dance. We endeavor to recognize and use all contributions of the past to the dance and will continue to use all new contributions in the future." (Sherman 11)

Between 1916 and 1928, composer/choreographer Louis Horst worked at the Denishawn School during which time he developed a choreographic theory aligned to the rules of music composition. He tutored the early moderns in his theories, notably Graham and Humphrey, after which he became the dance composition teacher for Graham's school of dance until 1948 (87). Horst's rigid laws of dance making became the paradigm for what could constitute a "good" dance, and remained uncontested until the postmodern influence appeared in the 1960s.

Shawn's and St. Denis' move to Jacob's Pillow may have seen the end of their marriage and collaboration, but it instituted the legendary Jacob's Pillow Dance Festival that has since been a driving force in the forward movement of dance in America. Dancer Mikhail Baryshnikov calls it "one of the America's most precious cultural assets -- a haven for choreographers and dancers and an environment that nurtures the creation of new work" (Baryshnikov, "Inside/Out"). True to the founders' beliefs, each summer a myriad of choreographers and dancers, representing every genre of dance, create and show their work at Jacob's Pillow (Jacobs Pillow Dance Festival).

It is also interesting to know that all of these modern dance performers, Duncan through Graham, diversified their involvement in dance opportunities, performing in vaudeville, choreographing musical comedies and revues, and working in the legitimate classical concert dance arena. While their vision and philosophical points of view seemed rigid and elitist toward popular dance, their associations were not.

IV. EARLY DOCUMENTATION OF POPULAR AND MUSICAL THEATRE DANCE FORMS

In musical theatre, as minstrelsy was winding down and after the introduction of the chorine in *The Black Crook*, theatre entrepreneur Florenz Ziegfeld took the form a step further by borrowing a diverse revue format from the French through which to present beautiful women, songs and comedy acts in his *Ziegfeld Follies* shows. From about 1907 through the teens and twenties, emphasis was placed on beauty and, for *Follies* and revue producers especially, a specific "look" was required that had strict height and weight allowances as well as guidelines for the hiring of chorus girls. The operetta was also a highly popular form at this time and while it placed emphasis on music and comedy, dance in operettas was also borrowing "whatever" from "wherever," popularizing and theatricalizing social and folk forms. In 1907, when *The Merry Widow* opened in New York, the waltz experienced resurgence in popularity across the country, as did "Merry Widow" clothing and hairstyles. America's "show dance" aesthetic, however, was gaining popularity through the *Follies* and other spectacular revues so popular at this time, as well as in vaudeville and burlesque shows and, of course, musical comedies.

Ned Wayburn's Documentation of Ensemble Staging

As the *Follies* went on and became more lavish and spectacular, production elements and performers took on more artistry. Sumptuous costumes and Joseph Urban's opulent art deco settings had to be populated with only the most perfectly proportioned, beautiful and capable women. Ziegfeld dance directors Julian Mitchell and Ned Wayburn began to demand at least some training and a professional attitude from the women who danced for them (Kenrick, 2003). They introduced precision chorus lines, kick lines, geometric patterns, even the famous Ziegfeld walk, and established these elements as musical theatre standbys that still have a huge fan base as seen by the existence and popularity of The Radio City Music Hall Rockettes, a modern day link to musical theatre's origins.

In the 1920s and 30s, dance director Busby Berkeley began to more skillfully "organize" the dances for large ensembles in Broadway musicals. Berkeley himself utilized ideas garnered from his work as a field artillery lieutenant in the army and his own affinity for geometrics to arrange complex formations in stage and early movie musicals. Albertina Rasch dressed up popular taste by incorporating her own classical training into musical staging and demanding that her dancers be classically trained. By doing so, she set a higher bar for dance and dancers on Broadway and became one of the first dance directors to be referred to as a "choreographer." Even Russian trained ballet dancer George Balanchine choreographed twenty Broadway shows between 1935 and 1951. This gradual raising of standards for crafting dance in Broadway musicals that began with Wayburn and Mitchell continued into the 1930s when artists George Balanchine and Robert Alton dominated Broadway choreography, the 1940s when Agnes DeMille and Jerome Robbins began choreographing the integrated musical, and the 1950s when we see the first work of choreographers Michael Kidd, Bob Fosse, and Gower Champion.

Barbara Stratyner's book *Ned Wayburn And The Dance Routine: From Vaudeville to the Ziegfeld Follies* scrupulously charts the life and work of dance director Ned

Wayburn by offering what she characterizes "a structural analysis, a methodology used in the late 1970s for analyzing postmodern dance and popular entertainments," an approach, she claims that made it possible to document individual movements, routines, and stage pictures seen in Wayburn's choreography (Stratyner ix). This text, along with Wayburn's own book *The Art of Stage Dancing* truly documents the dances themselves down to the steps, spatial patterns, and groupings of types of dancers and their purpose. Stratyner began this study as a professional biography of three women dance directors from the turn of the century, but turned her attention to Wayburn when she discovered that while there was very little information about the actual content of the women's work, Wayburn left a wealth of documentation not only of his career, but of the "specifics of his routines and dances—perhaps the most complete body of material for any choreographer in the commercial theatre" (ix). Statyner's text not only offers hours of reading for choreographers interested in the evolution of the form, but also potential historical or inspirational material to call upon when modeling popular choreography of this early theatrical time. Wayburn's writing can also be seen as the earliest choreographic theory for this field, and while it does not necessarily encourage individual creativity, like ballet it devises a vocabulary of steps and records of proven practices and standard compositional details used by working dance directors at that time.

The Influence of Jazz

In the 1920s the number of oft-working dance directors expanded to include Bobby Connelly, Sammy Lee, Seymour Felix, Earl Carroll, and George White, the latter two doing mainly revues, however, rather than book musicals. This distinction between genres is an important one, because it is with the book musical that musical theatre choreography evolved. Hischak states "As the books got better and reasons for dance arose, the choreography became more important" (viii). Also, jazz entered the equation in the late 1910's; it was ushered in by ragtime and made respectable by Irving Berlin in 1911 with the wildly popular "Alexander's Ragtime Band." Theatre scholar David Savran positions jazz music during the 1920s as "the most important and controversial form of cultural production in the United States" (459) and stresses the importance of both musical theatre and vaudeville to the development and dissemination of jazz music. Their intimate connection to jazz separated these two musical forms from an emerging legitimate literary theatre, which condemned jazz for being socially and morally depraved. Because of the extraordinary galvanizing effect that jazz had on difference in the United States, Savran states, "it became the symbol of a modernist revolt in a nation undergoing unprecedented change"

(459). He also points out the excesses of the time and of the music itself and makes clear that because of its sweeping and intimate connection to societal and cultural issues, it is not possible to discuss 1920s jazz as only a musical form, or only in terms of its musical particulars. Jazz challenged America's social, racial, and ethnic hierarchies and obsured traditional boundaries, not only within music, but those that defined culture, race, and morality, as well. Savran's research has to do with how jazz separated into hierarchies the less popular but established legitimate theatre practices in New York (the highbrow) from the very popular vaudeville and musical theatre genres (the lowbrow), which embraced jazz and popularized it. He argues that during the 1920s, jazz in its many manifestations caused playwrights and critics a vast amount of anxiety because they believe it undermined their efforts to legitimize theatre as "an elite cultural practice" (459-461). America began to identify itself with jazz, (whether or not it approved), and it became synonymous with urban culture. More specifically, jazz was thought to be centered in the theatre district in Manhattan. Jazz was a rhythmic expression of the times, but because it was associated with excess, decadence, and cultural miscegenation it was shunned by playwrights who "constructed disagreeable characters who loved jazz and sympathetic ones who held it in contempt" (463).

Savran's subsequent analysis of the considerable Jewish influence on New York theatre and musical theatre culminates with a discussion of George Gershwin, whom he calls "the hero of Broadway…the most famous composer the US has produced…a lightning rod of the conflicts swirling around race, ethnicity, and cultural legitimacy" and a musician who "personified the scandalous mixing of high and low" (464). A close reading of several Gershwin songs and an analysis of a few of his most popular theatrical works allows Savran to place Gershwin at the center of an emerging modernism that brings together the popular and the esoteric, as he has one foot in "the sacred precincts" (460) of Carnegie Hall and the legitimate theatre and the other in vaudeville, cabarets, and cheap dancehalls. Gershwin epitomizes for Savran the struggle for popular entertainment like musical theatre to gain status within the existing cultural hierarchy by acting as a foil and a frustration to legitimate playwrights and theatre critics of his time who desired a clear delineation of art forms. Critics working to establish an American art theatre continually reminded musical theatre of its position in the theatre hierarchy. Savran cites drama critic George Jean Nathan who said, "Problems arise when [musical theatre] forgets its place and takes itself with deadly seriousness" (473). In my experience, the predominant perspective on *theatre dance* by those in the concert dance world has also, traditionally, been one of condescension and a distancing caused by their differences as high art from low art. Savran claims, however, that theatre ultimately lost its struggle for cultural ascendency over jazz, which has since become "the substance of and the foundation for real American music," and that musical theatre has also found its place as part of American culture (473). I would argue that theatre dance has also found its place as an American cultural form.

In 1927, composer Jerome Kern and librettist/lyricist Oscar Hammerstein II were the first to venture beyond musical comedy norms, focus on better integration of music and drama and present adult, realistic themes with their groundbreaking musical *Show Boat*, the first time a musical was billed as "a musical play" rather than a musical comedy (Kislan 123). In the short run, this work made long term strides toward a progression of the form, but musical theatre on the whole did not immediately follow suit. During the 1930s, contradictory trends existed side by side as audiences still demanded the frothy escapism of a Cole Porter musical as well as musicals with a social conscience, such as *The Cradle Will Rock, Porgy and Bess*, and the Berlin revue *As Thousands Cheer*. By the beginning of the 1940s, the gritty, realistic, ahead-of-its-time Rodgers and Hart musical *Pal Joey* set the stage for a major step forward in the maturation of the musical form. A few years later when Richard Rodgers was pressed to change partners and hooked up with Oscar Hammerstein II, their first play set a new standard for the integrated musical. The evolution of musical theatre is based entirely on the idea of integration. Not only did *Oklahoma!* change the course of the relationship between music and drama for all musicals that followed, but because of choreographer Agnes DeMille, expectations also changed for dance in musicals. Pushing the art form past its function as pure entertainment to a medium that has something more to say was accomplished by turning attention to the primacy of the book. From here on, the purpose of every element that goes into the making of a musical must be only to serve the script and the story being told. Except as nostalgia, gone are the days when a chorus line of cuties appears out of nowhere to tap up a storm because the show needs a pick-me-up or because a certain tune must be featured. Choreographers became dramatists, and so aesthetic tricks such as the stage positioning of ensembles, precision tapping, and high-kicking chorus lines became only one part of a musical theatre choreographer's expertise.

Simultaneous Trends in Modern Dance

It is important to remember that from the 1920s through the 1940s movement exploration was also taking place in Europe that would influence dance making around the world. Influenced by Delsarte, Dalcroze and Rudolf Laban, the technique and choreography of Mary Wigman, who used tension and relaxation as a tenet of her movement philosophy, led to the development of the European model of modern dance known as Expressionism. In 1915, Laban's Choreographic Institute in Germany attracted students like Mary Wigman and Kurt Jooss who ultimately became independent choreographers and teachers with systems of training for young dancers. Disciples of Laban, such as Wigman herself, whom I recall having as a guest teacher at my college in the late 1960s, were responsible for the widespread communication of Laban Movement Analysis throughout the world. Laban's 1928 publication *Kinetographie Laban* introduced the dance notation system known as Labanotation, which later became a required course in the training of BFA dance students in many colleges and universities, such as my own. Laban's theories of movement and his teaching of choreography laid the groundwork for European modern dance and are still taught in specialized schools and programs around the globe. Laban's work has long been considered important foundational knowledge for all professional dancers and choreographers and is referred to in most texts written on the craft of choreography. In her book *Dance Composition: A practical guide to creative success in dance-making,* Smith-Autard states the following:

> The dance composer has [his or her own] movement language as a basis but requires a means of analyzing the content so that they may take the symptomatic human behaviour patterns, refine them, add to them, vary them, extract from them, enlarge them, [and] exaggerate parts of them according to the needs in composition. The movement analysis which is most useful and comprehensive is that which Rudolf Laban presents in his books. (2010, 18)

Choreographers on both fronts, concert dance and theatre dance, were crossing lines and bringing their influences with them. Ned Wayburn's work at the turn of the century was influenced by Delsarte (Stratyner, 1996), Holm studied with Wigman, and Balanchine and Rasch carried with them the physical perfection of the ballet world, while artists like Robbins and De Mille had not only ballet and modern dance histories, but also more eclectic dance backgrounds, creative minds, and a fearless sense of self. The influence of both modern dance and ballet on musical theatre was not only theoretical, but it was eminently practical and obvious as choreographers such as DeMille, Balanchine, Tamaris, Dunham, Holm and Robbins moved back and forth between both worlds all the time.

V. ACADEMIC DANCE AND EXPANDING ANALYSIS

The Growth of College Dance and Emerging Theories

When University of Wisconsin physical education teacher, young Margaret H'Doubler, went to New York in the summer of 1917 she was charged by her Chair to "look into dancing and maybe you could come back and teach dance" (Hagood 34). H'Doubler claimed to be "so disappointed," however, because she was unable to find any kind of dance worthy to teach in college. After many months of searching, H'Doubler had a revelation in a class run by Alys Bentley, a teacher of music who taught musical interpretation through movement. Working on detailed movement exploration exercises on the floor, H'Doubler thought that if college women were to find benefit in studying dance, "it must be grounded in knowledge of the body itself" (36). This revelation ultimately led her toward a more scientific study of dance and a teaching philosophy that produced dancers knowledgeable of physical anatomy and rhythmic structures. Her dancers were taught to generate "their own movement ideas to give life to art expression through dance performance" (40). Her teaching and the administrative leadership and support from her Chair, Blanche Trilling, led to the first university "Specialized Major of Dancing" in 1927. Later that year an M.A. in Physical Education with a Specialized Major of Dancing was also created (47). "Through her teaching and writing," notes Ann Dils, "H'Doubler's influence was unprecedented in college dance," and her 1940 book, *Dance: A Creative Art Experience*, oversold any other book on dance education (105). Since that time dance programs have spread to thousands of colleges and universities, and the teaching of dance and dance composition continues to be refined and re-defined as an art form.

Dance Professor Cathy Beckman wrote that, during the 1930s, the colleges were instrumental in the growth of modern dance in this country because "as the dancer tried to educate the public, the colleges were helping the dancers," not only by training dancers for the profession, but by providing knowledgeable audiences to support and promote dance performances commercially (Beckman 29). It was a full ten years from H'Doubler's introduction of dance into the physical education curriculum at Wisconsin to the realization of the first degree-granting program in dance, after which other colleges began to follow H'Doubler's lead. Modern dance was becoming established as gym teachers used their vacations to study in New York with Graham, Holm, Humphrey, and Weidman, and went back to their schools to incorporate that training into their college courses. In addition, colleges hosted dance companies who performed the "gymnasium circuit" during the school year (29). Modern dance was developing as an art form as well as an academic pursuit.

Although dance was being taught in universities because of H'Doubler's efforts, it seems it was still not considered a valid academic pursuit, evidenced by the way dance was "disguised" as a science rather than an art. Ann Dils wrote, "By the late 1940s and early 1950s, dance educators were in search of an academic identity. Dance in higher education was now primarily artistic training—technique and choreography—but labeled physical education. However, dance faculty pushed to have dance reclassified as a fine or performing art or as its own subject area" (107).

Regarding the teaching of choreography, H'Doubler's seminal text, mentioned above, had three chapters devoted to certain important theories of dance making and of dancing for creative discovery: "Form and Content," "Form and Structure," and "Dance and Music" (1940). But Hagood asserts that H'Doubler's focus was always planted firmly on the student and the developmental and liberating capacity of dance, not on the development of dance itself as an art form or on the dancer as artist. "Attention to professional, performance-based outcomes in dance education was not of interest to her; she felt strongly that students should not be concerned with professional preparation in dance, since there was ample time to attend to that after college" (49). Regardless of her educational goals, H'Doubler's dance curriculum was structured and taught as a professional pursuit, and because many professional dancers, choreographers and dance educators now are products of undergraduate dance programs, her influence seems paramount. Hagood claims that "core elements of H'Doubler's philosophy for dance education have had a lasting impact on the field; among these are the ideas that dance must be taught conceptually and that the individual learns best through structured experience" (49). There is some irony in the fact that H'Doubler's predominantly *scientific* approach to the comprehension and application of technique to the body was successful in training dance *artists,* but seems less incongruous when considering the significance of balance as a stabilizing factor in most aspects of life. Rather than considering science and art as binary concepts, her approach points out the ambiguous nature of artistic virtuosity, which is a command of technique (or the physical mastery of an art form) along with the constant interplay of less quantifiable objectives that are mental, emotional and spiritual. "There need be no antagonism between science and art," claims H'Doubler; "It is of the greatest importance, when we are working toward art expression, to know the conditions under which the mind creates and the nature of the medium through which it works" (94).

Further regarding this interplay between technique and creativity, educators like Jan Van Dyke and Elizabeth Hayes believed they are inseparably bound. "For me," Van Dyke avowed, "technique is not necessarily about imposing limits but acquiring a set of options, tools to explore and use according to need" (2005, 17). Hayes believed that the practice of "pigeonholing" dance technique and compositional expression contributes to "artistic sterility." Teachers who emphasize one element over the other, she maintained, risk either composing dances that cannot be effectively danced or are limited to a smaller range of movement choices. Or, they are limited to composing less meaningful dances that are only about the technical beauty of the movements and can only be performed by a few highly proficient individuals. Neither, she felt, were useful methods in an educational setting (3). Technique as the means to full expressivity was a tenet ingrained in me by my early mentors and a belief I still embrace. As a teacher for many years, I am aware of the complexity of maintaining the balance between technique and expression—or art and craft as I stated earlier—and the importance of refining pedagogical techniques that support my ability to do so.

During the 1930s and '40s, university teachers like H'Doubler and professional dancers like Humphrey and Graham were teaching dance composition as a profession and an art. Dance as an art was developing in both higher education and the commercial sphere and teachers of dance were gaining ground as "artists" whose individuality was respected and considered a crucial element to the teaching process. Former Gertrude Colby student and Graham dancer Martha Hill was the director of Vermont's Bennington College summer program in dance beginning in 1934, which was a peak time of the interaction between college and professional dance. Bennington boasted teachers such as Graham, Humphrey, Weidman, and German modern dancer Hanya Holm and was one of many colleges adding rigorous dance training programs to their summer curriculum at a time when dance was still residing within the physical education departments in higher education. In 1942, the summer dance program combined with an arts program which "expanded in the first years to include classes in stage design, music with Louis Horst, [and] criticism with John Martin," which allowed advanced students to dance in festival productions "and have the experience of working with one of the 'big four'—Graham, Humphrey, Weidman and Holm" (Beckman 29-30). In 1947, Hill went to Connecticut College where she designed a successful pilot program for dancers, dance teachers, and college dance groups. In 1948 it opened officially as the Connecticut College School of Dance/American Dance Festival. In 1951, seventeen years after initiating the first Bennington summer program, Hill founded the Julliard Dance Division, where dance finally came together with fine and performing arts. Besides connecting "dance techniques with a strong academic program of music theory, dance history and criticism, composition, anatomy and notation," Hill's approach to dance education "provided an enlightened academic model that signaled to other like-minded dance educators the coming break of dance away from physical education" (Nadel 177-78). In 1969, under the direction of Charles L. Reinhart, the Connecticut College American Dance Festival became known as the American Dance Festival or simply ADF, which in 1977 came south and "took over the sprawling green lawns, studios offices, and dormitories of Duke University in Durham, North Carolina" where it remains today as a prestigious and important training ground for dancers, choreographers, dance critics, and historians of dance (*American Dance Festival* [ADF], "History").

The Escalating Need to Document Choreographic Theory

Of those Bennington "big four" pioneers of modern dance, it was Doris Humphrey who eventually codified her teaching methods for young choreographers. Posthumously, her text was published on the craft of choreography entitled *The Art of Making Dances (1959)* and became required reading for college dance majors around the world. H'Doubler's text *Dance, A Creative Art Experience (1940)* was published before Humphrey's but the nature of these two books is vastly different. Humphrey's text is practical, conversational, and straightforward. She lays out the tools of the trade and comments on ideas with her opinions, which, generally speaking, are not scholarly analyses but grounded in her experiences as a choreographer. H'Doubler's text is a philosophical analysis of both the scientific and artistic natures of dance and how she perceives dance as an educator. It also strikes me as a phenomenological examination of the consciousness of, and the experience of, dancing and creating dances. Her target is the pedagogue, whereas Humphrey's target is the choreographer. Another author's texts also existed before Humphrey's, as well, although it has been difficult to discern if they enjoyed similar popularity during that time. As early as 1935, the young Wisconsin-Madison graduate student, Elizabeth Hayes, wrote and eventually published *The Emotional Effect of Color, Lighting, and Line in Relation to Dance Composition* (Hayes, 1935). In 1949, earning her Doctorate in Education at Stanford University, she wrote *Theory and Techniques for Motivating Choreographic Expression on the Secondary and College Levels* (Hayes, 1949), and in 1955 published *Dance Composition and Production for High Schools and Colleges* (Hayes, 1955). Finally, Princeton Books published her most recent books on the topic, *Dance Composition and Production*, first in 1981 and a revised edition in 1993 Hayes, 1981 & 1993). Besides D'Houbler's work, Hayes' writing also illustrates a depth of analysis given to the teaching of dance composition years before Humphrey's text. Hayes' first publication on the teaching of choreography, with which she earned her Ph.D. at Stanford in 1949, predated Humphrey's by 10 years and was most likely based, to a large extent, on her research and teaching as a dance professor at the University of Utah since 1940. Humphrey, on the otherhand began developing and teaching the methods found in her book in the early 1930's when Hayes was still a student. As an academe, Hayes was expected to write articles and books based on her work while Humphrey's work, of course, was all practical. Hayes studied under H'Doubler's mentorship in Wisconsin. She also studied at Julliard with Martha Hill, and at Bennington in 1939. During her Bennington summer, she studied with all the great modern dance pioneers: Holm, Graham, Humphrey, Weidman, musician/choreographer Louis Horst, and Martha Hill. Interesting is that she does not acknowledge Humphrey or Horst with some of these other influences (1993). Hayes remembered Humphrey as being "cold" and Horst "terrified" her. She thought he might have been an effective teacher had he not been so terrifying. Telling is this statement she made in an interview with Utah paper, *The Deseret Times:*

> Perhaps that's the big difference between dance educators and professionals; the former are concerned primarily with what experiencing dance will do for the human being, and the latter care most about the end result—dance performance. Professionals turned teachers often take shortcuts in their handling of people, sometimes damaging egos. (Stowe, 1988)

Hayes' work with H'Doubler was clearly more influential to her as a teacher than her work with Humphrey and Horst, who worked together in developing the choreographic theories that Humphrey advocates in her book. The tone of Humphrey's text is the tone of an established professional: matter of fact, confident, and often opinionated, whereas H'Doubler and Hayes write with the objectivity of academes. It is curious to me now that my teachers in Boston did not require all three existing texts on dance composition in my yearly choreography courses. I can only assume that Humphrey's historical importance and her star status as a professional dancer made her book both prominent and credible as soon as it was published, whereas H'Doubler and Hayes were college professors and less widely known than Humphrey. (Also, at that time there was a more obvious distinction drawn between teachers of dance and those who remained in the professional world.) Finally, it is also possible that the academic tone and level of scholarship of the professors' texts may have been considered too heavy reading for undergraduates in the late 1960s. Regardless, H'Doubler's research has become legendary, and Haye's books (and very many others) did eventually become recognized by university teachers and used as standard texts for teaching choreography over time (Hayes Obituary, 2007).

In stating their differences, I do not make value judgements on either Hayes or Humphrey, of course. They worked in two very different worlds for very different reasons, but both, in their unique ways, advanced the art of modern dance. Humphrey may not have been particularly warm, but she was brilliant in her study of dance. Sometime in the mid-1940s, Doris Humphrey was commissioned by the John Simon Guggenheim Memorial Foundation to, as she states, "commit my theory to paper." In October of 1958, just a few months before her death, Humphrey wrote those words in the Foreword of her new text, *The Art of Making Dances.* Less than a year later, her book on choreography was published, but her autobiography was left undone. Thirteen years earlier, dance historian John Martin wrote of Humphrey's work as a dancer: "Besides being a great artist and a great theorist, she is in this field unquestionably the most important figure who has yet arisen in the American dance" (Martin 128). Her work on the relationship of gravity to the behaviors and movements of the body were based on observation, knowledge of the body and of physics and "constitute one of the most important contributions that anybody has made to dance theory, and actually comprises what might be called the kinetic laws of dance" (124). These theories led to rich developments in dance training in general, in her choreography, and in the establishment of her theories of choreography. Since then, many of Humphrey's ideas have become not only part of the core knowledge of stage design and artistic structure for generations of choreographers and other theatre artists, but they are also the traditions to question and the rules to break for contemporary artists of each generation hoping to push the art form in new directions.

According to Humphrey, for hundreds of years the patriarchal conventions that formed ballet traditions frowned upon divergent thinking. "There were always a few gifted individuals who would undertake to put dances together and had a knack for dramatic sequence," so the idea was to leave well enough alone and rely on these chosen few (Humphrey 17). Early in the twentieth century, however, revolutionary dancers like Fuller, Duncan and St. Denis inspired Russian ballet choreographer Michel Fokine to break set and "declare that dancers should look like human beings, that technique should vary according to theme, and that music and décor should correspond in style to the period chosen, ideas which began to shake young dancers loose from the ties of conventional formulaic dance works (18).

Still it seems that theories for dance composition needed an even stronger impetus for coming into being because they did not begin to emerge until the 1930s. Reflecting on the impact of World War I, Humphrey surmised that it could have been responsible for the emergence of choreographic theory. "The shocks reached all the way down to the thoughtless lives of dancers," she wrote, "especially in

America. Everything was re-evaluated in the light of the violence and the terrible disruption, and the dance was no exception" (18). Interestingly, she notes that Germany and the United States reacted most strongly. "Dancers asked themselves some serious questions," says Humphrey, such as "'What am I dancing about?' 'Is it worthy in the light of the kind of person I am and the kind of world I live in?' 'But, if not, what other kind of dance shall there be, and how should it be organized?'" (18). Humphrey asked herself such questions, and as she searched for answers she developed into a probing, innovative, and prolific choreographer.

As a young teacher of choreography, I found that Doris Humphrey's philosophical reflections and her tenets of craft made a great deal sense to me, and so I began to teach with my "bible" of choreographic theory close by my side. Over the years her theories have held up well, but have also encountered questioning and even rejection as young dancers become bolder and more likely to question rules and defy expectations. New theories of choreography have emerged, but because Humphrey was one of the earliest artists to codify the teaching of choreography as a craft, it is Humphrey's text that I rely on as the "ground zero" of choreographic theory, considering it a starting position, a point of comparison and a place from which to divert. Writing down her methods seemed logical to her, but Humphrey never intended her text to be a rigid formula for how to create good choreography and said, "I always thought students should learn principles of movement and be encouraged to expand or embroider on these in their own way" (19). She thought of choreographic theory as a craft, "for I do not claim," Humphrey wrote in the preface to her text, "that anyone can be taught to create, but only that talent or possibly genius can be supported and informed by know-how" (19). It is with this same philosophy, and a healthy dose of humility, that I presume to write down my own principles of craft.

The Need for Guidelines and the Importance of Practice

Dance educators Gertrude Shurr's and Rachel Yocum's thorough and superbly illustrated text, *Modern Dance; Techniques and Teaching* (1949), is dedicated exclusively to teaching modern dance technique. The authors, however, state early on that they place the manner of teaching technique, as well as the teaching of choreography and creative dance, strictly in the domain of each individual teacher: "The responsibility for the use of technical and choreographic education rests entirely with each individual, for student and dancer can only communicate in terms of the known vocabulary" (Shurr and Yocum 16). This emphasis on the creativity and artistry of the teacher shows how the perception of dance from a form of physical exercise was changing during that time to the perception of dance as an art form.

Unlike Isadora's philosophy of shunning all restrictions of convention, Shurr and Yocum stress the importance of young choreographers learning what has already become established as the basis of modern dance composition before forming their own approach. "Once the fundamentals of choreography are mastered," they maintain, "the students, like the creative artists, may deviate from the learned pattern as the content or the mood of a dance demands" (16). Likewise, other teachers of dance composition note a similar need to first teach the fundamentals of the craft. Jan Van Dyke wrote that "once in possession of skills for crafting dances, students are equipped to begin other kinds of exploration...as they mature artistically and gain firm control of the skills covered, they can decide what to do with this knowledge (2005, 116-17). Prominent British dance educator and author Jacqueline Smith-Autard prefaced her book by writing, "[My] book focuses almost exclusively on traditional, formal approaches in dance composition because it is considered that artistic 'rules', established through generations of practice, need first to be learned and applied in many differing contexts before they can be broken, changed or ignored" (7). Again, I agree that the maturation process of an artist takes years and happens gradually; it is only achieved through "doing," and the "doing" happens in small, or what Humphrey refers to as "bite size," steps. She began by teaching her students the nature of dance, what "ingredients" make up movement and how one can use those ingredients in a knowledgeable and purposeful way. "Only then," she explains, "are considerations of form, construction, and real choreography undertaken" (Humphrey 46-47). Blom and Chaplin concur:

> You do not learn choreography by reading about it, hearing about it, or by watching the major companies in concert. You learn by choreographing, by experimenting, by creating little bits and pieces and fragments of dances and dance phrases, by playing with the materials of the craft over and over again until they become second nature. (3)

Supporting the need for young artists to learn the arts experientially, psychologist John Haworth examined Merleau-Ponty's embodiment theory of art, which characterizes a work of art "as an 'enriched being' in its own right" (Haworth cited in Sabo, 2009, 12). "Merleau-Ponty's focus on the origins of perceptual knowledge and consciousness claim that 'knowing and understanding are embodied action.' In other words, we know the world because of how our bodies react within it." and so, "works of art come about through the continuous interaction of the artist with the ideational and physical fabric of the world," as well as its intuitive component (12). Much earlier, in 1965, La Meri wrote in the introduction to her composition text:

> You cannot create choreography by sitting and brooding and commanding your heart to tell your brain to tell your body what to do...There must be the courage to travel the long, rough road of practical knowledge...I have seldom found a student willing to start at the beginning and to pursue without undue haste, to the end, the study of the elements herein set forth. (16)

I found this last statement to be true in my own experience with many of my own beginning choreography students. It is logical and comforting to some students that they begin their study of choreography with something specific and tangible and to be asked to adhere to specific guidelines. Other students, however, show resentment of restrictions to their creativity and resist pedagogical preferences that favor traditional methods and philosophies, even as means to an end. Balancing learning styles, learning expectations, and student receptivity is often daunting in courses stressing creativity and relying upon subjective response. In my estimation, rules can be useful, even if just to be broken.

Professors Blom and Chaplin claim that their text is not a set of rules, but "rather it offers an isolated and comprehensive exploration of each of the many elements that collectively comprise the process of choreography (xv). They are in accord with Van Dyke who states: "Techniques can be taught...that are focused on the "how to" of dance-making" (2005, 117). These techniques offer a starting place, a connection to, and familiarity with the past of one's art form. This knowledge of where it has been can help artists assess where they would like to take it next. In that vein, Hayes (1993) also intended her book to be "a stimulus to creative teaching rather than a crutch" (xiii) stating:

> [A teacher] cannot tell the dancer what or how to compose. On the other hand, he can assist the student by acquainting him with his art instrument—his body—and with his art medium...and be taught guiding principles of the art form which may assist him in composing and in judging his artistic efforts. (2)

Smith-Autard finds that the challenge in teaching young artists lies in guiding them to fulfill their own potential, and feels that learning the techniques of their craft give them the tools to make that happen.

> There are 'rules' or guidelines for construction, which need to be part of [the student's] awareness when he [or she] sets about making dance. They have to do with (a) the material elements of a dance, (b) methods of construction

which give form to a dance, (c) an understanding of style within which the composer is working" (1976, 13)

Regarding the "material elements," Humphrey succinctly names them in the first chapter of her text's section entitled "Craft," stating, "The four elements of dance movement [or choreography] are design, dynamics, rhythm, and motivation. These are the raw materials that make a dance" (46). Many teachers discuss dance as the combination of timespaceforce, which allows movement to stand on its own, or contend that dance does not need an intellectual reason to exist. Smith-Autard bases her study of choreography on the aspects of movement as laid out by Rudolf Laban, stating "The concepts identified in his analysis are fundamental because Laban categorized the total range of human movement into easily recognizable and descriptive frames of reference" (7). Her use of Laban elements is very useful in working through motif building and motif manipulation. They are excellent roadmaps to help choreographers navigate the creative process.

Finally, I will mention Jonathan Burrows' book, *A Choreographer's Handbook* (2010), a mostly philosophical exercise in the meaning of choreography and many tasks associated with it. It strikes me as a stream-of-consciousness diary or a transcript of notes taken during a lifetime of thinking and talking about making dances. Burrows' ideas can be inspirational to other artists and can also provoke further thinking and conversations about the craft. For instance, on stillness and silence, "Stillness and silence are as strong as any other material, and without them your audience will become exhausted." But then, "Maybe you want your audience to be in a state of exhaustion"? Or, "Our tolerance for stillness is greater than you might imagine" (91). His work as a contemporary dance choreographer seems to have refined his ability to think "out-of-the-box," the central feature that drives his text. Thinking "out-of-the-box is also a pivotal activity for developing an individual's creative instincts making Burrow's book a useful read for choreographers.

VI. DANCE IN MUSICALS OF THE 1940's AND 1950's

Thanks to the advent of the integrated musical in the early 1940s, choreography for the theatre had to follow suit and re-invent itself, as well. Hereafter began the most significant evolutionary time for theatre dance. While glimmers of this evolution began during the late 1930s, it was during the 1940s that the pace picked up and momentum took over. In her insightful article "The Influence of Modern Dance on American Musical Theatre Choreography of the 1940s," Lisa Jo Sagolla writes an account of how this evolution began, not only because of better librettos and more integrated music, but because of the crossover of modern dance choreographers from the legitimate dance world to the musical theatre world. Sagolla explains:

> Modern dance, with its abhorrence of virtuosic displays of technical feats, encouraged choreographers to search for movements that would emanate naturally out of the characters. Unlike ballet, modern dance is not based on a finite vocabulary of prescribed steps. Therefore, it more easily allows for the creation of movements which are uniquely expressive of individual characters and dramatic situations. This modern-influenced method of approaching musical theatre choreography led to a truer integration of dance, staging, music, and drama. (Sagolla 48)

Dance artists such as George Balanchine, Agnes de Mille, Hanya Holm, Jerome Robbins, and others began migrating between working in classical dance companies and creating dances for musicals. Dances began to develop a more hybrid, theatrical nature. Balanchine "moonlighted" from his work as a ballet master and ballet choreographer to choreographing musicals, most likely to help support his classical dance pursuits. His choreography for "Slaughter on Tenth Avenue" in the 1936 musical *On Your Toes* brought together ballerina Tamera Geva with hoofer Ray Bolger. This ballet's storyline, although solidly separate from the plot of the musical itself, was conveyed through well executed classical ballet movement combined with theatrically stylized jazz-type movement within a musical comedy. Also, the dance itself was a narrative. The dancers became specific characters with psychological and emotional conflicts. Rather than abstract steps presented in interesting formations, each movement had to be motivated and seem appropriate to the character performing it. It may be that dance elitists consider Balanchine's Broadway work "slumming" in comparison to the work he did for his several dance companies at the time, but by bringing classical ballet to Broadway, he was advancing the expectations for the kind of dance that would evolve there. Although it was a crossbreed of dance forms and not "pure" ballet, "Slaughter on Tenth Avenue" was considered legitimate enough to enter the New York City Ballet repertoire in 1968 when it was danced by *primo* and *prima* dancers Arthur Mitchell and Suzanne Farrell (NYCB Website, Repertory Index).

Despite these early attempts at elevating the level of dance in this popular entertainment genre, Agnes de Mille is generally credited with beginning the true integration of dance in musicals by putting movement to work developing the storyline in 1943's *Oklahoma!*. Her choreography in this show gave dance the significance of being integral to the telling of the story rather than simply being an entertaining *divertissement*. DeMille's insistence on using trained dancers rather than casting the women's ensemble on beauty alone mystified both Rodgers and Hammerstein, as well as their director Reuben Mamoulian, although they supported her or at least gave her enough rope to see her through to the end. What she achieved was stunning and surprised even her. DeMille biographer Carol Easton wrote:

> Until *Oklahoma!* most theatergoers had equated ballet with swan queens and princes, tutus and tights. Agnes's dancers wore jeans and gingham dresses; their leg movements were balletic, but they did not assume the classical ballet positions. They were characters in the play, not interchangeable members of an anonymous chorus, and their gestures were idiomatic American. Their dancing was sharp and focused, often funny, and sometimes quite beautiful…Agnes's work was so influential that forty-six of the seventy-two Broadway musicals to open during the next three and a half years would include ballets…[and] after *Oklahoma!* it was taken for granted that show dancing would include ballet and modern dance, in whatever proportions the show required. (Easton 208)

By the late 1960s, jazz or "modern jazz dance," as it was called during the 1950s and 60s, had not yet gained the same status in the academic dance world that modern dance had gained. Even so, the development of jazz dance as a serious technique *had* been introduced into the commercial dance consciousness during the 1940s when legendary jazz dance guru Jack Cole began to teach theatrical dance in a more methodical way. Dancer and dance professor Tom Ralabate, who characterizes Cole's legacy as "leaving an indelible mark," explains Cole's complex style:

> Cole borrowed from modern dance (Humphrey-Weidman), ballet (Cecchetti), *bharatanatyam* (a style of Indian dance), African and Caribbean dances and rhythms, and other world forms to create a new jazz hybrid. His style utilized African movements, such as deep pliés with explosive hip movements; East Indian isolations; the rhythm and syncopation of swing; athletic and acrobatic movements; and intricate floor work. The influence of his style, though redefined, is visible in current jazz choreography. (Ralabate, *Dance Studio Now,* 2008)

Rigorously and meticulously trained jazz dancers who studied with Cole, such as Gwen Verdon, Matt Maddox, Carol Haney, and Buzz Miller, became the new models for the Broadway, film, and cabaret theatre dancer. But, it should be remembered that just getting to *that* point took almost a hundred years of hokum-dance, "girls in tights," and dancing in musicals that was used mainly to break up the monotony of the script.

After *Oklahoma!*, DeMille and others such as Hanya Holm, Michael Kidd, and Jerome Robbins continued to push forward the idea of technicaldance-slash-storytelling-slash-classicallyrooted-slash-characterdriven movement in musicals like *Kiss Me Kate, Guys and Dolls* and *On The Town*. It was Jerome Robbins, however, who took the idea of "dance telling the story" to an extreme in the 1957 musical *West Side Story (WSS)*, thus becoming an innovator in how integral to the plot dance could potentially be. *WSS* is absolute integration. By the time the film was released in 1961, America was already familiar with the music; not only was it being played on the radio, but vocalists were covering songs from the show on recordings and performing them on television shows. My knowledge about musical theatre at the time was too limited to have understood the massive step forward this show took for the genre, but while there have been musicals created since then that center around dance, what Robbins did with *West Side Story*—its complete integration of the disciplines— has not been done since. *WSS* was special, which was obvious to anyone who cared about this kind of entertainment, but many of its *aficionados* did not really know why, nor were the artistic breakthroughs made by both Bernstein and Robbins completely understood by the common theatergoer. Bernstein's music inspired the dance created for *WSS*. Robbins' choreographic interpretation of the music was so thorough that it became significant not only to telling the story, but to the expansion of acting technique by utilizing dance movements that demonstrated the psychology, emotionality, and inner conflicts of the play's characters and relationships. Bernstein's music expressed the inner life of the characters and Robbins physicalized it. Through a seamless melding of the internal aesthetic of modern dance with the skill, beauty, and outward aesthetic of the ballet form—and working within the timely and popular be-bop jazz style—Robbins paid effective and valuable service to both the music and the story. Both the stage and film musicals are masterpieces of integrated storytelling, and nothing quite like it has been created since. For these reasons, *West Side Story* was, for me, the most important innovation in the evolution of dance in this genre since *Oklahoma!*, up to and through *A Chorus Line*, and beyond.

Beginning most significantly in the Golden Age of musical comedy, 1943 through the 1950s, the need also emerged for a choreographic technique to allow these innovations to flourish and develop. Today, dancers performing in Broadway musicals are classically trained (as are the singers) in addition to having technical training in the vast variety of musical and dance styles they will encounter in musicals. The singer/dancer/actor or dancer/actor/singer or actor/singer/dancer (etcetera) can potentially bounce back and forth between shows such as *Les Misérables* to

Rent to *Thoroughly Modern Millie*, and back again to a jukebox musical such as *The Jersey Boys*. A dancer could be hired to be a member of the ballet *corps* in *Phantom of the Opera*, move from there to performing the acrobatic shenanigans of *Cats*, become a safari animal in *The Lion King*, a depraved/deprived teenage bebopping-Manhattanite in a revival of *West Side Story*, cross the bridge and morph into a Brooklyn Latino hip hopper from *In the Heights* and wind up as an acro-jazz spectacle entertainer in Twyla Tharp's *Movin' Out*. And, like Albertina Rasch, choreographers now are often classically trained dancers with at least some training in modern dance choreography. Their work, although demanding, technical and often classically based, is subjugated to the needs of a musical, fulfilling the story's given circumstances concerning *where* it takes place, *who* is being depicted, *what* is happening, *when* it's happening, and *why* the dance exists within this storyline.

While Jack Cole began the movement to make jazz dance a recognized and technical dance form, subsequent teachers such as Matt Mattox, Luigi, and Gus Giordano created jazz techniques of their own beginning in the 1960s. These men led the crusade to "legitimize" jazz dance as a serious dance form that should have its own technique, which, like modern dance, would be based on the individual styles of its creators. Giordano's "classical jazz technique," his school, and his company, *Gus Giordano Jazz Dance Chicago*, began the crossover of jazz dance to the concert dance world in 1963. Now dancers are trained specifically in jazz techniques to dance in jazz dance companies throughout the world.

I began teaching Dance for Musical Theatre in the late 1970s to B.F.A. musical theater majors at Syracuse University. At the time we knew of only three other schools offering this same degree, so I am certain I was not the only person in academia teaching such a course, but I believe I was one of the first. Also, in New York, Broadway dancers and choreographers were teaching jazz classes featuring theatre dance combinations and Lee Theodore, in particular, focused a spotlight squarely on musical theatre dance with her company *American Dance Machine*, which reproduced the work of Broadway choreographers. Since that time, dance classes teaching styles and techniques used in theatre dance have proliferated. Under a variety of titles, such courses are offered by teachers throughout the world in college programs and professional schools alongside traditional dance technique classes. Much like jazz and modern dance, coursework takes on the personalities and proclivities of its teachers. Without question, the demands of becoming versatile in this type of dance, either as a performer or a choreographer, are considerable. Furthermore, I believe the rigorous, unique, and distinctive nature of musical theatre choreography warrants its consideration as a technique that can be documented, codified, and presented by teachers as a legitimate technique for students wishing to specialize in theatre dance.

Although this overview could not cover every book ever written on the topic of teaching choreography, my hope is that it does illustrate the sheer volume of existing documentation devoted to teaching modern dance choreography, as opposed to what is available in both the theory and practice of teaching musical theatre choreography.

The following section is a literature review, brief because the literature is brief, of the texts I have found having to do with teaching musical theatre choreography. If I have missed any that fit the type of content I describe, I apologize, and would like to know about them.

VII. EXISTING TEXTS ON MUSICAL THEATRE CHOREOGRAPHIC PEDAGOGY

There are a small number of texts that indicate musical theatre choreography in their titles, such as Matthew White's *Staging a Musical*, David Young's *How to Direct a Musical*, and the Novaks' *Staging Musical Theatre*. These texts, however, address the more encompassing idea of the full mounting of a musical and predominantly target either the producer, the director or the *entire* artistic staff, not solely the choreographer. These texts are valuable "how-to" resources for musical theatre choreographers, but they do not fully, or at all, address theory or artistic process. I use them as reference materials as I write, and they will be included in the bibliography at the end of this text, but I will not list them as pedagogical texts for teaching musical theatre choreography..

Until the late 1980s, only about 30 years ago, except for Ned Wayburn's *The Art of Stage Dancing* (1925, 1927), only a small smattering of instruction manuals or articles in early periodicals addressed the techniques that go into musical theatre staging and choreography. In this final section I intend to review the three available texts I was able to find that target this topic primarily, or at least secondarily, as an art form: Robert Berkson's *Musical Theatre Choreography: A practical method for preparing and staging dance in a musical show*, Joe Deer's book *Directing in Musical Theatre: An Essential Guide*, and Margot Sunderland and Kenneth Pickering's *Choreographing the Stage Musical*. I am not including Wayburn's text here because it is not as concerned with choreography as an art form as it is with recreating staging routines, formations, and spatial techniques created and perfected by Wayburn. As previously stated, I believe the value of this choreographer's documentation lies in its historical preservation of actual dance routines and ensemble choreography so popular in its time. Each of the aforementioned texts, particularly the first, addresses musical theatre choreography more from a practical point of view rather than theoretical. However, woven through each of them are certain philosophical approaches that, when significant, I will highlight. Finally, since this scholarship is so minimal, I would like to approach each text separately and more fully than the previous chronological overview of modern dance composition texts offered.

Berkson, Robert (1990). *Musical Theatre Choreography: A practical method for preparing and staging dance in a musical show.* New York: Back Stage Books.

Central Purpose of the Research and the Writing. Berkson shares his purpose and targets a broad audience early on, stating:

> My goal is to offer general approaches, starting points, considerations, and alternatives for dealing with common musical theatre situations. Professionals as well as amateur choreographers can benefit from this systematized presentation of duties, as will dancers branching out into the world of choreographic direction. (2)

Berkson also feels this book could potentially influence the work of other members of the collaborative team positively or at least they would better appreciate and understand the work of the choreographer. Berkson immediately positions the choreographer as an artist involved in a creative process, pointing out that while both the director and musical director are primarily interpretive artists working from previously written materials, the choreographer "must undergo a specific process to first *create* his material, structuring his dances to suit the dramatic context, and finalizing the steps to be used even before they can be taught to performers" (1). Berkson, clearly someone who worked professionally and extensively in this field, specifies his audience even more specifically by gently drawing a distinction between the *dilettante* and those with appropriate qualifications. He cites, for instance, that often in amateur situations people with no dance skills, or even skilled classical ballet or modern dancers with no background in the specific requirements of choreography in this genre, accept the task of choreographing a show. Such choreographers have little else to guide them except to dig in and learn through experience, in lieu of which he offers this text. His hope, he says, is to inspire developing choreographers to *create* (3).

Methodology and Overview of Contents. In Chapter 1 Berkson distinguishes the role of each member of the artistic staff, what he refers to as the production team, and goes through each duty through the eyes of the choreographer, whom he designates as "the movement expert who defines and supplies the "specialized movement needs of the entire project" (7). He discusses the importance of all of the collaborators conforming to and serving the vision of the director but feels that each collaborator should set with the director the scope of his own artistic freedom within certain boundaries. Berkson addresses choreographic theories and the dramaturgy behind the material throughout his text. Chapters 1 through 5 and the Appendix, entitled Theatrical Research Sources, deal predominantly with the creative process in discussions that cover such things as the choreographer's role, script and score analysis, score interpretation, and musical staging. In other chapters he addresses more practical problem-solving such as creating structure, choosing the steps, choosing and teaching lifts, staging fights, working with costumes, scenery and props, auditioning and casting, how to run rehearsals, and even how to take and give notes. While Berkson does not develop either the theory or the practice discussions to a great degree, he does concisely introduce, explain, and offer resolution to most of the major tasks, problems, and miscellaneous other factors that will present themselves to choreographers in the course of creating and teaching movement for a musical.

Conclusions. Berkson's text is presently the most useful of the three presented here, and I support it as required reading for beginning musical theatre choreographers because it is systematic in laying out the fundamentals. His approach to the musical is not external but instead he instructs the reader to begin within by analyzing the play for its overall message and each song as a mechanism to further serve the plot, motivate movement, and integrate the music and dance into the drama. Until Joe Deer's text, which I examine next, Berkson's is the only text I was able to find that applies this holistic approach, and it is why I find his contribution an important one.

Deer, Joe. *Directing in Musical Theatre: An Essential Guide.* London and NY: Routledge, 2014.

Central Purpose of the Research and Writing, Deer begins by stating his belief that readers will use his book for two different purposes, either to "help refine their directing process," or as a textbook in a "formal educational environment." In order to facilitate the latter, he has provided exercises, teaching ideas, lecture slides, syllabi, and checklists for assignments on the Routledge website (xvii). I like this book a lot. It is a meticulous resource not only for teachers and students of directing, but also for working directors and choreographers.

Deer's text divides the process of directing into five Phases, within which he houses nine chapters that chronologically follow the protocol for directing musicals. They are:

Phase 1 *Conception*
    Chapter 1. Preparing for collaboration   Chapter 2. Imagining the chorus

Phase 2 *Collaboration*
    Chapter 3. Collaborative partners   Chapter 4. Directing the design

Phase 3 *Rehearsal*
    Chapter 5. Auditions   Chapter 6. Staging and coaching

Phase 4 *Production*
    Chapter 7. Moving into the theatre

Phase 5 *Performance*
    Chapter 8. Shaping the production   Chapter 9. Etcetera—and all the rest

His introductory chapter lays out the nature of musical theatre and certain conventions established over the years, as well as a section on how to use the book (3-7). There are also useful appendices and photos to illustrate techniques discussed throughout.

Regarding staging and movement, (my primary concerns), in Chapter 6 "Staging and Coaching," Deer organizes his ideas around five concepts that address the following issues: using staging to tell stories, using available tools, understanding how blocking is like and unlike staging, coaching your cast, and the necessity for your work to have "entertainment" values (115-159). He expands on many of his ideas but, like Berkson, does not go into considerable depth in this volume. Staging is, after all, one subset of the director's task, which also comes under the purview of the choreographer. He does an excellent job of introducing it, however, which I examine in the next few paragraphs.

Methodology and Overview of Contents. Again, I will examine only Chapter 6 since its content is of greatest significance for choreographers.

After discussing the use of staging as a storytelling device, the author identifies three levels of staging in musicals: Blocking ("closest to real life"), Musical staging (heightened blocking or pedestrian choreography"), Choreography ("highly organized, often formalized or athletic danced behavior"), stating that they share a common value, which is that "they are external expressions of the internal action of the character" (117).

Deer offers a questionnaire to discuss the staging of action, posing and answering questions like "What is the dramatic action of the scene or song?" and "How can I express the dramatic action through the characters' physical behavior?" After a discussion on how to identify what level of staging to use, Deer identifies the types of musical numbers he finds in musicals. Again, these catagories are not engraved in stone like the names of the steps we do at the ballet barre, but even if some folks use different names, most work within the same categories, which are: a solo ballad, solo up-tempo or charm song, duet ballad/musical scene, Duet up-tempo or charm song, small-group staging, and full-scale group staging.

Deer's next heading, "Prompts to staging opportunities," introduces a section that offers a number of ways for choreographers to "find [their] way into a musical sequence" (126). This section is very useful for inexperienced choreographers because it offers something quite tangible to use as a starting point for staging. A few of the entry possibilities are, to analyze the storytelling requirements, to work with the musical style, or to research the historical period or geographical locale for customs, social behaviors, dances, etc. (122-124). The charts he includes that show how he analyzes storytelling in a song, "beat by beat," and the storyboards guiding readers through group staging notation used for the film *The Producers* are also excellent concrete examples illustrating the use of such diagrams during the creative process (127-133). This chapter also touches on images, stage pictures, and compositional structure. Deer discusses blocking more in depth and offers a wide range of "tools" to use when working with performers (134-156). He even devotes a short section to the idea that "dancers are actors, too," and discusses the more commercial aspect of being entertaining while also telling a story (157-160).

Conclusions. Deer's ability to break down and categorize the many right-brained and diverse ideas inherent in directing a musical the way he does is frankly awe-inspiring to someone like myself. (Given the opportunity, I will wallow in the primordial goo of my right-brain until I am forced to communicate with the world in a reasonable fashion.) I also believe that this book has been many years in the making, as portions of it have been journal articles, revised content from his book, *Acting in Musical Theatre: A Comprehensive Course* (Deer and Dal Vera, 2016), and from years of teaching, directing and gathering knowledge through experience. Deer's text is necessary sharing of his artistic process with loads of valuable information and many beneficial exercises; it is an excellent combination of theory and practice.

Sunderland, Margot with Pickering, Kenneth. *Choreographing the Stage Musical.* **New York: Theatre Arts Books/ Routledge, 1990.**

Central Purpose of the Research and Writing. In a preface the authors state their purpose for writing this book, but not until the end of a relatively brief discussion about the importance of musicals in the commercial sense, which they cite as: the ongoing popularity of live musical entertainment, the proliferation into the mainstream of songs from shows and the infusion of rock (or pop) songs into shows. All, they claim, have played a part in raising the standards of production. Increased demand has allowed the art form to evolve and now audiences have expectations of quality and "are less tolerant of the second-rate" (p. 9). The discussion switches to acknowledge the role of the director and the importance of the "balance of power" between the director, choreographer and musical director and then moves even more abruptly to the structure of rehearsals and scheduling. This "stream of consciousness" writing does come together in the end by concluding with a general statement of purpose: "This book is intended for all those who wish to create that unity between music, language and movement which is capable of generating so much excitement in the live performance of a stage musical" (10), and then stresses again the importance of solid collaboration. A more accurate statement might be that this text is intended to offer practical and specific solutions to choreographic problems presented to young or neophyte choreographers of musicals; and, even as they allow in their preface, the authors' methods assume "no previous experience in dance" and could even be made good use of by directors and musical directors, as well (10).

Methodology and Overview of Contents. The authors call upon their own experiences as choreographers of musicals and college instructors to identify potential questions, usable movement techniques, and ideas and ways to approach many of the practical aspects of choreographing a musical. Their concerns range from rehearsal preparation to the use of props while dancing. In the introduction following the book's preface, they briefly lay out several theoretical ideas about the use of choreography in a musical (11), and suggest distinguishing factors of this kind of choreography, such as the need to "[consider] pace, rhythm and drive....be neat [with] clear designs...be precise both temporally and spatially...be varied stylistically" and leave the singer enough "breath to sing loudly" (11). Following this is a glossary of the terminology they intend to use in the rest of the book.

Chapters follow through with what is promised in their headings, except for chapter one, which I thought would be primarily theoretical "How and when to move in songs," but although one or two mentions are made regarding context and plot, the writing does not look beyond surface elements and it positions dance as an isolated component. Remarks such as "…indeed one can over-dance a musical," or "First, it is important to identify the obvious 'excuses' and places for dance" (5) trivialize or generalize the material and detract from some of the helpful advice the authors do give later in the text. The authors do not approach the subject as an inherent aspect of the storyline nor do they stress the idea of seeing and analyzing the dance in context. Furthermore, I do not agree with certain of the information given in this initial chapter. For instance, under the heading "Gesture for the Singer" they suggest, "If it is important that the singer holds his arms still for a long time, he may feel more at ease by holding both hands in front of the body as shown in Figure 1." (Here two outlined figures are shown, one with arms at side and the other with hands clasped in front of the waist in a typical opera singer stance.) They continue, "Arms held by the sides often look unnatural and uncomfortable" (16). My immediate reaction to this bit of advice was to write in the margin, "Eeks! Don't say that!" For one thing, this advice goes against what is generally considered effective performance technique because it limits the actor's connection to his audience by cutting him off emotionally. Clasping hands at waist level in front of the body is a position of protection and uneasiness—not one of openness and confidence. Furthermore, this kind of ultra-specific advice for actual movement selection and invention that is given throughout the text is a clear sign that it may not be the best source for the autonomous choreographer, or performer, for that matter.

Chapter two deals with how to utilize the ensemble or chorus during a song or dance that features just one or two of the actors. Again, while headings like "Ways a Silent Chorus can Watch and Listen to Soloist Singers and Dancers" (20) tend to make me cringe a little, the accompanying advice about manipulating focus onstage is important practical information for choreographers; also the authors' profuse use of illustrations makes these ideas crystal clear to those reading it who may be (and most probably are) visual learners. A chapter on "general vocabulary" actually attempts to illustrate the myriad derivative movements seen often in theatre dances, but their initial advice in the beginning of the chapter is excellent. After mentioning the importance of capturing "the essence or flavour of a style," they offer a list of sources for textual or video materials in order to see these concepts in action—for six different musical and dance styles: ballet, country, disco, tap, ballroom and latin, and a "quick reference" category that lists some of the great old movie musicals, my personal favorite storehouse of excellent dancing.

Subsequent chapters give a great deal of information for dealing with different size groups, groupings and designs, contact and partner dancing, and utilizing and working with the music, properties, settings and costumes in a musical show. Again, with accompanying illustrations, they are giving the reader precise suggestions of actual movement choices. Their information is generally practical and correct, such as:

> A figure may become conspicuous the moment it starts to move…some colours are immediately more noticeable on account of their shorter wavelengths…people facing downstage are generally more conspicuous that those facing upstage…(87)

…and so on. At the end of the text is an appendix of examples of how the authors would pre-plan a musical number. Each example consists of the categories: 1) Choreographic Method I-Design/Vocabulary Division, and then 2) The Choreography Plan, which can be quite extensive as it plots through the music and the movements for principles and ensemble for that song.

Conclusions. As stated or implied above, overall this is an informative text for novice choreographers of musicals. Much like Stratyner's text outlining early dance director Ned Wayburn's dance documentation, this text gives specific formations and work on group design that can save much time if working on early and classic musical comedy material.

My primary concern lies in this book's approach to dance in musicals as an exclusively left-brained activity. The authors do not integrate their "nuts and bolts" information with the idea of creating the dance in context, nor as an integral storytelling component of the musical. Secondly, it does not address the choreographer as an imaginative and potentially innovative artist.

In addition to the three texts reviewed above, many others exist that are biographies or autobiographies of successful musical theatre choreographers. These studies are worthwhile resources for examining not only a prominent choreographer's artistic process, but also their philosophical ideas and how their individuality enters into their dances. Scholarly examinations of a choreographer's life, such as the relatively recent study of Agnes De Mille by Kara Anne Gardner, so closely examines De Mille's methods it might even be listed here with these other pedagogical texts. In the foreward of Gardner's book entitled *Agnes De Mille: Telling Stories in Broadway Dance*, Geoffrey Block states:

While there are a number of books on de Mille, I think it's fair to say that none engage the musical and dramatic content of a stage musical in such a fully realized manner as Gardner has accomplished in *Telling Stories in Broadway Dance*...Gardner demonstrates how de Mille pioneered the implementation of character and psychological development in dance and the invention of interesting and carefully drawn secondary characters that rescued the inhabitants of her dance lines from their customary anonymity. (Block in Gardner x-xi)

And so,

In musical theatre, the narrative or thematic identity of a work does not spring only from the mind of the choreographer but initially from the librettist, composer, and lyricist. In these ways and others, theatre dance is unlike modern dance, including and most particularly in its reason for being. In its most linear and representational manifestation, theatre dance is inextricably linked to a narrative, to the vision of the head interpreter of the narrative, and to the words and music that tell the story of the narrative in its very particular way. The musical theatre choreographer's personal vision is one among many, i.e. the visions of the director, musical director, scenic designer, lighting designer, and costume designer. Because of this diversity of ideas, a unifying vision must be devised by the director of the production and adhered to by all collaborators. This service to a collective goal is unlike the autonomy available to concert dance choreographers. Musical theatre choreographers have a solid working knowledge of the same techniques that guide choreographers of strictly concert dance forms, but must also possess the visual, analytical, organizational, and interpretive skills expected of theatrical play directors. In addition, these choreographers are musically savvy and diverse because, ultimately, it is *always* the music that drives and colors their work.

When I was in college, I typed the dedication from a book I was reading onto a notecard, and I taped the card inside the lid of my small wooden treasure box. I always have the box with me. I still use it for items I hold dear and I love to rummage through it from time to time. Here it is, the author's Dedication from *Dance-Drama: Experiments in the Art of the Theatre*:

This endeavor to extend the boundaries of
Dramatic Art, and the dance-dramas that
illustrate it, I dedicate to any young dancer
who is possessed of imagination and intelligence—
if there be such a one—who has the curiosity to
look over the walls that hem in his or her art, who
has sufficient of the spirit of adventure to explore
the horizon that lies beyond, one for whom dancing is
something more than its technique, one who is
not only a dancer but also an artist of the Theatre.
(Terence Gray, 1926)

In that same treasure box is a journal clipping of a short quote that I think of as a mantra. I used to believe it was something Martha Graham once wrote, but I can find no proof of that now. Regardless of who said it, I have kept it as an ongoing goal:

"...to be true, to convince, to enchant." (Anon.)

Each of these quotes charges artists to be true to themselves and to their work, and to keep stretching the boundaries of their art form "*...to explore the horizons that lie beyond…*".

Over the years, Gray's charge specified what mattered to me most as an artist—dance and theatre—and clarified for me an active standard to work toward. The latter provided me with a nutshell inside which the art I make strives to reside. In a nutshell, an artist should strive "*...to be true, to convince, to enchant.*" I love the last word the most. *Enchant!*

What is *your* nutshell, and what are the paths your art takes to live there?

APPENDIX
Documents A-M

Supplemental Material for Part One

I am sharing some of my material and methods for teaching a Musical Theatre Choreography course here. You will develop your own, but feel free to borrow anything you believe might be useful to you at the start.

APPENDIX A.   *Course Descriptions for Musical Theatre Choreography*

APPENDIX B,   *My Syllabus*

APPENDIX C.   *Requirements for my class*

APPENDIX D.   *Assignments before our first class meeting*

APPENDIX E.   *In-Class Assignment, Sample 1*

APPENDIX F.   *In-Class Assignment, Sample 2*

APPENDIX G.   *In-Class Assignment, Sample 3*

APPENDIX H.   *In-Class Assignment, Sample 4*

APPENDIX I.   *Other possibilities for in-class style work*

APPENDIX J.   *Song Analysis Form*

APPENDIX K.   *An Extended Scene and Song Breakdown*

APPENDIX L.   *A Rubric for Early Choreography Showings*

APPENDIX M.   *Checklist for the Final Showing*

APPENDIX A.
Course Descriptions

TITLE OF COURSE: MTE 320 G. Selected Topics in Music Theatre. Concepts in Staging and Choreography Techniques for Musicals: For Choreographers (4sh).

Directing and/or choreographing a musical each require knowledge of staging techniques that are unique to the musical theatre genre. This course will examine both the *overall* structure of choreographing a musical, as well as more *specific* techniques and the musical and stylistic requirements for staging a ballad, a character/comedy song, a small group work, and/or a production number, if resources allow the latter. Reading and listening assignments will be required (analysis of assigned musical) as well as practical in-class projects and a semester length project. In-class improvisations and spontaneous projects will be assigned on a regular basis. Performers from our companion course (for performers) will be made available to choreographers and will earn credit for participating. Permission of instructor is required based on dance background, previous study, and readiness of the student.

TITLE OF COURSE: MTE 320 H. Selected Topics in Music Theatre. Concepts in Staging and Choreography Techniques for Musicals: For Performers (1sh).

This course is for performers interested in gaining experience performing musical theatre repertory and will commit to being available to choreographers in MTE320G throughout the semester. This course will require availability during weekly class hours, as well as some outside hours to rehearse with your choreographer, when necessary.

Depending upon the number of people in the class, each performer will most likely be responsible to 2 choreographers. It is important for the performers to know that once they commit to the course, the expectation is that these commitments be honored and performers will be available to their choreographers during all class periods or outside class, when needed. *This opportunity is open to any dance, acting or musical theatre major in the performing arts department, freshman to senior.* You should feel comfortable singing with others onstage, not be afraid to improvise and learn movement, and have the ability to remember and accomplish movement and staging and/or technical dance, depending on the requirements of the choreography.

APPENDIX B.
A Syllabus

SYLLABUS
Selected Topics in Musical Theatre

Concepts in Staging and Choreography Techniques for Musicals:
For Choreographers (4sh)

Pre-requisite: Permission of Instructor. Class meets:
Professor: Linda Sabo Office Hours:
Phone/email: TA:

Course Description. Directing and/or choreographing a musical each require knowledge of staging techniques that are unique to the musical theatre genre. This course will examine both the *overall* structure of choreographing a musical, as well as *specific* techniques for staging a ballad, a character/comedy song, and a small group work or production number, depending upon available resources. Reading and listening assignments will be required as well as specific weekly in-class projects. For potential choreographers it is advisable to have dance and some improvisation or choreography experience. For potential directors, some dance, movement and acting/directing experience is advisable. **Pre-requisite:** Permission of instructor is required based on year of study, previous experience, and readiness of the student.

Goals. This course will not attempt to be a "how to" course of absolutes, but a mentoring process for students of dance and music theatre to approach musical theatre staging and choreography with a clearer understanding of its unique needs, based on the particulars of the material and the conventions and traditions of this theatrical form. My overall goal for the course is for potential directors and choreographers to better understand the importance of the visual storytelling component inherent in musical theatre and to make them aware of useful techniques to facilitate their own artistic process.

Objectives. Goals of the course will be met through both theory and practice.

- Students will be expected to read, reflect upon, research, theorize, and discuss outside readings, their own and peer work, and practice theories through creating actual staging and choreography.

- Weekly reading and discussion assignments to introduce new concepts with class practice.

- Regular mentoring sessions with Linda, some one on one, to facilitate ongoing projects.

- Rehearsal sessions with performers to create new choreography

- Periodic informal showings of in-class projects.

- Three formal dance showings during second part of semester with dancers and classmates to perform and critique in-context choreography.

Materials.

- You will need to have easy access to our Moodle site, where I will post readings.

- You will be responsible for getting copies of the libretto, score and cast recording of your assigned show. .In many instances, I have access to the librettos and scores that I suggest.

- I will assign your individual shows during the first week of classes.

- You will cast your final project first from the performers taking this course, after which you may also procure your own performers. If you have outside performers, you will have to create outside rehearsal times. Choreographers can also be available to perform in one of the other choreographers' project.

- Any props or items needed to create your staging.

- Recording device to record your music with an accompanist.

Requirements for Grading

1. In-class discussions based on assigned readings: These will be more prominent in the first few weeks of the term. I expect you to take notes while reading so you will have questions and observations to share with the class.

2. Weekly assignments, written and practical based on readings. <u>Important:</u> Until your initial plot breakdown is complete, and you've finalized your

analysis for your in-context assignments, you will not be permitted to show your choreography.

3. In-class improvisation work and "instant" choreography assignments.

4. Preparation for mentoring sessions and systematic progression of large choreography assignments.

5. Choreography: Attention to details of class rubrics; conducting rehearsals and motivating your performers; rehearsal logs; research notes, reflections. (Some of this is inherent in the above-mentioned assignments that follow your readings.)

Attendance

Attendance is expected during all class sessions. Any choreography that cannot be completed during class hours will have to be scheduled by you for out of class hours. Follow the calendar to know when you are expected to show your choreography in class and when to complete reading and choreography assignments. I will expect you follow the schedule diligently with all work completed on time.

On a personal note…

Please remember your honor code commitment and be aware that as your professor I am obliged to respond appropriately if I suspect it has been violated. Feel free to call or email if you have questions or difficulties with the course, or otherwise. I hope that you feel comfortable enough to make me aware of problems so that I can help you through them. Good luck with all of your courses this term!

SYLLABUS
Selected Topics in Musical Theatre

Concepts in Staging and Choreography Techniques for Musicals:
For Performers (1sh)

Pre-requisite: Permission of Instructor. Class meets:
Professor: Linda Sabo Office Hours:
Office Phone: Cell:
Email: **Additional rehearsal & Showing times: TBA**

Course Description. Student painters require paint to learn and practice making paintings; student choreographers require performers to learn and practice making dances and staging for musicals. This course is for performers interested in gaining experience performing musical theatre repertory and will commit to being available for students in MTE320 J throughout the semester. This course will require availability during weekly class hours when necessary, to learn and perform small in-class spot assignments and during set evening or weekend times each week with their choreographers. Each performer will be responsible to 2 choreographers. It is important for the performers to know that once they commit to the course, the expectation is that these commitments be honored and all hours are treated as class hours. You should feel comfortable singing onstage and have the ability to accomplish movement and staging, or dance, depending on the requirements of the choreography. Since all hours are in-class or rehearsal times, students will be expected to commit to a minimum of 4 hours during the week to this class.

Goals. This course will not attempt to be a "how to" course of absolutes, but a mentoring process for students of dance and music theatre to approach musical theatre staging and choreography with a clearer understanding of its unique needs, based on the particulars of the material and the conventions and traditions of this theatrical form. My overall goal for student performers is to better understand the importance of the visual storytelling component inherent in musical theatre, to make them aware of useful techniques to facilitate their own artistic process, and to gain an appreciation of and patience with choreographic process.

Objectives. Goals of the course will be met primarily through practice.

- Performers will be expected to attend class when scheduled to learn and perform in-class choreography assignments, or for choreography showings of semester assignments.

- Performers will be expected to attend all rehearsals agreed upon with their choreographers; learn the material, perfect it between rehearsals, and participate willingly and with a positive frame of mind.

- Performers must be available at least 4 hours each week for class or rehearsal purposes. Anyone desiring to offer more time may do so of their own accord.

- Performers are responsible to be familiar with and have a good understanding of the entire show they are working with and the characters they are performing.

Materials

- You will need to have easy access to our Moodle site, where your choreographers can post communications with you about scheduling or materials pertinent to their dances.

- A recording device to record your music so that you can learn songs and lyrics between rehearsals.

Requirements for Grading

1. Participation in In-class improvisation work and "instant" choreography assignments.

2. Regular and positive rehearsal attendance.

3. Taking notes and directives given to you by your choreographers and performing them to the best of your ability.

4. Attendance at all required choreography showings for Linda.

Attendance

- Attendance is expected. Because of outside rehearsal hours, we will be on different schedules. Follow the calendar to know when you are expected in class together during class hours. I will expect you to be at those diligently.

- Excuse from any rehearsal sessions should be only for illness and should be accompanied by a doctor's note, OR must go through Linda when going to the doctor is not needed (i.e. migraine, fever, flu). Email your choreographer and me as soon as you know you will be unable to attend. This should happen very seldom. Remember that without your presence in rehearsal, the choreographers can only "imagine" what will happen or might be able to happen.

On a personal note...

Please remember your honor code commitment and be aware that as your professor I am obliged to respond appropriately if I suspect it has been violated. Feel free to call or email if you have questions or difficulties with the course, or otherwise. I hope that you feel comfortable enough to make me aware of problems so that I can help you through them. Good luck with all of your courses this term!

APPENDIX C.
Requirements for My Class

COURSE REQUIREMENTS – Choreographers only

Participate in all in-class assignments; graded for 4 at 15 pts each.	20% -- 60 points total
Prepare for and participate in mentoring meetings, including discussions of assigned readings. 4 at 15 pts each	20% -- 60 points total
Participate in class critiques. 3 at 10 points each.	10% -- 30 points total
Submit written assignments when required. (You will not be able to show your dances until your written work is up to date. Complete it BEFORE you begin rehearsing).	25% -- 75 points total
Show your dances on required days. There will be 3 total showings at 25 points each	<u>25% -- 75 points total</u>
	100% **300 points total**

APPENDIX D.
Assignments Before Our First Class Meeting

Because the initial chapters of my text examining play structure and analyzing musicals are based on the musical <u>110 in the Shade</u>, it will be necessary for students to have a working knowledge of this play and its non-musical incarnation, <u>The Rainmaker</u>, both written by N. Richard Nash.

1. Watch the 1950s film *The Rainmaker* starring Burt Lancaster and Katherine Hepburn. I have a copy of this I can lend you, and you can probably find it in the library. You can also get the script and read it, if you prefer.

2. Read the musical *110 In the Shade* (this is the musical version of *The Rainmaker*) and listen to the cast recording. Your can find the libretto and score in the library.

3. Look through the list of shows uploaded on Moodle and give me your first and second choice of a show to analyze and work on throughout this semester. This is important to the theory part of the class. You will share and analyze the show with a partner, but when it comes to choosing numbers from the show to stage, you will have the option to work on those alone.

4. Read the libretti and listen to the cast recordings of your two choices.

APPENDIX E.
In-class Assignment, Sample 1

1st In-class assignment- Improvise and Create
Dance Elements and Motif

Review of basic dance composition tools using Laban-based prompts to explore the elements.

Teachers, use your own tried and true methods here. These are suggestions.

Design (Space)

Create with one or two other people 4 designs. Progress with any prompts, i.e. use symmetry and asymmetry…. create transitions…add music…add text… add meaning, expand on transitions, etc.

Action and Space- *Suggested prompts*

Create a floor pattern. Again, progress with any prompts, such as use directional changes…make it a particular length…time signature…add jumps and turns… levels…work with one other dancer to make a short study combining both dancers' travels. Each dancer's choice of pattern should try to complement or contrast the other dancer's choices.

Traveling ideas:

- running
- walking
- turning
- jumping, hopping, leaping
- sliding, galloping
- diagonals
- straight paths forward, backward, sideways
- circular

Effort: Incorporate quality changes on the continuum. Improvise first with just effort prompts using descriptive words, progress to acting-like prompts using emotions and situations.

Weight: strong……………………..……to……………………….light

Time: sudden……………………………to…………………….sustained

Tension: bound OR free

Space: direct OR indirect

Time in musical scores is set but I often add time prompts to the final study or assign music to be added to the study with prompts of how to relate to the music in various, unexpected ways. (See below)

If time permits, dividing the class into 4 or 5 groups and asking them to pull from the work already created to create a final study incorporating all of these elements is also recommended, because now you can have them create a story to tell, characters to express through movement who are dealing with some sort of dramatic conflict, etc. The possibilities are endless. Unlike in modern dance choreography class, this course objective IS to tell stories through movement, so we can start by using these foundational elements.

Finally: Decide upon a title which will convey the overall meaning of your study.

Motif

Create a Motif Phrase: 16 counts in length

  Incorporate at least one:

- Clear isolation movement
- Jump or some airborne movement
- Rest or hold
- Traveling movement
- Floor-bound movement

Repeat motif:

- Traveling in an indirect way
- Traveling in a direct way
- As Bound/heavy movement
- As Free/light movement
- Contrasting quick/fast tempos with slow/sustained ones

APPENDIX F.
In-Class Assignment, Sample 2

In-Class Assignment – Find my personal style response

Style—how does *this* music make you move? Improvise first and create phrases you can work with later. Pay attention to the music and its arrangement as you invent and then organize your movement with your dancers. Teachers and choreographers: use modern dance composition prompts to discover motif variations. Make choices. Apply, Modify, Refine.

COME TOGETHER- Beatles

Trevor

- Lexi
- Reagan
- Cara
- Corrine
- Joe
- Patrick

Deshawn

- Nasia
- Jess
- Meagan
- Mercer
- Jake
- Nick

APPENDIX G.
In-Class Assignment, Sample 3

In-Class Assignment-Working in time periods- 60's & 70's

Choreographers are highlighted:

(Jersey Boys) SHERRY:	**Jacob Trevor** Joe Patrick
(Mamma Mia) MAMMA MIA:	**Jess** Lexi Cara
(Mamma Mia) MAMMA MIA:	**Reagan** Corinne Mercer

The choreographers will choose and craft movements and steps into a finished performance. If desired, choreographers may have their dancers participate in movement invention. You will have the rest of today's class to listen to the music and begin to improvise. You can begin anyway you like, but my suggestion would be to organize your music early on so you can see the song as a whole and begin to think of it in sections or segments. Look at:

- the song form: Verse/Refrain, ABA, AABA, ABAC, etc.? (Breaking down the work)

- the counts in each section

- the lyrics and how you will use them-your performers will have to mime or sing them with the recording.

These are songs from jukebox musicals and although they have plots and characters, the songs were not written to serve the book, nor the characters or situation. It was the other way around. The book of the musical was written as an excuse for the songs. For this assignment, you can either consider the dance as being staged in-character for the musical, or not. I don't expect you to incorporate character or situation in this assignment unless you want to and know the show well enough to do that. You *should* consider period, however, and the kind of movement that would be appropriate for that period. You can go back and view actual videos of the Four Seasons and Abba, but you most likely won't find them dancing. These **musicals** do have the singers dancing as they perform because it is a musical, but the actual groups were singers and musicians, not dancers. The songs were socially danced to during specific decades, however, and so I expect that you will research and incorporate those social dance styles into your choreography. Start, however, with how it feels to you. That will come through as you improvise with the music. Then get ideas by doing a little online research of movements and dance styles done during those periods and add or incorporate some of them into your own ideas. Mainly, have some fun with it, but give it a little extra thought for the appropriate style of movement.

On Wednesday you'll come in and use the space to work with your groups. On Friday, you'll have the first 15 minutes of class to run through and touch up. Then we'll show the dances to each other. You can work on your own outside of class, as well, if you choose to do so.

APPENDIX H.
In-Class Assignment, Sample 4

In-Class Choreography Assignment
…from *Grease* – "We Go Together" – 1950s

JACOB CHOREOGRAPH – (The Blue-Man Group)
Cara
Mercer
Reagan
Patrick
Joe
Jake

<u>Nasia</u>—You can join the above group to perform with them, but you can also be available to mentor each group (as I will) throughout the process.

JESSIE CHOREOGRAPH – (The Pink Lady Group)
Nick
Deshawn
Trevor
Corrine
Meagan
Lexi

I'd like you to use the song from the film version of *Grease*, not the Broadway cast recording. It is about 3 minutes long. Try to plot out the entire number using the characters in the show, where are they, why do they sing the song, what are their present points of view, etc. Find a synopsis of the film. I think you can probably try pulling together the whole number. Lots of 50s dance moves available for you to use in different ways. Research them.

You will have the weekend to prep, and two classes with your performers to choreograph the song. Final day next week you will review your groups for 30 minutes, then we'll show the dances and critique them after that.

APPENDIX 1.
Other possibilities for In-Class Assignments

Additional Possibilities for Style Work

These are endless, of course. Because of time restraints, it does help if the student has some familiarity with the show the song is from. I will also assess if the assignment can be accomplished within the time allotted and adjust expectations, if necessary. It is often too brief a process to work with character and situation, as well, so unless your choreographers are familiar enough with context or can adjust quickly, stick primarily with style work over context for these in-class assignments.

For the most part, I rely on classic repertory to facilitate students' ability with diverse styles of music and movement they are less familiar with. Modern jukebox musicals or period pieces like *Hairspray* and *Crazy for You* are very good at working on style over content at this stage of the process. Study should include contemporary styles, as well, such as those used in *Legally Blonde*, *In the Heights*, and *Hamilton*. While some songs do emphasize character and relationship, the musical style should be the guiding force.

"When I'm Not Near the Girl I Love"
"Little Shop of Horrors"
"Fit as a Fiddle"
"Brush Up Your Shakespeare"
"Friendship"
"When Mama Gets Married"
"Won't You Charleston with Me"

Some shows where you can find songs for in-class assignments:

Big River
Little Women
Peter Pan
Chicago
Ain't Misbehavin'
Wonderful Town
Thoroughly Modern Millie
Guys and Dolls
1940s Radio Hour

APPENDIX J.
Song Analysis Form

Helping Choreographers to Analyze the Song: Process[4]

Your Name: _____

Song Title: _____

1. WRITE OUT THE LYRICS OF THE SONG YOU ARE STAGING BELOW. Mark with a slash (/) where the acting beats change in the song. You may use my breakdown of "Another Hot Day" as a template for this initial discussion. (Also indicate the song form: Verse, Refrain, is it AABA, ABA, ABAC, etc.?)

2. Cite any words or phrases that are unfamiliar to you. Look them up and write down their meanings. The context may change the meaning later.

3. Cite any repeated words, words that change, poetic words or phrases, and any unusual words or phrases. Also, does the song have qualifying/descriptive words (or phrases) that add depth or detail to the word(s) that follow?

4. Cite any references to:

    a) Age (Could the song be sung by any age?)

    b) Gender

    c) Time period

    d) Place (urban, rural, etc.)

    e) Indications of economic background

    f) Words that indicate a part of the country (dialect) or any other references, which tell you about the speaker's ethnic and/or occupational background

    g) Educational background

---

[4] Adapted from a loaned document from R. Brent Wagner, University of Michigan.

5. What is the song about—in your own words?

6. Cite the progression of the song. Use the ***song form*** to show the arc of the song. How does each unit relate to the overall topic/theme of the song? Of the show? Of the character singing it?

7. Listen to the accompaniment only (with no singing) and cite these other FACTS: (Key, tempo, range, modulation, dissonance, syncopation, accents suspensions, characteristics of the melody,)

8. Analyze the melody and discuss/interpret how it interacts with the lyrics.

9. Note your emotional response to the music.

10. Identify elements in the music, including orchestration if you are working with it, that are valuable for the interpretation of the song (accents, lyricism, syncopation, accompaniment, etc.).

11. Identify and describe the situation in which the song takes place. What is its function in the play? What does the singer want? Where does this take place and when? How does it further the plot?

APPENDIX K.
An Extended Scene and Song Breakdown

THE LIGHT IN THE PIAZZA
Director, Linda Sabo

ACT ONE
1953, Florence, Italy, summer. Early morning.

Music 1: Overture

SCENE 1. Piazza Della Signoria—outside in piazza– statues, pillars, large architectural pieces.

SCENE AND SONG: "Statues and Stories," pp. 1-1-1 to 1-1-9 (or 1-2-9). MARGARET, CLARA, FABRIZIO, and ENSEMBLE. This opening song is to establish place and background—an American mother and daughter are in Florence, Italy on vacation. The lyrics, diaglogue, staging and their interactions with each other and the ensemble should give us enough information about Margaret and Clara so that by the end of the song, the audience knows them pretty well. The end of the scene when Fabrizio enters initiates the plot and is the action upon which the show is centered. We need to see Margaret's apprehension about Clara making friends with this young man, see the young peoples' strong attraction to each other, and become aware that there is more to the story than meets the eye. The ensemble will be part of the environment from the beginning through the end of the scene. Once the scene with Fabrizio begins, there should be only 2 or 3 people lingering on stage.

Music 2D. Transition to Uffizi—set change

SCENE 2. The Uffizi: An English tour guide appears followed by a small tour group. This is the same day, early in the afternoon.

SCENE pp. 1-2-9 to 1-2-10: MARGARET, CLARA, TOUR GUIDE, TOURISTS. In this scene we see that Clara and her mother have separate objectives. Margaret is only interested to continue sightseeing, but Clara wants to go to Fabrizio's shop because she said she would meet him there. Margaret is trying to downplay the whole situation as one would with a child but is frustrated that Clara is behaving in a more adult fashion than she is used to.

SONG "The Beauty Is," p 1-2-11, CLARA. At the beginning of this song, Clara is puzzling over the naked statues of the male figure in Italy and delighting in being among friendly people and feeling at home there. As the song progresses, it acts a lot like "Something's Coming" in *WSS*, except instead of her singing it to another person, she is really considering this and working it out in her mind—we see her projecting in a positive way that something very good may be coming her way. She feels it and tells us she is open to it.

SCENE pp. 1-2-12 to 1-2-13: CLARA, FABRIZIO, MARGARET. C & F meet again, but Margaret pulls Clara away. Clara calls back to Fabrizio that they will come to his shop. This small scene is important in pushing the plot along. It also intensifies the relationship of the young lovers, as well as Margaret's agitation and conflict with it.

Music 4.

SONG "Il Mondo Era Vuoto (Part 1)": FABRIZIO. Fabrizio sings about how he never realized how much he lived in the "dark" until he met Clara who brought light to him. She has become the essence of his life, but he is convinced she cannot love him because he is so immature. "She cannot love a little boy." The set is changing around him from the Uffizi to Nacarelli's Tie Shop while he sings this part of the song. Like the song "Maria" in *WWS,* this song makes the audience aware of how young and worked up he has become about this girl. He is over-the-top emotional about her after one meeting. This song is emotionally charged.

SCENE3: The Naccarelli Tie Shop. *(Fabrizio arrives at the shop, still singing. Fabrizio's father, Signor Naccarelli, sits and reads the newspaper, not responding to the agony of his child.) This is the same day; it is end of the workday in the late afternoon.*

SONG/SCENE pp. 1-3-13 to 1-3-16: FABRIZIO, SIGNOR NACCARELLI, GIUSEPPE. As the song and dialogue continue into the scene, we meet Fabrizio's father and older brother and learn that their family dynamics are normal, loving and they have a sense of humor. He begs them to help him because he cannot look like a little boy; he needs to dress like a man. At the end of the song, Signor agrees to help.

Music 5. American Dancing/ Duomo

His older brother Giuseppe (very suave and socially savvy--a playboy), tries to teach him to dance, but only to point up his own ability and show off a little. Signor finally promises to help and leads Fabrizio out of the shop by the end of the scene.

SCENE 4: <u>The Duomo</u>. *Fabrizio approaches his father who is meeting with a Priest. When he sees Margaret and Clara entering, looking up into the dome, he hides, flowers behind his back. I think of this as the next morning.*

<u>SCENE only, pp. 1-4-17 to 1-5-19: SIGNOR, PRIEST, FABRIZIO, MARGARET, CLARA.</u> The plot moves forward when Fabrizio again runs into the Johnsons at the Duomo, sightseeing. His father is there also and invites them both for a walk later in the day at the Piazzale Michelangelo.

Music 5B.

SCENE 5: <u>Piazzale Michelangelo.</u> *Sunset. A café. Franca is helping Fabrizio with his English -- This is the same day in the late afternoon.*

<u>SCENE pp. 1-5-20 to 1-5-21: FRANCA, FABRIZIO, GIUSEPPE, WAITER, PEOPLE ON THE STREET, GIUSEPPI GIRLFRIEND.</u> This scene introduces us to Franca and tells us about her relationship with both Fabrizio and her husband, Giuseppe, who walks in with a woman he has spent the afternoon with. We're seeing the breakdown of their relationship in contrast to the growing relationship of Fabrizio and Clara. Franca storms out on Giuseppe; he exits pursuing her. During the remainder of the scene, our focus moves between Fabrizio and Clara walking and Margaret and the Signor walking and talking or singing. The following breaks down those scene shifts.

<u>SCENE pp 1-5-22 to 1-5-23: FABRIZION and CLARA, ENSEMBLE.</u> They meet first and she shows him her scar and they make conversation. They are

getting to know each other. They see their parents and begin to walk independent of them.

Music 5C. *Punctuation*

SCENE pp 1-5-23 to 1-5-24: SIGNOR and MARGARET, ENSEMBLE. They continue to talk and walk. They are getting to know one another.

Music 6. *Passeggiata (Part 1)*

SCENE and SONG "Passagiata": pp 1-5-24 to 1-5-25: FABRIZIO and CLARA, ENSEMBLE. He tells her about where he grew up and how well he knows this place and loves it.

Music 6A. *Passegiatta (Part 2)*

SCENE and SONG pp. 1-5-25 TO 1-5-26 FABRIZIO, CLARA, MARGARET, SIGNOR, ENSEMBLE. All 4 couples are in view now. Margaret and Signor move out after scene.

Music 6B. *Passegiatta (Part 3)*

END OF SONG: "Passegiatta" p 1-6-27: FABRIZIO, CLARA, ENSEMBLE Fabrizio finishes the song down stage; they exit at end of song.

Music 6C. *Transition to Tea Scene -set change into the Nacarelli home.*

SCENE 6. The Nacarelli Home—the time is, most likely, a few evenings later.

SCENE pp 1-6-27 to 1-6-30: GIUSEPPE, SIGNORA, AND SIGNOR NACARELLI,

FRANCA, MARGARET, CLARA, TWO SERVANTS. People are trying to get to know each other. During her conversation with the Nacarelli's, Margaret keeps trying to tell them the problem with Clara, but she keeps getting interrupted. At some point Franca and Clara leave so Franca can show her the paintings in the corridors of the house.

An Extended Scene and Song Breakdown

Music 7. *The Joy You Feel* - Scene shifts focus to a corridor in another part of the house.

SONG "The Joy You Feel, pp. 1-6-31; FRANCA, CLARA. In this song, Franca tells Clara how unhappy she is and how men change after you marry them. She warns Clara, saying she remembers feeling how happy she and Giuseppe used to be, like Clara and Fabrizio, but to beware because that will change. Clara is confused at the end of the song and runs out to return to the others.

SCENE continues, pp 1-6-32 to 1-6-36 Back in the living room. MARGARET, SIGNOR NACCARELLI, SIGNORA NACCARELLI, GIUSEPPE, FABRIZIO, SERVANTS. Margaret's objective in this scene is to tell the Naccarelli's about Clara's accident, but she is unable to find the right moment. When she finally gets the chance, she decides not to say anything. The Naccarelli's all like Clara and are happy that her mother is so close to her and proud of her. Clara runs back into the room upset, Fabrizio calms her down; Signora explains to Margaret what a good boy Fabrizio is, as opposed to his brother Giuseppe. They like Clara very much and even suggest possibly Clara will stay and marry Fabrizio. Margaret says they must move slowly.

Music 7B. *After Tea*

SCENE 7 -- Margaret & Clara's Hotel Room. After dinner at the Naccarelli's – about 11:00-ish that evening.

SCENE pp 1-7-36 to 1-7-39: MARGARET & ROY. Margaret calls her husband Roy back in NC. We meet him in this scene and learn that he is busy, on his way for a dinner engagement and is not really interested in speaking with her at the moment. She tries to tell him about Clara, he tells her to end whatever is starting and hangs up. She is left feeling very alone and realizes that their relationship no longer has love or even regard for each other. It prompts her thoughts in the following song.

Music 8. *Dividing Day*

SONG "Dividing Day" pp 1-7-39 to 1-7-40: MARGARET. It is in this song that Margaret becomes resigned to the fact that she will have to deal with this situation with Clara on her own. She looks for Clara but realizes she has left the room and runs out to find her.

Music 9. *Hysteria/Lullaby*

SCENE 8. On the Street late that same night (after midnight)

SCENE and SONG 1-8-40 to 1-8-41: CLARA, FABRIZIO, PEOPLE ON THE STREET, MARGARET (at end of scene.) Clara leaves to meet Fabrizio but gets lost on the streets. There are strange & frightening people, she gets lost and becomes panicky. Fabrizio cannot find her but by the end of the scene her mother finds her, and she collapses into her arms. They walk back to the Hotel room, as the set is changing. A foreshadowing of her and Fabrizio's coming together & the turmoil that causes.

SCENE 9. The Hotel Room. – Even later, into the morning hours

SCENE and SONG, "Lullaby" p 1-9-42: MARGARET, CLARA. Margaret comforts Clara by singing a Lullaby.

Music 9A: *Hotel Bar-* Clara falls asleep and Margaret leaves for the Hotel Bar.

Music 9B. Fabrizio arrives at the door. He knocks. Pause. He comes in, looks for Clara. She wakes.

SCENE and SONG, 1-9-42 to 1-9-45: FABRIZIO and CLARA. They talk, Fabrizio has trouble expressing himself. She tells him to talk anyway and that she will understand. They sing and during the song she proposes to him. He says he must do it, so he proposes to her, they continue to sing and at the end of the song, they are about to make love. Margaret enters and finds them as the lights come down.

END OF ACT ONE

APPENDIX L.
A Rubric for Early Choreography Showings

This rubric contains tasks the choreographers should start to think about as they are preparing for and beginning the rehearsal process. A Song Analysis Form should be submitted sometime prior to this showing with any additional notes on character, situation, and place. Mention, also, any specific goals you were working toward.

PURPOSE: Does your choreography/staging take into account the song's purpose to the plotline of the musical and how it functions in the story? Does your choreography/staging help clarify and facilitate the performers' objectives and is it a clear and appropriate statement of each character's state of mind/point of view?

BODY PLACEMENT and TRAVEL: SPATIAL PATTERNS FOR MUSICAL STAGING AND DANCES. Do you make effective use of the stage for group design; appropriate use of stage to create meaning making conscious use of strong or weak areas, diagonals, directional choices, etc.? Do you choose design elements such as symmetry, asymmetry to create meaning and balance, or imbalance, etc.?

CLEAR AND EFFECTIVE CHOICES TO CREATE APPROPRIATE FOCUS. Are you aware of the focus you are creating as you create your staging or choreography? Do your movement choices and use of space effectively address dramatic elements in the song and move focus during a song when necessary so that the audience is paying attention to what you do not want them to miss? In large group dance numbers, focus on smaller moments can be more difficult to focus, but necessary to the telling of the story of the song, or fulfilling its purpose. Are you paying attention to those smaller and more specific themes as well as to the bigger picture?

BODY LANGUAGE. Is there effective and appropriate use of physicality, primarily with naturalistic, pedestrian, or non-stylized movements used in scenes, ballads, and character songs? Are differences in physicality seen in different characters? Are you getting ideas from your performers that you can/should use in your piece?

MOVEMENT INVENTION FOR DANCES. Are there visual, dynamic, and rhythmic variations within movement choices; are they innovative vs. derivative?

Is style used appropriately and is period style effectively used? Are movement choices appropriate for the characters and situations being depicted?

PACING/TEMPO and OTHER MUSICAL CONCERNS. Will the score be altered in any way, i.e. will dances be shortened or lengthened? Other considerations to pay attention to are 1) the stylistic intentions of the composer, 2) getting lyrics across clearly and effectively, 3) using orchestration effectively, 4) demonstrating overall musicality in your physical interpretation of the music and achieving that musicality in your dancers? Do your choices enhance and interpret the music effectively?

STYLE OF MOVEMENT. Is the style of the movement appropriate to the period of the show and the music, and are historical/social/ethnic movement styles being researched?

CONSIDERATIONS of SINGING and SINGERS. Does the movement compromise the singing of the song in any way, or does it enhance it? Are you considering the needs of your performers so that they can give you their best work?

ACTING ELEMENTS. Do the dancers understand the meaning of the piece and what the choreographer would like to convey? Are they getting the jokes? Do they understand all of the words and lyrics of the song? Does staged movement enhance or integrate well with acting choices or does it seem anachronistic?

USE OF PROPS, COSTUMES, AND SCENIC ELEMENTS. If you are using props are they necessary or aesthetic choices? Either way is fine. If aesthetic, will they also help to tell the story? Do they fit into the overall themes of the piece? Are you rehearsing enough with your props or scenic additions to make the most creative use out of them, as well as to make them natural extensions of the dancers' bodies?

APPENDIX M.
A Rubric for Final Showings

A Level: Exemplary/Exceptional level of work. All considerations covered and evident. Extraordinary level of creativity, skill, and knowledge of libretto. Intended character and emotional content is believable and compelling showing original, deep, and specific choices throughout. Preparation of performers is at a high level and shows polish and professionalism.

B Level: Very Good to Excellent level of work. Most considerations covered and evident. High level of creativity, skill, and knowledge of libretto is shown. In most cases, intended character and emotional content is believable and interesting. Choices are motivating and specific in most cases. Preparation performers is above average with only a few incidents of more rehearsal time needed.

C Level: Average to Good level of work. Some or many considerations of rubric are not dealt with in a visible way. Conventional level of creativity, skill and knowledge of libretto is shown. Character and emotional content are, at times, ambiguous and non-specific. Performers seem under-rehearsed or unclear about their motivations and intentions.

The Story

Purpose:

- Is the purpose of the song clearly realized in the staging?
- Are character objectives clear as well as their individual points of view?

Considerations of Singing and Singers:

- Is the singer comfortable, sounding in control, and able to enjoy performing the material?
- Does the movement come naturally out of the character?
- Is the movement stylized or pedestrian; is the choice appropriate; is the choice honored consistently throughout the song; if not, can you justify it?

Acting Elements:

- ➤ Do the dancers understand the meaning of the piece and all the lyrics and what the choreographer and writers would like to convey?

- ➤ Does staged movement enhance or integrate well with acting choices or does it seem anachronistic and unnatural?

- ➤ Has the choreographer been able to get what he/she needs to from the performers or reworked the choreography until that point is reached?

Body Language:

- ➤ Is there effective and appropriate use of physicality, primarily with naturalistic, pedestrian, or non-stylized movement used in scenes, ballads, and character songs?

- ➤ Are appropriate blocking/staging choices made that reveal the character in some way?

Technical Elements

Body Placement and Travel--Spatial patterns for Staging and Dances:

- ➤ Effective use of stage for group design;

- ➤ Appropriate use of stage to create meaning, i.e. strong vs. weak areas/ use of diagonals/direct vs. indirect; etc.;

- ➤ Balance of large groups on stage, effective use of symmetry/asymmetry to create meaning;

- ➤ Effective use of body types in ensemble staging.

Focus:

- ➤ Are stage values considered when placing actors and dancers?

- ➤ Do movement choices specifically address dramatic elements in the song or scene?

- Are appropriate and effective focus solutions applied either in small or large group numbers?

Movement Invention for Dances:

- Is attention paid to design, dynamic and rhythmic variation within movement choices made?

- Are specific choices made is using innovative vs. derivative movement?

- Are stylistic considerations appropriate (including use of historical/social/ethnic movement styles)?

- Is consideration given to character & situation-appropriate movement choices?

Musical Concerns:

- Are the pacing and tempo appropriate and effective for the scene and the song?

- Does the shortening or lengthening of dances retain the integrity of the score and the composer's intention?

- Are the stylistic intentions of the composer worked with and enhanced?

- Is the song able to be sung well by the performers—does the movement facilitate the singing or diminish it?

- If working with a cast recording, is the orchestration used effectively when making movement choices?

- Does the dance and staging show an overall musicality?

Props, Costumes, Scenic Elements:

- Is there effective and creative use of these elements in the work?

- Have the actors been sufficiently rehearsed using props or working on scenic pieces.

BIBLIOGRAPHY

Anthony, Joseph (Director). *The Rainmaker* (Motion Picture). Paramount, 1956.

Banes, Sally. "The Choreographic Methods of the Judson Dance Theater. *Moving Histories/Dancing Cultures,* edited by Ann Dils & Ann Cooper Albright, Wesleyan University Press, 2001, pp. 350-361.

Barranger, Millie S. *Understanding Plays*. 3rd ed., Allyn & Bacon, 2003.

Barry, Sarah. M. "A Somatic Approach to Education and the Creative Process: Seeking integration across boundaries." Thesis, University of Utah, 2005.

Baryshnikov, Mikhail. "Inside/Out." *Jacob's Pillow Dance*, 2009, http://www.jacobspillow.org/festival/events/inside-out. Accessed on 7/15/14.

Bayles, David, and Orland, Ted. *Art and Fear: Observations on the perils (and rewards) of Artmaking.* 1st ed., Image Continuum Press, 2001.

Beckman, Cathy. "Performance and Education: Survey of a Decade." *Dance Scope*, (15:1), 1981, pp. 26-32.

Berkson, Robert. *Musical Theatre Choreography: A Practical Method for Preparing and Staging Dance in a Musical Show*. New York: Back Stage Books, 1990.

Bernstein, Leonard (Music), Sondheim, Stephen (Lyrics). *West Side Story* (Score), 1956, pp. 54-59. New York: Boosey and Hawkes Inc.

Bertolt Brecht 1898-1956: Epic Theatre Using Verfremdungseffekt. Collection of web sources to compile lists outlining distancing rules & contrasting artistic philosophies, 2005. http://web.mit.edu/allanmc/www/brecht.pdf. Accessed on June 30, 2017.

Blom, Lynn A. and Chaplin, L.Tarin. *The Intimate Act of Choreography.* University of Pittsburgh Press, 1982.

Bock, Jerry (Music) and Harnick, Sheldon (Lyrics). *She Loves Me (*Original Cast Recording, 1963). Audio CD, Verve Records, September 19, 1988.

Brecht, Bertolt and Willett, John, ed. and trans. *Brecht on Theatre: The Development of an Aesthetic* [1st edition]. NYC: Hill and Wang, 1964.

Bricusse, Leslie. *Jekyll & Hyde, the Musical.* (Libretto). NYC: Music Theatre International, 1997.

Bucchino, John. "A Glimpse of the Weave." *It's Only Life* (Original Cast Recording-Audio CD). P.S. Classics, 2006.

Buckroyd, Julia. *The Student Dancer: emotional aspects of the teaching and learning of dance.* London: Dance Books, 2000.

Burrows, Abe & Swerling, Jo. *Guys and Dolls.* (Libretto). NYC: Music Theatre International, 1950.

Burrows, Jonathan. *A Choreographer's Handbook.* London & NY: Routledge, 2010

Butterworth, Jo. "Teaching choreography in higher education: a process continuum model." *Research in Dance Education*, 5 (1), April 2004, pp. 45-67.

Butterworth, Jo, et al. *Contemporary Choreography: A Critical Reader*. London: Routledge, 2009.

Caird, John (Book) and Gordon, Paul (Music/Lyrics). *Jane Eyre, the musical* (Libretto). Music Theatre International, 2000.

Chorea. In Wikipedia, the Free Encyclopedia. March 21, 2017, https://en.wikipedia.org/w/index.php?title=Chorea&id=771436720. Accessed on July 15, 2017.

Conner, Lynne and Gillis, Susan. "*The Solo Dancers: Isadora Duncan.*" The Early Moderns, 1996a, http://www.pitt.edu/~gillis/dance/isadora.html. Accessed on June 12, 2009.

_____. "The Solo Dancers: Loie Fuller." *The Early Moderns,* 1996b, http://www.pitt.edu/~gillis/dance/loie.html. Accessed on June 12, 2009.

Conrad, Christine. *Jerome Robbins, That Broadway Man, That Ballet Man.* 1st ed., London: Booth-Clibborn Editions, 2000.

BIBLIOGRAPHY

Cramer, Lyn. *Creating Musical Theatre: Conversations with Broadway Directors and Choreographers*. Bloomsbury Methuen Drama, 2013.

Davis, Amy K. *Dance-making online: teaching choreography in virtual space.* Thesis: Texas Women's University, 2006.

Deer, Joe. *Directing in Musical Theatre: An essential guide.* London & NY: Routledge, 2014.

DeFoe, Ryan. "An Interview with Adam Guettel." *Talkin' Broadway*, 2001, file:///C:/Users/Owner/Desktop/Boston%20%20'An%20Interview%20with%20Adam%20Guettel'%20-%202_12_01.html. Accessed 1/10/20.

De Mille, Agnes. *America Dances.* New York: MacMillan Publishing Co., 1980.

Dewar, Torron-Lee. *50 Ways to Become a Better Choreographer.* CreateSpace Independent Publishing Platform; 1st ed., 2015.

Dils, Ann. "Social History and Dance as Education. *International Handbook of Research in Arts Education,* edited by Liora Bresler, 2007, pp. 103-112.

Dodworth, Allen. *Dancing and its relations to education and social life with a new method of instruction, including a complete guide to the cotillion (German) with 250 figures.* Harper & Brothers, New York, 1900, monographic.

Doughty, Sally, et al. "Technological enhancements in the teaching and learning of reflective and creative practice in dance." *Research in Dance Education*, Dec. 2008, 9 (2), pp. 129-146.

Douglass, Frederick. "Gavitt's Original Ethiopian Serenaders." *The North Star*, Rochester, VA, 6/29/1849. http://utc.iath.virginia.edu/minstrel/miar03at.html. Accessed on 6/19/2018.

Easton, Carol. *No Intermissions: The Life of Agnes de Mille*. Toronto: Little Brown and Company, 1996.

Eberson, Sharon. "A New 'Evita' Returns Che to His Roots." *Pittsburgh Post-Gazette*, July 6, 2014, p. 17, Questia, https://www.questia.com/newspaper/1P2-8149455/a-new-evita-returns-che-to-his-roots. Accessed on 5/26/18.

Edwards, Sherman (Music/Lyrics). *1776* (Original Cast Recording 1969). (Audio CD, Masterworks Broadway, 1992.

Ellfeldt, Lois. *A Primer for Choreographers.* Palo Alto: Mayfield Publishing, 1967.

Fergus, Kerry Auer. "*West Side Story*: The Tritone and the 7th," *From Score To Stage*, 5/17/17. https://www.fromscoretostage.com/single-post/2017/05/17/West-Side-Story-The-Tritone-and-the-7th. Accessed 1/16/2020.

Foulkes, Julia L. *Modern Bodies: Dance and American Modernism from Martha Graham to Alvin Ailey.* University of North Carolina Press, 2002.

Fraleigh, Sondra H. "Dance and the Other." *Dance and the Lived Body: A Descriptive Aesthetic,* 1st ed., pp. xii-xix, 57-70, University of Pittsburgh Press, 1987.

Frankel, Aaron. *Writing the Broadway Musical.* (Revised and Updated). DaCapo Press, Inc., 2000.

Freedley, George. "The Black Crook and the White Fawn" (1945). *Chronicles of the American Dance: From the Shakers to Martha Graham,* edited by Paul Magriel. DaCapo Press, Inc., 1948, pp. 65-80.

"From This Moment On," Bob Fosse (Choreographer). *Kiss Me Kate* (Motion Picture, 1953). *YouTube,* Uploaded by Nikolaus Thieme, July 25, 2014. https://youtu.be/YTBrVuEvZbg. Accessed on May 26, 2018.

Fuchs, Thomas. The Memory of the Body. University of Heidelberg, 2004. https://www.klinikum.uniheidelberg.de/fileadmin/zpm/psychatrie/ppp2004/manuskript/fuchs.pdf. Accessed June 26, 2011.

Gallwey, W. Timothy. *The Inner Game of Tennis: The Classic Guide to the Mental Side of Peak Performance.* Penguin Random House, 1997.

Gardner, Kara Anne. *Agnes De Mille: Telling Stories in Broadway Dance.* NYC: Oxford University Press, 2016.

Gardner, Sally. "Notes on Choreography." *Performance Research,* 2009, v.13, no. 1, pp. 55-60.

BIBLIOGRAPHY

Gilvey, John. *Before the Parade Passes By: Gower Champion and the Glorious American Musical.* Macmillan, 2005.

Gombrich, Ernst. (2005). "Press statement on The Story of Art." The Gombrich Archive. Metropolitan Museum of Art, 2005, https://gombricharchive.files.wordpress.com/2011/04/showdoc68.pdf. Accessed June 5, 2018.

Gordon, Paul, and Caird, John (Original Cast Recording). *Jane Eyre, the Musical* (Audio CD). München: Sony Classical, 2000.

Gray, Terence. *Dance-Drama: Experiments in the Art of Theater.* Cambridge: W. Heffer & Sons Limited, 1926.

Green, Jill. "Choreographing a Postmodern Turn: The Creative Process and Somatics." *Impulse,* 1996, v. 4, pp. 267-275.

Green, Stanley. *Broadway Musicals: Show by Show, Fifth Edition.* Hal Leonard, 1996.

Grody, Svetlana, and Lister, Dorothy. *Conversations with Choreographers.* Heinemann, 1996.

Gruen, John. "American Dance Machine: the Era of Reconstruction." *Dance Magazine,* February 1978. Theatredance.com: http://www.theatredance.com/dancemachine.html. Accessed 7/15/14.

Guettel, Adam (Composer). "Let's Walk." *The Light in the Piazza,* Original Cast Recording-Audio CD). Nonesuch Records, 2005.

_____. "Let's Walk." *The Light in the Piazza,* Vocal Score. Williamson Music, 2005, pp. 53-56.

Hagood, Thomas K. "Moving in Harmony with the Body: The Teaching Legacy of Margaret H'Doubler, 1916-1926." *Dance Research Journal.* 32/2, winter 2000/01, pp. 32-51.

Hamlisch, Marvin (Composer) and Kleban, Edward (Lyricist). "At the Ballet," *A Chorus Line* (Score). Tams-Whitmark, 1975.

Hammerstein II, Oscar (Book, Lyrics). *Carousel* (Libretto). Rodgers & Hammerstein Organization, 1945.

Hawkins, Alma. *Moving From Within: A New Method for Dance Making.* A Cappella Books, 1991.

Haworth, John. "Beyond Reason: Pre-Reflexive Thought and Creativity in Art." *Leonardo,* 1997, v. 30 no. 2, pp. 137-145.

Hayes, Elizabeth R. *The Emotional Effect of Color, Lighting, and Line in Relation to Dance Composition.* University of Wisconsin—Madison, 1935.

_____. *Theory and Techniques for Motivating Choreographic Expression on the Secondary and College Levels.* Stanford University, 1949

_____. *Dance Composition & Production for High Schools and Colleges.* John Wiley and Sons, 1955.

_____. *Dance Composition & Production.* Princeton Book Co., 1981 & 1994.

"Hayes Obituary." *Deseret News,* 9/15-16/2007.

H'Doubler, Margaret N. *Dance: A Creative Art Experience.* Madison, WI: University of Wisconsin Press, 1940.

Hilliard, Peter. "Part 1: Landmarks of Guettel's Style." *The Light in the Piazza: A rough guide for the M.D.* 2014. https://peterhilliard.wordpress.com/2014/07/15/the-light-in-the-piazza-a-rough-guide-for-the-m-d-part-1-landmarks-of-guettels-style/. Accessed: 6/12/2018.

Hischak, Thomas. *Enter the Playmakers: Directors and Choreographers on the New York Stage.* Scarecrow Press, 2006.

Humphrey, Doris. The *Art of Making Dances.* Hightstown: Princeton Book Company, 1959.

BIBLIOGRAPHY

ibdb.com. "The Black Crook," *Internet Broadway Database.* The Broadway League, 2001-2018, https://www.ibdb.com/broadway-production/the-black-crook-12518. Accessed June 20, 2018.

ibdb.com. "Shows, 1860-1865" *Internet Broadway Database.* The Broadway League, 2001-2018. https://www.ibdb.com/shows. Accessed, June 20, 2018.

imbd.com. "The Wizard of Oz." *Internet Movie Database.* MGM, 1939. https://www.imdb.com/title/tt0032138/. Accessed June 20, 2018.

Jacob's Pillow Dance Festival. *Home Page,* 2018, http://www.jacobspillow.org/festival/, 1933-2009. Accessed on 6/8/09 and 6/22/18.

Jeffries, Sean. *Life on the Line: An analysis of the lighting design for A Chorus Line.* Thesis, Kent State University, Kent, OH, 2012.

Kander, John (Composer) and Ebb, Fred (Lyricist). *Kiss of the Spider Woman* (Audio CD). Masterworks Broadway, 1997, BMG Music, 1995.

_____. "Anything for Him" (Sheet Music). *Kiss of the Spider Woman.* Warner- Tamerlane Publishing Corp. (BMI): 1992, 1993.

Kelly, Kevin. *One Singular Sensation: The Michael Bennett Story*. Doubleday, 1990.

Kenrick, John. "Dance in Stage Musicals, Part II." Musicals 101.com: *The Cyber encyclopedia of musical theatre, film, and television*, 2003, http://www.musicals101.com/dancestage2.htm. Accessed on July 7, 2017.

_____. *Musical Theatre: A History*. Continuum, 2010.

_____. "The Black Crook." *Musicals 101.com: The Cyber encyclopedia of musical theatre, film, and television,* 2014a. http://www.musicals101.com/1860to79.htm. Accessed June 20, 2018.

_____. "1700-1865: Musical Pioneers." *Musicals 101.com: The Cyber encyclopedia of musical theatre, film, and television*, 2014b. http://www.musicals101.com/1700bway.htm. Accessed on June 20, 2018.

Kirkwood, James, Dante, Nicholas. *A Chorus Line* (Book). Tams-Witmark, 1975.

Kislan, Richard. *The Musical: A Look at the American Musical Theatre.* Applause Theatre & Cinema Books, 2000.

Kisselgoff, Anne. "Jerome Robbins, 79, Is Dead; Giant of Ballet and Broadway." *New York Times,* July 30 1998. https://www.nytimes.com/1998/07/30/theater/jerome-robbins-79-is-dead-giant-of- ballet-and-broadway.html. Accessed on May 26, 2018.

Laban School. *History: Rudolf Laban.* http://www.laban.org/php/news.php?id=20. Accessed on June 10, 2009.

La Meri. *Dance Composition: The Basic Elements.* Lee, MA: Jacob's Pillow Dance Festival, 1965.

Lapine, James (Book) and Sondheim, Stephen (Composer/Lyricist). *Sunday in the Park with George.* (Libretto). NYC: Music Theatre International, 1984.

Laurents, Arthur (Book) and Sondheim, Stephen (Composer/Lyricist). *West Side Story.* Libretto. NYC: Music Theatre International, 1957.

Lavender, Larry. "Dialogical Practices in Teaching Choreography." *Dance Chronicle,* 2009, v.32, no. 3, pp. 377- 411.

_____. "Facilitating the choreographic process." In J. Butterworth & L. Wildschut (eds.), *Contemporary Choreography: A Critical Reader,* pp. 71-89, London: Routledge, 2009.

_____. "Intentionalism, Anti-Intentionalism, and Aesthetic Inquiry: Implications for the Teaching of Choreography." *Dance Research Journal,* 1997, v. 29, no. 1, pp. 23-42.

_____. *Dancers Talking Dance: Critical Evaluation in the Choreography Class.* Champaign: Human Kinetics, 1996.

_____. "Standing Aside and Making Space: Mentoring Student Choreographers," *Impulse,* 4 (3), 1996.

_____. "Critical Evaluation in the Choreography Class." *Dance Research Journal*, 1992, v. 24, no. 2, pp. 33-39.

Lavender, Larry and Sullivan, B.J. Transformative Systems for Teaching and Learning Choreography. In Hagood, Thomas (ed.), *Legacy and Dance Education: essays and interviews on values, practices, and people.* Amherst: Cambria Press, 2008.

Lazarus, Frank, Vosburgh, Dick, et al. (Original Cast Recording 1980). *A Day in Hollywood, A Night in the Ukraine.* (Audio CD). Port Washington: DRG Records, Inc., 1992.

Lee, Carol. *Ballet in Western Culture: A history of its origins and evolution.* Allyn & Bacon, 1999.

Leijen, Äli, et al. "Pedagogical Practices of Reflection in Tertiary Dance Education." *European Physical Education Review,* 2008, v. 14, no. 2, pp. 223-241.

Loesser, Frank. *Guys and Dolls* (Original Cast Recording-Audio CD, 1950). Santa Monica: Verve Records. June 27, 2000.

Lott, Eric. *Love and Theft: Blackface Minstrelsy and the American Working Class*, New York: Oxford University Press, 1993.

Lucas, Craig (Book) and Guettel, Adam (Composer/Lyricist). *The Light in the Piazza* (Libretto). Rodgers and Hammerstein Organization, 2005.

Magriel, Paul, Editor. *Chronicles of the American Dance: From the Shakers to Martha Graham.* DaCapo Press, Inc., 1948.

Mandelbaum, Ken. *A Chorus Line and the Musicals of Michael Bennett.* 1st ed., St. Martin's Press, 1989.

Martin, John. *The Dance: the story of the dance told in pictures and text.* Tudor Publishing Co., 1946.

Masteroff, Joe (Book) and Harnick, Sheldon (Lyrics). *She Loves Me* (Libretto). Music Theatre International, 1963.

McCarthy, Erin. " 'Maria'/*West Side Story* (1957)," *The Stories Behind Six Classic Stephen Sondheim Songs*, 3/22/15. https://www.mentalfloss.com/article/62387/stories-behind-6-classic-stephen-sondheim-songs. Accessed on February 6, 2020.

McCutchen, Brenda Pugh. *Teaching Dance as Art in Education*. Champaign, Human Kinetics, 2006.

McNally, Terrence, and Fred Ebb. *Kiss of the Spiderwoman* (Libretto). Samuel French, Inc., 1993.

Miller, Scott. "Inside Evita: Background and analysis," 2010. http://www.newlinetheatre.com/evitapage.html. Accessed July 10, 2017.

_____ . "Inside Bare: Background and analysis," 2011. http://www.newlinetheatre.com/barechapter.html, in section: "Hear My Voice." Accessed July 14, 2017.

Minton, Sandra C. *Choreography: A Basic Approach Using Improvisation*, Champaign: Human Kinetics, 2007.

Moore, Lillian. "Mary Ann Lee—First American Giselle." *Chronicles of The American Dance: From the Shakers to Martha Graham,* edited by Paul Magril, DaCapo Press, Inc., 1948, pp. 103-118.

_____ . "George Washington Smith." *Chronicles of the American Dance: From the Shakers to Martha Graham,* edited by Paul Magril, DaCapo Press, Inc., 1948, pp. 139-190.

Nachmanovitch, Stephen. *Free Play.* 1st ed., G.P. Putnam's Sons, 1991.

Nadel, Myron and Strauss, Marc. *The Dance Experience: Insights into history, culture and Creativity.* Princeton Book Company, 2003.

Nagrin, Daniel. *Choreography and the Specific Image.* University of Pittsburgh Press, 2001.

Nash, N. Richard. *The Rainmaker* (Script). Random House, 1955.

Nash, N. Richard, and Jones, Tom. *110 in the Shade* (Libretto). Tams Witmark, 1963.

BIBLIOGRAPHY

Neil, James. "John Dewey: The Modern Father of Experiential Education." *Weilderdom: Outdoor Education Research and Evaluation Center*, 2005, http://www.wilderdom.com/experiential/ExperientialDewey.html. Accessed July 25, 2017.

Novak, Elaine and Novak, Deborah. *Staging Musical Theatre: A Complete Guide for Directors, Choreographers, and Producers.* OH: Betterway Books, 1996.

NYCB Website, Repertory Index, http://www.nycballet.com/company/rep.html?rep=166. Accessed July 25, 2014.

O'Neill, Rosetta. "The Dodworth Family and Ballroom Dancing in New York." *Chronicles of the American Dance: From the Shakers to Martha Graham,* edited by Paul Magriel, pp. 81-102, DaCapo Press, Inc., 1948.

Palmer, Parker J. "Teaching in Community: A Subject-Centered Education." *The Courage to Teach,* pp. 115-141, Jossey-Bass Inc., 1998.

Pavis, Patrice. *The Dictionary of the Theatre: Terms, Concepts, and Analysis.* Translated by Christine Shantz, 1st ed., Toronto and Buffalo: University of Toronto Press, February 5, 1999.

Payne-Carter, David and McNamara, Brooks. *Gower Champion: Dance and American Musical Theatre.* Greenwood Press, 1999.

Pomer, Janice. *Dance Composition: An Interrelated Arts Approach. Human Kinetics*, 2009.

Powers, Harold S. "Lydian." *The New Grove Dictionary of Music and Musicians*, 2nd edition, 29:15, 2001, pp. 409-10. Edited by Stanley Sadie & John Tyrrell. London: Macmillan Publishers.

Ralabate, Tom. "Exploring the Tapestry of a Uniquely American Art Form." Common Ground/Defining Jazz Dance in *Dance Studio Now*, December 3, 2008. https://www.dancestudiolife.com/common-ground-defining-jazz-dance. Accessed on January 12, 2011.

Robbins, Jerome (Director/Choreographer) and Wise, Robert (Director). *West Side Story* (Motion Picture), United Artists, 1961.

Rogosin, Elinor. *The Dance Makers: Conversations with American Choreographers*. Walker, 1980.

Rosenthal, Bethana. *Dance Production: the effect of the dance creative process on student choreographers.* Thesis: California State University, Northridge, 2005.

Sabo, Linda. *Made in America: The cultural legacy of jazz dance artist Gus Giordano.* Thesis: Iowa State University, Ames, 1998.

_____. Conference Presentation "Efva Lilja's Movement as the Memory of the Body: Curating as a documentation of process and a critical examination of this artistic research project." *American Dance Festival, Screendance: The State of the Art, Curating the Practice/Curating as Practice*. Durham, NC. 2008.

_____. "Making Connections: Steering performers toward their authentic selves." Unpublished article, University of North Carolina at Greensboro, 2008.

_____. "The Mystery of Creativity; Scything through the underbrush." Unpublished article, University of North Carolina at Greensboro, 2009.

Sagolla, Lisa J. "The Influence of modern dance on American musical theatre choreography of the 1940s." *Dance: Current Selected Research, vol. 2,* edited by Lynnette Y. Overby & J.H. Humphrey, Ams. Press, Inc., 1990, pp. 47-68.

Savran, David. The Search for America's Soul: Theatre in the Jazz Age. *Theatre Journal,* 58.3, 2006, pp. 459-476.

Schmidt, Harvey (Music) and Jones, Tom (Lyrics). *110 in the Shade.* (Original Cast Recording, 1963). (Audio CD). RCA, June 12, 1990.

Schmidt, Harvey and Jones, Tom. "Another Hot Day." *110 in the Shade* (Score). Tams-Witmark Music Library, 1963.

Shurr, Gertrude and Yocom, Rachael D. *Modern Dance; Techniques and Teaching.* The Ronald Press, 1949.

Silén, Charlotte and Uhlin, Lars "Self-directed learning - a learning issue for students and faculty!" *Teaching in Higher Education*, 13:4, 2008, pp. 461- 475.

BIBLIOGRAPHY

Smith-Autard, Jacqueline. *Dance Composition: A Practical Guide to Creative Success in Dance Making*, 6th Edition. London: Methuen Drama, 2015.

_____. *Dance Composition: A Practical Guide to Creative Success in Dance Making*, 5th Edition. London: A&C Black Publishers, Ltd., 2004

_____ (as Smith, Jacqueline). *Dance Composition: A Practical Guide for Teachers.* 1st Printing, London: Lepus Books, 1976.

Smith, Holly. "Spoon-feeding: or how I learned to stop worrying and love the Mess." *Teaching in Higher Education,* 13 (6), 2008, pp. 715-718.

Sofras, Pamela A. Dance *Composition Basics: Capturing the Choreographer's Craft.* Champaign: Human Kinetics, 2006.

Sondheim, Stephen (Composer/Lyricist) and Lapine, James. (Librettist). *Sunday in the Park with George* (Libretto). Music Theatre International, 1984.

Sondheim, Stephen. *Finishing the Hat: Collected lyrics (1954-1981) with attendant comments, principles, heresies, grudges, whines, and anecdotes,* 1st ed., Knopf, 2011.

Sotiropoulos, Karen. *Staging Race: Black Performers in Turn of the Century America,* Harvard University Press, 2006.

"Steam Heat." *The Pajama Game* (Film 1954), Choreographer, Bob Fosse. *YouTube,* Uploaded by BroadwayJLM, March 29, 2011, https://youtu.be/eQdyDlSie0Q. Accessed May 26, 2018.

Stein, Joseph (Book) and Schwartz, Stephen (Lyrics). *Rags: The New American Musical* (Libretto). Rodgers & Hammerstein Organization, 1986.

Stone, Peter (Book) and Edwards, Sherman (Lyrics). *1776* (Libretto). Tams Witmark Library, 1969.

Stone, Peter (Book) and Yeston, Maury (Lyrics). *Titanic, the Musical* (Libretto). Tams Witmark Library, 1997.

Stratyner, Barbara C. *Ned Wayburn and the Dance Routine: From Vaudeville to the Ziegfeld Follies.* Studies in Dance History, No. 13. Madison: The Society of Dance History Scholars, 1996.

Strausbaugh, John. *Black like You: Blackface, Whiteface, Insult, & Imitation in American Popular Culture.* The Penguin Group, 2006.

Strouse, Charles (Music) and Schwartz, Stephen (Lyrics). "Children of the Wind" (Score). *Rags.* Rodgers and Hammerstein Org., 1986.

Strouse, Charles and Schwartz, Stephen. (Original Cast Recording) *Rags: The New American Musical* (Audio CD). Masterworks Broadway, 1991.

Stowe, Dorothy. "She Nurtured Modern Dance from Bud to Blossom at the U." *Deseret News,* May 1, 1988.

Sunderland, Margot, and Pickering, Kenneth. *Choreographing the Stage Musical.* Theatre Books/Routledge, 1989.

Tharp, Twyla. *The Creative Habit.* Simon & Schuster Paperbacks, 2005.

Toll, Robert C. *Blacking Up: The Minstrel Show in Nineteenth-Century America.* New York: Oxford University Press, 1977.

Tune, Tommy. *Footnotes: A Memoir.* 1st ed., Simon & Schuster, 1997.

Turner, Marjery. *New Dance; Approaches to Nonliteral Choreography.* University of Pittsburgh Press, 1971.

U.S. Bureau of Labor Statistics. "Occupational Employment and Wages," *Choreographers,* May 2017. https://www.bls.gov/oes/current/oes272032.htm. Accessed May 28, 2017.

U.S. Bureau of Labor Statistics. "Occupational Employment and Wages," *Dancers,* May 2017. https://www.bls.gov/oes/current/oes272031.htm. Accessed June 4, 2018.

U.S. Census Bureau. "Population Clock." *Homepage,* https://www.census.gov/. Accessed on June 4, 2018.

Van Dyke, Jan. Teaching Choreography: Beginning with Craft. *Journal of Dance Education*, vol. 5, no. 4, 2005, pp. 116-124.

_____. Intention: Questions Regarding Its Role in Choreography. *Journal of Dance Education*, vol. 1, no. 3, 2001, pp. 96-101.

Värlander, Sara. The role of students' emotions in formal feedback situations. *Teaching in Higher Education*, vol. 13, no. 2, 2008, pp. 145-156.

Viagas, Robert, Lee, Baayork, and Walsh, Thommie. *On the Line: The Creation of A Chorus Line.* William Morrow and Company, Inc., 1990.

Vertinsky, Patricia. "Isadora Goes to Europe as the 'Muse of Modernism': Modern Dance, Gender, and the Active Female Body. *Journal of Sport History*, vol. 37, no. 2, Spring 2010, pp.19-39.

Vosburgh, Dick (Book & Lyrics), Lazarus, Frank (Music), et al. *A Day in Hollywood, A Night in the Ukraine* (Libretto). Samuel French, 1980.

Warner, Jack L. (Producer), Hunt, Peter H. (Director). *1776* (Motion Picture). Columbia Pictures, 1972.

Wasson, Sam. *Fosse.* Reprint edition, Eamon Dolan/Mariner Books, 2014.

Wayburn, Ned. *The Art of Stage Dancing.* New York: Ned Wayburn Studios of Stage Dancing, 1925, 1927.

Webber, Andrew L. (Music) and Rice, Tim (Book & Lyrics). (Original Broadway Cast Album) *Evita* (Audio CD). Santa Monica: Verve Records, 1979.

Webber, Andrew L. and Rice, Tim. (New Broadway Cast Recording) *Evita* (Audio CD). NYC: Masterworks Broadway, 2012.

"Whatever Lola Wants," from *Damn Yankees* (film 1958), Choreography by Bob Fosse. *YouTube,* Uploaded by hardballget, November 21, 2010. https://youtu.be/6kjQmgm0r4g.

White, Matthew. *Staging a Musical.* New York: Theatre Arts Books/Routledge, 1999.

Wildhorn, Frank, Bricusse, Leslie, Cuden, Steve. *Jekyll & Hyde, the Musical* (Audio CD). NYC: Atlantic Records, 1997.

Willett, John, ed. and trans. *Brecht on Theatre: The Development of an Aesthetic.* NYC: Hill and Wang, 1964.

Winter, Marian H. "Juba and American Minstrelsy." In Paul Magriel (Editor), *Chronicles of the American Dance: From the Shakers to Martha Graham,* 39-64. New York: DaCapo Press, Inc., 1948.

_____. (1948). Augusta Maywood. In P. Magriel (Ed), *Chronicles of the American Dance: From the Shakers to Martha Graham,* 119-138. New York: DaCapo Press, Inc.

Yeston, Maury (Music/Lyrics), et al. *Titanic, the Musical.* (Audio CD). Masterworks Broadway, 1997.

Yeston, Maury (Music/Lyrics), Stone, Peter (Book). *Titanic, the Musical.* (Piano-Conductor Score). Cherry River Music Co. (BMI), Tams Whitmark, 1997.

Young, David. *How to Direct a Musical.* New York: Routledge, 1995.

www.ingramcontent.com/pod-product-compliance
Lightning Source LLC
Chambersburg PA
CBHW042226010526
44111CB00046B/2973